I CARE About You

THE CONSCIENCE OF

James Joyce

THE CONSCIENCE OF

James

Joyce

by DARCY O'BRIEN

PRINCETON NEW JERSEY

1968

PRINCETON UNIVERSITY PRESS

pReface

Twenty-five years after James Joyce's death, readers, critics, and scholars agree on his literary greatness and on the facts of his biography but on little else. We have had Joyce the Yea-sayer and Joyce the Nay-sayer; Joyce the relativist and Joyce the scholastic; Joyce the democrat, the bourgeois, the aristocrat; Joyce the Freudian, the Jungian; Joyce the Irish Dante, the Irish Ben Jonson, the Irish Walt Whitman. To range through the more than two thousand items in that ever-fattening behemoth, the Joyce bibliography, is to invite madness, so bewildering are the contradictions in interpretation. Joyce himself encouraged such confusion, because he believed that the best way to insure his immortality was to keep the professors busy for centuries. Perhaps he has succeeded too well. Potential readers are doubtless frightened away by the scholarly brawl which surrounds and obscures him, and there seems to be little possibility of reconciling the oppositions.

To the single question, "what moral judgments, if any, are embodied in the writings of James Joyce?" at least three incompatible answers have been given: Joyce judged man harshly; Joyce celebrated the moral worth of the ordinary man; and to Joyce not moral questions but only aesthetics mattered. Joyce was nauseated by life, we are told, and, like Flaubert, wanted to drown the world in his vomit. His treatment of man resembles Swift's treatment of the Yahoos. Yet other voices assure us that Joyce affirms the essential goodness of common life, that he is an apostle of love, compassion, and pacifism. Still others insist upon Joyce's moral neutrality, his exclusive devotion to his craft, his amoral experiments with shifting perspectives and points of view.

I hope to add another dimension to the reading and criticism of Joyce. Joyce's comedy and his conscience are equally the concerns of this book. But I have given the title to Joyce's conscience because I believe that his comedy derives from his moral sense, just as Swift's amusing proposal that Irish children be stewed, roasted, baked, and boiled derives from his moral indignation at human greed and folly.

Certain of Joyce's attitudes are curious in a writer who proclaimed himself an enemy of the Church. For all his literary experiments and innovations, he retained a vision of human frailty closer in spirit to his Irish Catholic background than to the moral relativism characteristic of our age. Although he became, as he himself said, "an Irish clown, a great joker at the universe,"[1] he did not put on cap and bells with ease. He began as an Irish Catholic youth well-schooled in contempt for the weight of Adam's flesh. Eventually he left the Church, but the Church did not altogether leave him. He broke away from priests and masses and confessional boxes; he ceased to believe that God would punish him for not making his Easter duty; but he continued to believe that human nature was irreconcilably divided between spirit and flesh, between ideal and actual, between good and evil. The sexual emphasis of Irish Catholic morality left an indelible mark on his thinking. Sex remained for him a manifestation of the actual brute in man, the constant rival of the potential angel in man.

Out of this background, out of this Irish, puritanical, self-lacerating, conscience-stricken view of life came Joyce's satiric comedy. While his convictions remained remarkably unchanged, he developed or shifted from bitterness to satiric delight in man's folly. Thus the contrast between the coldness of *Dubliners* and the warmth of *Finnegans Wake*: the one reflects Joyce's early disgust with Irish moral paralysis, while the other is animated chiefly

[1] Quoted by Jacques Mercanton, "The Hours of James Joyce, Part I," *Kenyon Review*, XXIV (Autumn 1962), 728.

by his later amusement at human failings. Joyce's felicitous comic mode in *Ulysses* and *Finnegans Wake* evokes laughter and, like the humor of all great comic satire, revels in the ridiculous side of man.

Professor Lawrance Thompson, of Princeton University, first nurtured my interest in Joyce and has aided me at every stage of composition. My dedication of this book to him expresses both friendship and indebtedness. Professor John Henry Raleigh, of the University of California at Berkeley, read the manuscript in an earlier version, suggested numerous improvements, and broadened my perspective with ideas often different from my own. Professor Thomas B. Flanagan, also at Berkeley, aided me with his vast knowledge of things Irish and was a matchless guide to Dublin when I met him there by chance in 1964. Mr. V. S. Pritchett, when he visited Berkeley in 1962, regaled me with information, anecdote, and opinion on Ireland, and I learned more from him than books have taught me. Professor Edwin Fussell, of the University of California at San Diego, read the manuscript with scholastic thoroughness and helped me immensely in matters of form and style. And my colleague at Pomona, Professor Ray Frazer, sharpened my arguments against his own and saved me from a great many confusions and embarrassments.

My research was aided by a Fulbright Fellowship to Pembroke College, Cambridge University, where I benefited from the advice and encouragement of Mr. Matthew Hodgart, now of the University of Sussex. While in England I was able to examine manuscripts of *Ulysses* and *Finnegans Wake* in the British Museum. I must thank Professor George Harris Healey, Curator of Rare Books at the Cornell University Library, who allowed me to read and to record the important correspondence from Joyce to his wife, still partially unpublished.

For permission to quote from Joyce's works I must thank

the Society of Authors in England for quotations from *A Portrait of the Artist as a Young Man, Dubliners, Finnegans Wake, Collected Poems, Exiles, The Critical Writings of James Joyce*, and *Letters of James Joyce*, Volumes I, II, and III. I am also grateful to the Purdue Research Foundation for granting me permission to reprint, in somewhat revised form, my article, "The Twins that Tick *Homo Vulgaris*—A Study of Shem and Shaun," *Modern Fiction Studies* (Summer 1966), as Chapter VI of this book.

If the extent of my wife Ruth Ellen's contribution to this study were known, its authorship might be in doubt. Suffice it to say that she has been responsible for the altering of more phrases than I care to remember.

D. O'B.

Pomona College
Claremont, California
1967

Acknowledgments

ACKNOWLEDGMENTS

Reprinted by permission of Random House, Inc., and John Lane The Bodley Head

From THE DUBLIN DIARY OF STANISLAUS JOYCE
Copyright © 1962 by George Harris Healey
Reprinted by permission of George Harris Healey

contents

ABBREVIATIONS AND EDITIONS
OF JOYCE'S WORKS USED IN THE TEXT

CW *The Critical Writings of James Joyce.* New York: The Viking Press, 1959.

D   *Dubliners.* New York: The Viking Press, 1958.

E   *Exiles.* New York: The Viking Press, 1951.

FW *Finnegans Wake.* New York: The Viking Press, 1958.

P   *A Portrait of the Artist as a Young Man.* New York: The Viking Press, 1964.

SH *Stephen Hero.* New York: New Directions, 1955.

U   *Ulysses.* New York: The Modern Library, 1961.

Collected Poems. New York: The Viking Press, 1957.

Letters. Volume I, Stuart Gilbert ed.; Volumes II and III, Richard Ellmann ed. New York: The Viking Press, 1957 and 1966.

THE CONSCIENCE OF
james joyce

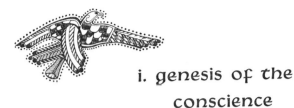

i. genesis of the conscience

First novels are often self-portraits, and they are usually flattering. But *A Portrait of the Artist as a Young Man* breaks the conventional pattern by scrutinizing rather than glorifying its subject. The book is a piece of self-analysis, and it displays both self-respect and self-criticism. To distinguish between what Joyce respects and what he criticizes in Stephen Dedalus is to discover the genesis of Joyce's conceptions of life and of art.

Some readers admire Stephen; others despise him. Some praise his fierce defiance of authority; others decry his presumption and pride. And as for Joyce's own view, like a painter or a dramatist he refrains from direct comment, thus inviting charges of inscrutability.[1] But if we observe Stephen's habits of mind, it becomes clear that Joyce reveals his own attitude in the very exposition of Stephen's. His art is his voice. He portrays Stephen as a young man brave and afraid, aware and self-deceived, slowly awakening to his Joycean conscience.

· I ·

Even as a child Stephen Dedalus is in quest of beauty: not the wild, fiery beauty of passion, but a serene, exalted

[1] See Wayne C. Booth, "The Problem of Distance in 'A Portrait of the Artist,'" in his *The Rhetoric of Fiction* (Chicago, 1961), pp. 323-36.

beauty. The beauty which Stephen seeks is like the mysterious loveliness of the Blessed Virgin as she is venerated in Catholic ritual: radiant and sexless. Stephen himself makes the comparison, for he thinks of the Virgin when he contemplates Eileen, the young girl who so allures him: "Eileen had long thin cool white hands too because she was a girl. They were like ivory; only soft. That was the meaning of *Tower of Ivory* but protestants could not understand it and made fun of it. . . . Her fair hair had streamed out behind her like gold in the sun. *Tower of Ivory. House of Gold.* By thinking of things you could understand them" (P42-43). Yet few theologians would agree that Stephen has reached a doctrinal understanding of those phrases from the litany of the Blessed Virgin. Instead he reveals his attitude toward the beauty of Eileen. He thinks of Eileen as soft and cool and pale, as a gentle Madonna who "had put her hand into his pocket where his hand was and he had felt how cool and thin and soft her hand was. She had said that pockets were funny things to have: and then all of a sudden she had broken away and had run laughing down the sloping curve of the path" (P43). A pure and passionless encounter: the young Madonna runs gaily down the path, away from passion. Stephen has not even noticed, or perhaps has repressed, the sexual provocativeness of her slipping her hand into his pocket. And he takes pleasure in recalling that sunny day because such thoroughly spiritual beauty is the object of his youthful quest.

But an occasional moment with this golden-haired little virgin is not enough for Stephen. Perhaps he fears that this house of gold will tarnish with time, for he cherishes too a timeless image of beauty—Mercedes, the heroine of *The Count of Monte Cristo.* He conjures up for himself numerous romantic interludes with Mercedes, all of them quite innocent of sexuality but suffused with a mystical, religious kind of beauty. Stephen's silent worship of Mercedes intensifies our awareness of his tendency to harbor within himself ideals of transcendent beauty. Fate prevented Monte Cristo from marrying Mercedes: she is thus appropriately elusive, inaccessible, and almost ethereal as an ideal of feminine beauty for the romantic Stephen. At times, brooding upon her image, he is led to wander about the avenues of Dublin in a state of emotional disquiet, yearning actually to grasp his ideal and to end his feverish longing: "He wanted to meet in the real world the unsubstantial image which his soul so constantly beheld. He did not know where to seek it or how: but a premonition which led him on told him that this image would, without any overt act of his, encounter him. They would meet quietly as if they had known each other and had made their tryst, perhaps at one of the gates or in some more secret place. They would be alone, surrounded by darkness and silence: and in that moment of supreme tenderness he would be transfigured. . . . Weakness and timidity and inexperience would fall from him in that magic moment" (P65).

Stephen's faith in this "unsubstantial image" of beauty is like that of a saint certain that he will someday see God: even the language describing Stephen's image is religious in tone. But his faith in spiritual beauty paradoxically destroys his more conventional religious faith. Strangely, it is not the flesh which quenches the spirit but a more powerful spiritual force which supersedes formal religious doctrine. The provincial dogmatism of the Irish Catholic Church begins to offend Stephen's intuitive spirituality. As religion fades, spirituality continues to flourish, and a yearning which has been a part of Stephen since childhood obscures and finally obliterates his orthodox Catholicism. Stephen seems to be longing for something close to the Roman Catholic idea of the Virgin, but the Church itself can only impede his quest by weighing down his soul with tedious rituals and restrictions, with ponderous doctrines, fears of ghostly punishments and, perhaps worst of all, with the provincialism of the Irish clergy.[2] When he must begin his day "with an heroic offering of its every moment of thought or action for the intentions of the sovereign pontiff. . . ." (P147), he cannot allow his soul to linger near the tower of ivory or house of gold that is Eileen, nor to flutter about the pagan if sexless image of Mercedes. The Church stifles him, and consequently not until Stephen actually encounters his "unsubstantial image" does he feel that "weakness and timidity and inexperience" have at last fallen from him, freeing him to leave the Church for good. Stephen happens upon his epiphany of beauty just when he is beginning to perceive his destiny as an artist. The search for beauty which has long preoccupied his soul becomes the artistic quest itself, and his new-found sense of artistic mission makes possible his rejection of the Church. Wandering on the strand, he hears his name called out across the dunes: "Now, as never before, his strange name seemed to him a prophecy. . . . Was it a quaint device opening a page of some medieval book of prophecies and symbols, a hawklike man flying sunward above the sea, a prophecy of the end he had been born to serve and had been following through the mists of childhood and boyhood, a symbol of the artist forging anew in his workshop out of the sluggish matter of the earth a new soaring impalpable imperishable being?" (P168-69)

The "unsubstantial image" of beauty which he had sought even "in the mists of childhood and boyhood" now becomes the object of the artistic mission: Stephen will create beauty "out of the sluggish matter of the earth." And even as he contemplates this seemingly foreordained task, his "premonition" about someday meeting an image of beauty, "in the real world . . . without any overt act of his," is fulfilled: "A girl stood before him in midstream,

[2] Hugh Kenner writes of Stephen's "flirtation with Christ" in *Dublin's Joyce* (London, 1955), pp. 129-31. Mr. Kenner sees Stephen as torn between the Bride of Christ and the Whore of Babylon.

alone and still, gazing out to sea. She seemed like one whom magic had changed into the likeness of a strange and beautiful seabird. Her long slender bare legs were delicate as a crane's and pure save where an emerald trail of seaweed had fashioned itself as a sign upon the flesh. Her thighs, fuller and softhued as ivory, were bared almost to the hips where the white fringes of her drawers were like featherings of soft white down. Her slateblue skirts were kilted boldly about her waist and dovetailed behind her. Her bosom was as a bird's soft and slight, slight and soft as the breast of some darkplumaged dove. But her long fair hair was girlish: and girlish, and touched with the wonder of mortal beauty, her face" (P171). The salient fact about this beautiful passage is that it is quite sexless, for all its bared legs and thighs and drawers.[3] In addition to describing the girl as a graceful bird—a seabird, a crane, a dove—Joyce reminds the reader of the passionless, mystical nature of Stephen's ideal of beauty by interweaving religious imagery with the bird imagery. Her legs are "pure," save for one "sign upon the flesh"; her "ivory" thighs bring to mind again the Tower of Ivory; and one need not explicate the importance of the dove in Christian symbolism. Three colors predominate: ivory flesh, blue skirts, "fair" yellow hair; these are the Virgin's colors. Surely the effect of this sexless, passionless, religious imagery is to reaffirm that Stephen's constant quest is for an ideal, unsubstantial, extraterrestrial beauty, a beauty which henceforth is to be the guiding force of his art. "Heavenly God!" is the silent cry of Stephen's soul—and the appeal to otherworldly powers seems appropriate. "Her image had passed into his soul for ever and no word had broken the holy silence of

[3] Cf. Kristian Smidt, *James Joyce and the Cultic Use of Fiction* (Oxford, 1955), p. 40, for a further analysis of the religious imagery of this episode. As Robert Scholes and Richard M. Kain have shown in their *The Workshop of Daedalus* (Evanston, 1965), pp. 255-81, the influence on the *Portrait* of the mystical aestheticism of such writers as Pater and D'Annunzio was considerable.

his ecstasy" (P172). Truly "a wild angel had appeared to him," for she is described in superhuman terms. His quest appears fulfilled; it will now be his mission not simply to seek beauty but to bring beauty into the world.

Stephen formulates an aesthetic creed quite naturally out of his obsession with beauty. This nascent poet's definition of art constitutes his justification, to himself and to others, of his own aesthetic longings. With the help of certain passages from Aristotle and Aquinas, he attempts to prove that beauty alone must be the object of art; the artist himself becomes a priest of beauty, who transforms the matter of life into beauty even as the priest of the Church changes bread and wine into the body and blood of Christ. In at least one passage free from the encumbrances of scholastic diction, Stephen propounds his definition of art: "To speak of these things and to try to understand their nature and, having understood it, to try slowly and humbly and constantly to express, to press out again, from the gross earth or what it brings forth, from sound and shape and colour which are the prison gates of our soul, an image of the beauty we have come to understand— that is art" (P206-207). The beauty to which Stephen thinks that art, including his own potential art, must be dedicated is still the cool, sexless beauty of Eileen and Mercedes and the wading, dovelike girl. For it is a "static" beauty, one which does not excite desire; neither does it move the beholder toward an emotional enthusiasm for itself, but rather causes an immediate apprehension and comprehension of beauty, the image of truth (P207). Stephen rejects any art which excites desire or loathing because such art neither serves nor reflects the "unsubstantial image" of beauty for which he has been searching since a child, the image which he now feels certain is truth itself: "Plato, I believe, said that beauty is the splendour of truth. I don't think that it has a meaning but the true and the beautiful are akin" (P208).

Stephen's rejection of formal religion has not made of him a sensualist but the reverse: an apostle of a lofty concept of beauty, an ascetic aesthete, whose long-nurtured love of undefiled beauty has now become the focus of his ambitions as an artist.[4] Joyce provides a sample of Stephen's poetry, a villanelle which begins,

> Are you not weary of ardent ways,
> Lure of the fallen seraphim?
> Tell no more of enchanted days.

The most striking thing about this poem, whatever its artistic merits, is its religious imagery, an imagery intended to serve the theme of a rejection of the flesh. Lustful thoughts of a girl awakening from sleep, "radiant, warm, odorous and lavishlimbed," incite Stephen to composition, but the poem itself is a call to chastity, intensified by religious symbols:

> Our broken cries and mournful lays
> Rise in one eucharistic hymn.
> Are you not weary of ardent ways?
>
> While sacrificing hands upraise
> The chalice flowing to the brim,
> Tell no more of enchanted days.
>
> (P223)

Though it constitutes an appeal to a woman, the poem conforms to Stephen's aesthetic specifications: it is *static*, for its language is intended to cause a direct apprehension of beauty, not to excite either desire or loathing. Its languid

---

[4] In his "Stephen Dedalus, Poet or Esthete?" *PMLA*, LXXIX (September 1964), 484-89, Robert Scholes contends that the villanelle marks Stephen's poetic birth and the end of his aestheticism. The poem seems to me mannered, precious, and aesthetic in the negative sense. In his *Workshop of Daedalus*, pp. 255-63, Mr. Scholes places Stephen's poem against the relevant background of such late Victorian poets as Ernest Dowson and Francis Thompson. But like his contemporaries Ezra Pound and T. S. Eliot, Joyce broke away from the affectations of this sort of writing.

syllables contribute to its static atmosphere, and its religious imagery reveals how close the world of Eileen, Mercedes, the dovelike girl, and the "unsubstantial image" is to the world of religion. The cult of the Virgin has simply given way to the cult of the virginal. A thin line indeed separates the chanting of litanies to the Tower of Ivory, House of Gold, Star of the Sea from the desire which Stephen confesses in his diary, "to press in my arms the loveliness which has not yet come into the world" (P251). Stephen has cast off the yoke of Catholic dogma, but the supernal purity of his aesthetic concepts—so long fermenting within him before being articulated as theory—would hardly make a choirboy blush.

Partly because Joyce himself appears to have held to Stephen's aesthetic tenets for a time, many readers and critics have taken these tenets as Joycean gospel and have even attempted to apply them to Joyce's later works.[5] The assumption that Joyce's artistic concerns were primarily aesthetic may in fact have been partly responsible for the enormous outpouring of highly technical scholarship on Joyce, scholarship unrelated to any possible world-view or moral vision in Joyce's writings: if one accepts Stephen's aesthetic theory as Joyce's, then Joyce's artistic purpose cannot be moral; his conscience cannot play a significant role in his art. Stephen's theory dissociates art from life.[6] The kind of art which he advocates is as remote from everyday existence as the kingdom of heaven and in fact bears many of the characteristics of that elusive domain. And Stephen's restrictive theory applies to so small a portion of the literature of the Western world that one would marvel at the narrowness of Joyce's taste had he subscribed to it. The lyrics of Shelley, Coleridge, and Keats

[5] Cf. two interesting criticisms of the theory: William York Tindall, *A Reader's Guide to James Joyce* (New York, 1959), pp. 94ff., and S. L. Goldberg, *The Classical Temper* (London, 1961), pp. 41-91.
[6] See Tindall, *A Reader's Guide*, pp. 95ff., for a similar view of the theory but a different view of Joycean morality.

are presumably art by Stephen's standards, but *Gulliver's Travels* certainly is not. Nor can a great many masterpieces be said to induce Stephen's description of proper aesthetic appreciation: "the luminous silent stasis of esthetic pleasure, a spiritual state very like to that cardiac condition which the Italian physiologist Luigi Galvani . . . called the enchantment of the heart" (P213). None of Joyce's own works, moreover, with the exception of the early poems, conforms to Stephen's theory.

It remains true, however, that very early in his literary life Joyce appears to have formulated Stephen's aesthetics for himself. The central propositions of the theory may be found in his notebooks of around 1903, and often the phrases are identical to Stephen's, as in this excerpt: "Art is the human disposition of sensible or intelligible matter for an aesthetic end" (CW145). This precept is the heart of Stephen's theory, even if it seems more appropriate to Oscar Wilde than to Joyce. Indeed, resemblances between Stephen's aestheticism and the art for art's sake movement of the eighties and nineties are obvious enough in the search for the beautiful; in the scorn of bourgeois society; in the love of the languorous, the self-conscious, the elegantly eccentric; even in Stephen's (and Joyce's) walking-stick. Joyce's notebook suggests that some strength for his rebellion against ordinary Irish life came to him from the example of the irreverent Wilde and his associates, who insisted that the only bad book was a badly written one. Like Stephen, Joyce in these notebooks identifies the beautiful as the end of all art, tragic or comic. The reader or audience must be moved neither toward desire nor toward loathing (CW144). The mingled loathing and sympathy one feels toward Shakespeare's villains—these emotions and the perceptions they might inspire are irrelevant and improper to art.

In an early essay on James Clarence Mangan (1902), Joyce speaks of the proper realm of poetry in a vein con-

sistent with Stephen's otherworldly aesthetics. "Poetry,"
Joyce writes, "even when apparently most fantastic, is
always a revolt against artifice, a revolt, in a sense, against
actuality. It speaks of what seems fantastic and unreal to
those who have lost the simple intuitions which are the
tests of reality" (CW81). The intuitions to which Joyce
refers are those apprehensions of beauty which in his
aesthetics are the essence of art. Although it is a revolt
against "actuality," beauty may yet be found within or
without the individual, in the life around us or in the
human soul: "Beauty, the splendour of truth, is a gracious
presence when the imagination contemplates intensely the
truth of its own being or the visible world" (CW83). Presumably, then, Joyce was uttering his own sentiments
when he permitted Stephen, in a draft of the *Portrait*, to
say of the artist, "He alone is capable of absorbing in himself the life that surrounds him and of flinging it abroad
again amid planetary music" (SH80). True art was to resound with the mystical harmony of the spheres.

Still further evidence of Joyce's early commitment to
Stephen's aesthetics appears in *Chamber Music*.[7] These
poems of the apprentice artist constitute Joycean attempts
at planetary music, at the capturing of the beautiful in
words, as in poem XI:

> Bid adieu, adieu, adieu,
> > Bid adieu to girlish days,
> Happy love is come to woo
> > Thee and woo thy girlish ways—

[7] These poems were undoubtedly written before 1904, when Joyce
met Nora. Joyce's own view of the poems as expressed in a letter to
Nora of 21 August 1909, quoted below in Chapter II, suggests that
William York Tindall's reading of the poems is over-ingenious. Mr.
Tindall, in his edition of *Chamber Music* (New York, 1954), finds
the poems full of the double-entendre characteristic of *Ulysses* and
the *Wake*. Joyce no doubt saw the pun of chamber music/chamber
pot, but only after he had written and titled his verses. For a more
plausible reading of the poems, see James R. Baker, "Joyce's *Chamber Music*: The Exile of the Heart," *Arizona Quarterly*, xv (Winter
1959), 349-56.

The zone that doth become thee fair,
The snood upon thy yellow hair.

When thou has heard his name upon
    The bugles of the cherubim
Begin thou softly to unzone
    Thy girlish bosom unto him
And softly to undo the snood
    That is the sign of maidenhood.

Not desire, nor loathing, but a static apprehension of the beautiful is at least the intention of these rather precious lines by the young Joyce. The poem is an epithalamium, and so chaste is its conception of sexuality that even cherubim make a discreet appearance. Its archaic language ("zone," "snood") adds to an air of otherworldliness; it might have been inserted into the *Portrait* as an example of Stephen's cult of the virginal. And a passage from Stephen's essay in *Stephen Hero* serves nicely as a comment on the poem: "Here the imagination has contemplated intensely the truth of the being of the visible world and . . . beauty, the splendour of truth, has been born" (*SH*80).

Thus an impressive lot of evidence suggests that Joyce embraced Stephen's theory and even put it into practice in *Chamber Music*. But if he accepted it at all, Joyce accepted Stephen's aesthetic theory for a time only. He held to it most probably while he was writing *Chamber Music* and perhaps during the period of *Stephen Hero* as well. But by the time he was engaged on the mature version of the *Portrait* and on *Dubliners*, he had discarded the theory as quite inadequate, as irrelevant to the moral concerns of his works.[8] Only if beauty can be taken loosely as a metaphor for the unity of a work of art can Joyce be said to have accepted Stephen's theory. And beauty does not mean

---

[8] Joyce was probably never as thorough an aesthete as Stephen but exaggerated his attitudes somewhat for the sake of vividness and drama. Joyce differed from Stephen at least in permitting the ugly to be included in an aesthetically coherent work of art (see *CW*147-48).

⟨   13   ⟩

only that to Stephen. To him the word *beauty* connotes all of the otherworldliness, indeed all of the escapism of his youthful quest for an unsubstantial image.

But merely because Joyce rejected beauty as the sole end of art, it would be a mistake to infer that Joyce therefore abandoned beauty itself as an ineffable ideal. The *Portrait* certainly does not damn Stephen Dedalus for his worship of ethereal beauty. Joyce himself did not—and probably did not want to—eradicate all traces of his youthful frame of mind. He continued to be drawn toward the spiritual, the transcendent, the ideal. But unlike Stephen he refused to shrink from the grimmer sides of life, confronting them in his mature writings and giving his conscience voice in so doing. He began by providing escape for his spirit in the romantic form of *Chamber Music*, but he went on to mirror even the most unpleasant truths in *Dubliners*. That plain-spoken group of stories is proof enough of Joyce's rejection of merely Dedalian aesthetics.

· 2 ·

Dubliners can hardly be said to exemplify Stephen's sort of static art. Apart from one's appreciation of their harmonious form, the stories excite not merely loathing but disgust, revulsion, and, far from an "enchantment of the heart," a disenchantment with the Emerald Isle. The point of view of the book is not so obscure as that of the *Portrait*, and *Dubliners* serves as an enlightening introduction to Joyce's detached view of Stephen Dedalus and of his countrymen. *Dubliners* is perhaps the most overt fictional manifestation of Joyce's conscience.

The Dubliners who populate these stories are of two main types: the perverse and the paralyzed. The former include a dissolute priest; a masturbating homosexual; a mother who deals with morality "as a cleaver deals with meat"; a father who beats his son; and a lower-class gigolo. The paralyzed among the Dubliners are those who, though morally well-intentioned, have not the strength of will to extricate themselves from the slough of despond which is Dublin. Through sheer inertia, they allow themselves to be held back from the escape for which they long. Little Tommy Chandler is typical of the paralyzed. He dreams of writing poetry but "he felt how useless it was to struggle against fortune, this being the burden of wisdom which the ages had bequeathed to him" (D71). Joyce's heavily ironic use of "wisdom" is unmistakable in that context. Later, one of the central themes of all the stories is articulated in terms of Tommy Chandler: "There was no doubt about it: if you wanted to succeed you had to go away. You could do nothing in Dublin" (D73). But instead little Tommy Chandler escapes only vicariously through the wild tales of his traveling friend, the sottish Ignatius Gallaher, and unwittingly takes out his frustrations on his baby boy, only to crumple with remorse. "He was a prisoner for life" (D84)—like so many other Dubliners; like the girl Eveline, who cannot run away with her lover because she is "passive, like a helpless animal" (D48).

Helpless animals: in writing about them, Joyce gives no hint of a static, unsubstantial image of beauty. The stories strike the emotions with moral force. We recoil as the "gallant" gigolo, Corley, displays with pride the gold coin he has gotten with his labors. In "Grace" another "helpless animal," this time a drunkard, is raised from the ooze of a lavatory floor to the exalted atmophere of a cathedral, where a Jesuit preaches salvation in ambiguously commercial terms. Joyce's Dubliners appear unusually deficient in moral fiber. One doubts that so hopeless, helpless a group could possibly be representative of its native city. Yet Joyce himself seemed sure: "I call the series *Dubliners*," he said, "to betray the soul of that hemiplegia or paralysis which many consider a city."[9] To those who would ques-

9 Letter to C. P. Curran, July 1904, *Letters*, ɪ, 55.

⟨ 15 ⟩

tion the prevalence of sordidness, the emphasis on moral
failure and weakness in *Dubliners*, Joyce himself answers,
"It is not my fault that the odour of ashpits and old weeds
and offal hangs round my stories. I seriously believe that
you will retard the course of civilization in Ireland by preventing the Irish people from having one good look at
themselves in my nicely polished looking-glass."[10] This
remark was directed to a publisher who had complained
about the negative emphasis in *Dubliners*.

Joyce wrote these stories not with any idea of finding
beauty in the gross matter of the earth, but from a desire
to lay bare the soul of a culture which he considered
morally vacuous. "My intention," he wrote, again to a publisher, "was to write a chapter in the moral history of my
country and I chose Dublin for the scene because that city
seemed to me the centre of paralysis."[11] In the last and
finest of the *Dubliners* stories, Joyce turns from this extreme sort of paralysis to the more subtle inertia of a Dublin Christmas party. The occasion is the "annual dance"
given by three spinsters, the Misses Morkan, at their home,
and several elements of Dublin life are present. Although
the atmosphere is redolent with the accoutrements of hospitality—a fat goose, ham, beef, jellies, jams, custard,
sweets, nuts, fruits, port, sherry, and "three squads of
bottles of stout and ale and minerals"—this same atmosphere loses most of its charm if one takes the simple pre-
caution of reading the story on a full stomach.[12] For any-

[10] Letter to Grant Richards, 23 June 1906, *ibid.*, I, 63-64.
[11] Letter to Grant Richards, 5 May 1906, *ibid.*, II, 134.
[12] Richard Ellmann, in his *James Joyce* (New York, 1959), pp. 252-
53, seems to suggest that Joyce praises Irish hospitality in "The
Dead" partly by way of making amends for being so rough on Ireland elsewhere. Mr. Ellmann also appears to identify Gabriel with
Joyce, Gretta with Nora. There are some parallels, but the biographical fallacy may be at work here in slighting the changes Joyce
wrought on life when he translated it into art. Gabriel surely lacks
Joyce's openly defiant spirit; and if his insensitivity to Gretta is an
autobiographical touch, then the story is self-satire. In a letter to
Stanislaus of 25 September 1906, Joyce considered the possibility of

one who does not care a great deal for talk about the weather, about the omission of women from church choirs, about whether Freddy Malins will turn up drunk, or about whether the singers in Dublin were better in the old days—anyone who cares little for such prattle finds the party tedious in the extreme. Mr. Browne, a boorish character whom Joyce displays at great length, epitomizes the story's aura of enervating vacuity with his reply to Miss Julia's concern over a pudding's not being brown enough: " 'Well, I hope, Miss Morkan,' said Mr. Browne, 'that I'm brown enough for you because, you know, I'm all brown.' " (D200).

The party in "The Dead," then, is a party of the meta-phorically dead. These dead Dubliners have contracted what Joyce identifies as the fatal Irish disease, paralysis; and into their midst steps a man who himself is victim-ized by Irish pathology but who considers himself some-how separate from or above his fellow sufferers. Like a few of the characters in the other stories—Tommy Chandler, Eveline, and, most notably, the boy in "Araby" who bears his "chalice safely through a crowd of foes"—Gabriel Con-roy senses that he must extricate himself from the Dublin morass. But he cannot goad himself to the task. Joyce makes clear Gabriel Conroy's mental dissociation from his holiday surroundings; Joyce also makes clear Gabriel's inability to make a clean break with Dublin. Gabriel en-joys music but the piece which Mary Jane plays at the party "had no melody for him." Tedium hangs heavily upon him. Drearily he turns to the window: "How cool it must be

---

being more generous to Irish hospitality and the beauty of the Irish countryside, but he concluded characteristically: "And yet I know how useless these reflections are. For were I to rewrite the book . . . I am sure I should find again what you call the Holy Ghost sitting in the ink bottle and the perverse devil of my literary conscience sitting on the hump of my pen." *Letters*, II, 166. In other words, his natural bent was moralistic. For a fuller treatment than I can afford here, see Jack B. Ludwig's excellent analysis in his *Stories British and American* (Cambridge, Mass., 1953), pp 387-91.

outside! How pleasant it would be to walk out alone, first along by the river and then out by the park! The snow would be lying on the branches of the trees and forming a bright cap on the top of the Wellington Monument. How much more pleasant it would be there than at the supper table!" (D192) But Gabriel does not have the will to leave this place. He too is paralyzed into acquiescence, though in a moment of desperation he blurts out to the nationalistic Miss Ivors, " 'O, to tell you the truth . . . I'm sick of my own country, sick of it!'

" 'Why?' asked Miss Ivors.

"Gabriel did not answer for his retort had heated him" (D189). In fact Gabriel does not answer because an occasional outburst is all he will allow himself. Instead of acting upon his rebellious impulses, he himself becomes the focal point of the evening's attention as he delivers a foolish after-dinner speech in praise of Irish hospitality: "I feel more strongly with every recurring year that our country has no tradition which does it so much honour and which it should guard so jealously as that of its hospitality." And so on: "As long as this one roof shelters the good ladies aforesaid . . . the tradition of genuine warmhearted courteous Irish hospitality, which our forefathers handed down to us and which we in turn must hand down to our descendants, is still alive among us" (D203).

We have all, to our mutual chagrin, sat through such speeches. Its tedious, all too familiar tone, its trite appeal to tradition, its windy and cliché-larded rhetoric—all combine to make a mockery of whatever sentiment it might express. Obviously Gabriel Conroy need not stoop to such oratory. He is evidently a man of some talent and sensitivity; he does not feel a part of this wearisome gathering. But on he drones, dwelling now upon those Dubliners "gone beyond recall" whom the supposedly living Dubliners still cherish in memory, but advising with painful obviousness that "we all of us have living duties and living affec-

tions which claim, and rightly claim, our strenuous endeavors" (D204).

Gabriel Conroy's reference to the living and the dead
evokes the central question posed by this story: "Which are
the living, which the dead?" In a metaphorical sense the
Dubliners gathered at this party, like the Dubliners scattered throughout the other fourteen stories, are dead, their
vitality stilled by hemiplegia of the soul.[13] But the first part
of that question is not answered until Gabriel's wife, Gretta,
is moved by the strains of a melancholy song—

> "O, the rain falls on my heavy locks
> And the dew wets my skin,
> My babe lies cold . . ."

—and then, alone later in a hotel room with Gabriel, recalls
that song and falls upon the bed in tears. When Gabriel
learns that the song has brought back to Gretta memories
of Michael Furey, he sees himself for what he is, "a ludicrous figure, acting as a pennyboy for his aunts, a nervous,
well-meaning sentimentalist, orating to vulgarians and
idealising his own clownish lusts" (D220). He knows that
he can never mean to Gretta what the dead Michael Furey
means to her, and Gabriel realizes that he himself is really
dead, he who has never loved, who has "never felt like that
himself towards any woman, but . . . [knows] that such a
feeling must be love" (D223).

The image of Michael Furey which haunts Gretta's mind
is of a mystically beautiful kind. She remembers his delicate singing of "The Lass of Aughrim"; his dark, expressive
eyes; his standing in the rain beneath a dripping tree, only
to see her. "I think he died for me," she says (D220). Hers
is a poetic memory, notably devoid of lust. It contrasts
significantly with Gabriel's sexual craving for her: "his

[13] See Kenner, *Dublin's Joyce*, pp. 62-68, for the same point made
differently, although Mr. Kenner places no evident emphasis on the
Joycean value of Gretta's (and Stephen's) devotion to chaste love
and beauty.

arms were trembling with desire to seize her and only the stress of his nails against the palms of his hands held the wild impulse of his body in check. . . . He was in such a fever of rage and desire . . . the dull fires of his lust began to glow angrily in his veins" (D215, 217, 219). He admits to himself that he has never loved any woman, that the chaste passion of Gretta for her dead lover is lamentably beyond his capabilities. "His own identity was fading out into a grey impalpable world" (D223). Ironically the dead Michael Furey is a more vital figure than the metaphorically dead Gabriel Conroy. Gretta's image of beauty lives in a way which Gabriel cannot.

The resemblance between Gretta's image of beauty and Stephen Dedalus' own multiple images—Eileen, Mercedes, the dovelike girl—is clear and important. Gretta and Stephen both shelter their secret images of beauty within themselves as talismans against the outside world. Gretta's talisman protects her from the paralyzing dullness of her life with Gabriel; Stephen's not only shields him from the coarseness of everyday life in Dublin but will also, he believes, form the basis of his art. Gretta and Stephen are kindred in that each has kept alive the life of the spirit by sheltering an ideal of chaste beauty.

But as the satiric force of *Dubliners* shows, Joyce considered an ideal of beauty more a means of preserving sensitivity and purity of spirit than a sound basis for art. Joyce's own art was directed far more at a revelation of the sordid than the beautiful in life: as he said himself, it was a "general indictment" of Ireland, "a chapter of the moral history of my country."[14] In *Dubliners* he exposed what he felt to be some of the more insidious elements of corruption in Ireland; and he castigated as well those "helpless animals" like Gabriel Conroy—too weak to rebel, to escape. "No one," Joyce asserted in 1907, "who has any

[14] Letter to Stanislaus Joyce, 12 July 1905, *Letters*, ii, 96; letter to Grant Richards, 5 May 1906, *ibid.*, ii, 134.

self-respect stays in Ireland, but flees afar as though from a country that has undergone the visitation of an angered Jove" (*CW*171). Stephen Dedalus may have planned to direct his art toward a purely aesthetic end, but Joyce, for all his aesthetic concern, was by his own admission writing moral satire.

Still, Stephen should not be dismissed as a mere aesthete. His reveries remain to him what Michael Furey is to Gretta, an affirmation of the beautiful and noble capabilities of the human spirit, something to be treasured and preserved, to be carried like a "chalice safely through a crowd of foes." But Joyce's art encompassed the crowd of foes as well as the chalice.

· 3 ·

Stephen's devotion to beauty frees him from weakness and timidity, aids him in his flight from the Church, and is therefore essential to his development as an artist; but some of the effects of this devotion must themselves one day be overcome. It is not that Joyce scorns the chaste, the virginal, the beautiful. Rather, he considers Stephen only half an artist, unable as yet to face life whole. For Joyce begins to establish at an early stage of the *Portrait*, through an oblique kind of authorial commentary, that the very sensitivity which enables Stephen to resist environmental pressures and to shelter within himself a vision of chaste beauty, causes him at the same time to hide from and even to attempt to deny life's baser aspects.

Not only does Stephen try to drench his imagination with the ideal: he is troubled from earliest childhood by a seemingly irreconcilable opposition between the ideal and the actual. Joyce represents him as shocked and dismayed by the ugliness, the bestiality of the life around him and of his own mind. Happening upon the word "Foetus" carved into a student's desk, he imagines a boy, surrounded by his grinning fellows, cutting the word into the wood: "The sudden legend startled his blood . . ." and he hurries away, repelled. One does not ordinarily think of foetus as a particularly disagreeable word, but to Stephen it evokes thoughts which shame him: "But the word and the vision capered before his eyes as he walked back across the quadrangle and towards the college gate. It shocked him to find in the outer world a trace of what he had deemed till then a brutish and individual malady of his own mind. His recent monstrous reveries came thronging into his memory. . . . He had soon given in to them and allowed them to sweep across and abase his intellect, wondering always where they came from, from what den of monstrous images, and always weak and humble towards others, . . . sickened of himself when they had swept over him" (P89-90). Certain aspects of the life around him and within him repel Stephen; he attempts to dismiss these aspects from his mind but is unable to do so. His natural bent is toward contemplation of the beautiful, but often the sordid intrudes: "Aubrey and Stephen had a common milkman and often they drove out in the milkcar to Carrickmines where the cows were at grass. . . . But when autumn came the cows were driven home from the grass: and the first sight of the filthy cowyard at Stradbrook with its foul green puddles and clots of liquid dung and steaming brantroughs sickened Stephen's heart. The cattle which had seemed so beautiful in the country on sunny days revolted him and he could not even look at the milk they yielded" (P63).

Joyce concentrates distasteful elements here—"foul green puddles," "liquid dung," "steaming brantroughs"—deliberately in liquid images. He attributes to Stephen a kind of hydrophobia, a fear and dislike of liquid which varies in significance as the *Portrait* progresses. Liquid often becomes for Stephen—and for Joyce—a gathering metaphor of sordidness, an expansive symbol of the baser elements of life which Stephen detests and attempts to shun. One of his most unpleasant childhood experiences is associated with liquid, the "cold slimy water" of the ditch into which the bully Wells pushes him: "How cold and slimy the water had been! A fellow had once seen a big rat jump into the scum. . . . It was a mean thing to do; all the fellows said it was. . . . That was the way a rat felt, slimy and damp and cold. Every rat had two eyes to look out of. Sleek slimy coats, little little feet tucked up to jump, black shiny eyes to look out of" (P10, 14, 22). The sinister bestiality of these imaginary rats is associated in Stephen's mind with Wells's brutality, with the unpleasantness of the ditch-water, which like liquid dung and foul puddles of the cowyard represents for Stephen the side of life he must try to avoid.

Stephen attempts with great energy to escape these slimy, sordid, liquid aspects of existence. And it is just this attempt which draws Joyce's first clear criticism: he implies the futility of any effort to flee from reality. The sordid must be confronted, accepted if still reviled, understood rather than shunned. Instead, Stephen tries to bring an ideal order into his life, when disorder is bound to overcome him. He has won a literary prize. He is filled with good resolutions. He will bring his life into perfect order, with the help of his prize money. The money runs out; his rules collapse. He can control neither life nor himself: "How foolish his aim had been! He had tried to build a breakwater of order and elegance against the sordid tide of life without him and to dam up . . . the powerful recurrence of the tides within him. Useless. From without as from within the water had flowed over his barriers: their tides began once more to jostle fiercely above the crumbled mole" (P98).

Stephen for a time recognizes his own futile tendency, but so strong are his habits of mind that he persists in his efforts to elude life's fetid waters. Stephen's aim is "foolish," but it is also compelling to him, particularly as an attempt to obliterate the evident opposition between lust and love, the conflict between his worship of beauty and his distaste for the obscene: "A figure that had seemed to him by day demure and innocent came towards him by night through the winding darkness of sleep, her face transfigured by a lecherous cunning, her eyes bright with brutish joy. Only the morning pained him with its dim memory of dark orgiastic riot, its keen and humiliating sense of transgression" (P99). Nothing troubles Stephen more than this intrusion of lust into his vision of pure, sexless beauty—his cult of the virginal. He continues to flee from lust and continues also to be overtaken by it.[15] The Jesuit retreat, with its meditations upon death, judgment, hell and heaven, intensifies to a maximum degree Stephen's already poignant feelings of guilt, as he comes to despise even his own genitals: "What a horrible thing! Who made it to be like that, a bestial part of the body able to understand bestially and desire bestially? Was that then he or an inhuman thing moved by a lower soul than his soul? His soul sickened at the thought of a torpid snaky life feeding itself out of the tender marrow of his life and fattening upon the slime of lust. O why was that so? O why?" (P139-40) Struggle though he might, Stephen cannot, as Joyce makes clear, evade the "slime of lust," the "sordid tide of life." Such an aim is "foolish" because futile.[16]

In attempting to banish lust, Stephen is, of course, following the teachings of the Church as well as heeding his own sickened conscience. The Jesuits who are his mentors warn him against any submission to sexuality for its own sake as contrary to the will of God and, if persisted in, as likely to result in eternal damnation. But Stephen's aversion to the "slime of lust" outlasts any adherence to Roman

[15] Kenner, *Dublin's Joyce*, pp. 130-31, discusses this opposition in a somewhat different way, arguing that Stephen is not attempting to shut out the lustful but is torn with equal force between two poles.

[16] Tindall, *A Reader's Guide*, p. 93, writes that Stephen's problem is "to find someone who, at once Virgin and whore, pleasingly embodies the actual and the ideal. Mrs. Bloom does that." But Joyce never reconciled the ideal and the actual. And Molly Bloom a virgin?

Catholic doctrine: even after Stephen has left the Church, even after he has determined that the Church is too restrictive for him to remain within it, he continues in precisely the same way to attempt to erect barriers against the sordid and ineluctable tides of life. The overtly religious imagery of the villanelle which Stephen writes in Chapter V has already been cited as evidence of the consistent purity of Stephen's outlook. The manner in which Joyce pointedly comments on Stephen's poetic composition has not, however, been considered as yet. Joyce's implied judgments are highly significant, for they inform the reader that Stephen, though he has left the Church, still persists in his energetic efforts to evade sordid aspects of reality.

Joyce begins by establishing beyond the doubt of any careful reader that Stephen is trying to hide from ordinary life: "The full morning light had come. No sound was to be heard: but he knew that all around him life was about to awaken in common noises, hoarse voices, sleepy prayers. Shrinking from that life he turned towards the wall, making a cowl of the blanket and staring at the great overblown scarlet flowers of the tattered wallpaper. He tried to warm his perishing joy in their scarlet glow, imagining a roseway from where he lay upwards to heaven all strewn with scarlet flowers. Weary! Weary! He too was weary of ardent ways" (P221-22). By shrinking from common life, Stephen makes of himself a recluse: the "cowl" with which Stephen hoods himself signifies his still foolish evasions. Tattered wallpaper becomes for Stephen a "roseway" to heaven, but through Joyce's subtle commentary the reader is able to see that it remains tattered wallpaper, imprinted not with roses but with "great overblown scarlet flowers." We are made aware that Stephen is deceiving himself even about the very nature of his commonplace surroundings. And when he goes on to create a religious hymn out of an erotic dream, his self-deceiving pattern of thought becomes even more evident. "A glow of desire kindled . . . his soul and fired and fulfilled all his body," but soon he transforms this insistent glow of desire into an appeal for chastity, a denigration of the "lure of the fallen seraphim":

> *While sacrificing hands upraise*
> *The chalice flowing to the brim,*
> *Tell no more of enchanted days.* (P223)

Here Joyce makes new use of water imagery, as the waters of common life are transformed into the insubstantial: "her nakedness . . . enfolded him like water with a liquid life: and like a cloud of vapour or like waters circumfluent in space the liquid letters of speech, symbols of the element of mystery, flowed forth over his brain" (P223). The "element of mystery" drives sordidness from the mind. Seraphic rhythms and sounds lead Stephen away from any direct confrontation of lust, and his erotic dream is metamorphosed into a hymn, just as his tattered wallpaper had been transformed by his imagination into a heavenly roseway. Stephen is represented as having donned the "cowl" of self-deception, and he has made of it his mode of thought. He has in fact made this obscuring cowl the basis of his aesthetic theory, which would exclude the sordid tide of life from art. Ugliness seeks persistently to invade his thoughts, but again and again he shunts it aside, almost as a zealous parent snatches pornography from a child. He imagines "the poxfouled wenches of the taverns and young wives that, gaily yielding to their ravishers, clipped and clipped again," but he admonishes himself for these lustful contemplations, chiding inwardly, "That was not the way to think of her. It was not even the way in which he thought of her. Could his mind then not trust itself?" (P233). Indeed it cannot, or should not: it exhibits a persistent fondness both for hiding from life's unpleasant side and for building from hellish stuff a heavenly vision.

Joyce emphasizes Stephen's aptitude for self-deception

by the technique of juxtaposition. Romantic, Pateresque passages are deliberately, pointedly alternated with physically repulsive passages. The appearance of the dovelike, wading girl is generally thought to be not only the most beautiful passage in the *Portrait* but also the turning point in Stephen's growth as an artist: the girl represents the ultimate call to the life of art, the rejection of the deadly entanglements of family, nation, and Church; and the chapter of which she is the dominant figure ends on this romantic note: "A rim of the young moon cleft the pale waste of sky like the rim of a silver hoop embedded in grey sand; and the tide was flowing in fast to the land with a low whisper of her waves, islanding a few last figures in distant pools." Read aloud, these words slip with liquid ease from the tongue; their tone and the images which they evoke form together a paean to beauty, and the last word, "pools," emitted like the low moaning of the wind, fixes in the mind the luminous wetness of that sandy shore. But Joyce, in the passage immediately following, abruptly roots up the memory of those moonlit pools by substituting for them a different kind of pool: "He drained his third cup of watery tea to the dregs and set to chewing the crusts of fried bread that were scattered near him, staring into the dark pool of the jar. The yellow dripping had been scooped out like a boghole and the pool under it brought back to his memory the dark turfcoloured water of the bath in Clongowes" (P174). No moonlit pools but the greasy pool in a jar of dripping is thrust under Stephen's and our eyes. The mention of Clongowes indicates that Joyce continues here to employ water-imagery to restate his central theme. The effect is not to destroy altogether the beauty of Stephen's epiphany by the sea but rather to reemphasize the coexistence of ugliness with beauty. Through this juxtaposition of images Joyce reminds us that a vision of beauty is only a partial vision of life.

Stephen does not accept stoically the double nature of existence which Joyce tries to make clear to his readers. Instead he attempts to close his mind to all fearful or repulsive elements. As he trudges down a Dublin lane, he hears "a mad nun screeching in the nun's madhouse beyond the wall.

"–Jesus! O Jesus! Jesus!

"He shook the sound out of his ears by an angry toss of his head and hurried on . . . He drove their echoes even out of his heart with an execration: but, as he walked down the avenue and felt the grey morning light falling about him through the dripping trees and smelt the strange wild smell of the wet leaves and bark, his soul was loosed of her miseries" (P175-76). Stephen will not allow his mind to dwell upon the screeching of a mad nun because such agony is incompatible with his search for and obsession with beauty: yet the nun screeches. And just as Joyce balanced moonlit pools with a pool of grease, so he continues to temper Stephen's imagination with reality: Stephen's "morning walk across the city had begun; and he foreknew that as he passed the sloblands of Fairview he would think of the cloistral silverveined prose of Newman; that as he walked along the North Strand Road, glancing idly at the windows of the provision shops, he would recall the dark humour of Guido Cavalcanti and smile; that as he went by Baird's stone cutting works in Talbot Place the spirit of Ibsen would blow through him like a keen wind, a spirit of wayward boyish beauty; and that passing a grimy marine dealer's shop beyond the Liffey he would repeat the song of Ben Jonson which begins:

"*I was not wearier where I lay*" (P176).

As this passage shows, Stephen tries to escape the common life, to don his now familiar cowl of self-deception by thinking of "cloistral" prose. The ordinariness of a stone cutting works causes him to fill his mind with the romantic poetry of the early Ibsen, and at a shop he repeats the rhythms of Jonson. Notably Stephen does not think of the later Ibsen—the rather icy, rational Ibsen of *Ghosts* or *An Enemy of the People*—but of the earlier, romantic Ibsen; nor does he think of Ben Jonson the satirist, but rather of Jonson the lyricist, author of "The Vision of Delight," from which the song is taken. Stephen shuts out a part of these writers, just as he banishes a part of life; and one is reminded of his restrictive aesthetic theory, which cannot be made to include *Dubliners*.

Joyce in fact undercuts Stephen's aesthetic theory even in the exposition of it. Just after Stephen renders into the clearest language his definition of art as an image of beauty, Joyce remarks that Stephen and his companion, Lynch, "had reached the canal bridge and, turning from their course, went on by the trees. A crude grey light, mirrored in the sluggish water, and a smell of wet branches over their heads seemed to war against the course of Stephen's thought" (P207). The very setting or surroundings of Stephen's aesthetic proclamations "war against" them and underline their inadequacy. If art is to be an image of beauty it must avoid, even as Stephen attempts to avoid, "crude grey light" and "sluggish water," the hideous screeching of a nun, and the dullness of a stone cutting works. As Stephen continues to expound upon the beautiful and the duty of art to represent it, "a long dray laden with old iron [comes] round the corner of sir Patrick Dun's hospital covering the end of Stephen's speech with the harsh roar of jangled and rattling metal" (P209). A jangling and rattling reality intrudes upon Stephen's aesthetic and, thus juxtaposed, undercuts it. Again and again material surroundings "war against the course of Stephen's thought" and deflate it.

Lynch, the coprophagous companion to whom Stephen addresses his discourse, objects to Stephen's thesis at every turn. Not the logic of Lynch's arguments, however, but their illogicality, their banality and, most of all, the bumptious fatuity of their speaker mock Stephen's own arguments. While Stephen ascends toward the heavenly spheres, Lynch whinnies, guffaws, rubs his hands over his groin, admits that he once ate cow dung, speaks of "flaming fat devils of pigs," and brags of having inscribed his name upon the backside of the Venus of Praxiteles. In effect Joyce here expands his already familiar technique of juxtaposition: Lynch himself is contrasted with Stephen. Joyce establishes a kind of counterpoint between Stephen's supernal definitions of art and Lynch's crudely earthbound definitions of life—common, ordinary life, which the monkish Stephen attempts to avoid in thought and in art. By his very inclusion of Lynch, Joyce is commenting negatively upon Stephen's restrictive aesthetic theory: Lynch is comically loathsome, his eyes "lit by one tiny human point, the window of a shrivelled soul, poignant and selfembittered" (P206). Lynch could not be a part of Stephen's static art, but Joyce pointedly makes him a part of Stephen's life. Stephen addresses him as though he were not present, ignoring his barbs, treating him for the most part as a mute audience; Stephen does not cease discoursing even when Lynch grimaces and says, "If I am to listen to your esthetic philosophy give me at least another cigarette. I don't care about it. I don't even care about women. Damn you and damn everything. I want a job of five hundred a year. You can't get me one" (P207).[17]

A negative judgment on certain aspects of Stephen's behavior need not mean a dismissal of him as a downright detestable young man, nor yet as a "dead" young man. Many critics have condemned Stephen on counts of pride and egoism—and have of course assumed that Joyce con-

[17] For contrasting analyses of Joyce's use of juxtaposition, see Kenner, *Dublin's Joyce*, p. 99; Tindall, *A Reader's Guide*, p. 94; Tindall, *James Joyce, His Way of Interpreting the World* (New York, 1950), p. 17; and Robert S. Ryf, *A New Approach to Joyce* (Berkeley and Los Angeles, 1962), pp. 156-70.

curred in their verdict. But Joyce does not simply make of Stephen a Miltonic Satan and then take the role of God for himself. Stephen's youth is excuse enough for his admitted imperfections; indeed, were he an octogenarian we would be no more justified in condemning him because of certain flaws in his outlook or because he shows signs of an arrogance not uncommon to an artistic temperament. Moreover, Stephen is at least partially conscious of his own deficiencies. He may appear quite sure of himself, quite prideful, but in fact Joyce informs us that "his thinking was a dusk of doubt and selfmistrust . . ." (P177). If he is naively obsessed with beauty and with his own somewhat narrow "lightnings of intuition," it is because those lightnings are "of so clear a splendour that in those moments the world perished about his feet as if it had been fireconsumed" (P177). The world is simply obliterated by his vision—or rather, Stephen thinks it is obliterated. He is unsure. He gazes at birds swirling overhead and questions, "What birds were they? . . . Symbol of departure or of loneliness?" (P225-26). The birds remind him of Thoth, the god of writers, but somehow the god's image appears to him as "a bottlenosed judge in a wig, putting commas into a document which he held at arm's length and he knew that he would not have remembered the god's name but that it was like an Irish oath. It was folly. But was it for this folly that he was about to leave for ever . . . ?" (P225). This comical image of Thoth reminds us that literature, like life, must be filled with folly as well as beauty. Though he does not want to, Stephen is capable at times of seeing life as Joyce sees it, in its duplicity: its nobility and its commonness. Duplicity is probably a better word than duality for the Joycean vision, because duplicity implies something sinister as well as something double; and life to Joyce had something of a sinister quality along with its beauty: poxfouled wenches lurking behind dovelike maids.

Stephen is uncertain, tortured, tormented by self-doubt

and by the sordidness which he is trying to elude. But to his credit he refuses to be paralyzed by the tenuousness of his position. He strikes out boldly. He acts, rather than despairing of action like so many of the immobile characters in *Dubliners*. Anyone who wishes to condemn Stephen for pride or egoism might keep in mind that Joyce's flaccid Dubliners could use a dose of Stephen's pride and egoism. Action often requires a measure of pride. Stephen's aesthetic theory, his self-deceived attempts to see beauty where there may be only cow dung or tattered wallpaper—these are but the first brave if awkward sallies of a fledgling artistic consciousness. Of his initial ideas Stephen himself says, "I need them only for my own use and guidance until I have done something for myself by their light. If the lamp smokes or smells I shall try to trim it. If it does not give light enough I shall sell it and buy another" (P187).

Joyce leaves Stephen at the end of the *Portrait* on the brink of disillusion, a disillusion foreshadowed by Stephen's own self-doubts and by Joyce's subtle criticisms of his protagonist. Though a rebel from the Church, Stephen is really following with religious fervor a tendency marked in him since childhood, when first he worshiped the Madonna and then those multiple personifications of spiritual beauty—Eileen, Mercedes, the wading girl, and even the mysterious E.C. He constructs an aesthetic theory which would exclude from art the loathsome aspects of existence. If his art is to comprehend life, Stephen must confront the motley nature of reality, just as Joyce does in *Dubliners*. He must make room for the wretchedness of life as well as its beauty, just as he must come to accept the existence of lust as well as spiritual love within himself. He cannot continue to transform erotic dreams into religious villanelles, nor to treat the reptilian Lynch as though he didn't exist, nor to turn away from Dublin slums to the silvery prose of Newman. If Joyce himself entertained for a time the aesthetic theory which he attributes to Stephen, he must either have believed in it halfheartedly or soon have rejected the heart of it. *Dubliners* and the *Portrait* can be said ultimately to induce in the reader a static apprehension of beauty if by beauty one means admiration for the aesthetic whole, for balance and unity, for wholeness and harmony. But clearly Stephen means by beauty both an absence of moral content and the showing forth of a loveliness as ethereal as that of the Virgin. Instead, both *Dubliners* and the *Portrait* impart a sense of life's inevitable duplicity. In Gretta's mind, Michael Furey still stands under the dripping tree; but Gabriel Conroy, "in a fever of rage and desire," longs to sully that image with his lust. Stephen has pressed the image of the dovelike girl into his soul forever, but nighttown awaits him still. Joyce's two-sided vision of life is not "balanced" as some critics have claimed, but embattled. Life to Joyce is a war of contraries, balanced only in the sense that neither contrary ever entirely vanquishes the other.

It is not surprising that Joyce tried to prevent his *Chamber Music* from being published.[18] These gentle lyrics might, as has been suggested above, be included in the *Portrait* as further examples of Stephen's verse. But Joyce knew, as Stephen only fitfully suspects, that the beauty of *Chamber Music* represents but a half-truth, but half of life, and surely but half of himself. "I wrote *Chamber Music* as a protest against myself," Joyce once confessed,[19] and he came to feel that as an expression of life and of himself the poems were incomplete, even dishonest, and therefore not fit for publication.[20] By the time Joyce came

[18] See Ellmann, *James Joyce*, p. 270.
[19] Quoted in *ibid.*, pp. 154-55, with reference to the papers of Joyce's first biographer, Herbert Gorman.
[20] Joyce would not have wanted to withhold the poems had they contained the amusing punning which William York Tindall suggests. See note 7 above and the further discussion of Joyce's poetry in Chapter II.

to write the final version of the *Portrait*, he had changed and grown until he could write about his youth with detachment. Stephen's exultant "Welcome, O life!" really means "Welcome, O beauty!" And Joyce himself could by that time not bid life unqualified welcome.

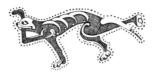

ii. the conscience examined

If the portrait Joyce draws of Stephen is that of an idealist tortured by the persistent intrusions of reality, then it is a self-portrait. Physical details are altered, time sequences rearranged, self-ironies introduced; the compression and exaggeration which translate life into art are brought into play, and as we have seen, Joyce is critical of Stephen's attempts to elude reality. But Stephen's characteristic obsessions and convictions remained Joyce's own. Like Stephen, Joyce nurtured within himself a fragile idealism and, again like Stephen, he was vexed to see his ideals obscured by a depraved environment and sullied by personal lust. Virginal beauty and whorish allure; the prose of Newman and the slums of Dublin; a noble will to escape and a spineless inability to do so: these were the kinds of contradictions and oppositions which occupied Joyce's thoughts. From them he shaped the moral heart of his writing. From his own troubled conscience, to paraphrase Stephen Dedalus, he forged the uncreated conscience of his race.

The only solid justification for this conception of Joyce as an idealist and a moralist must come from Joyce's books themselves. Yet when biographical evidence substantiates this view, it too ought to be considered as an aid to our understanding of the writer's mind. Late in 1909, during two brief business trips to Ireland,[1] Joyce wrote sev-

[1] For background to this period, see Richard Ellmann, *James Joyce* (New York, 1959), pp. 283-318.

eral letters to his wife which clarify his moral values. He reveals himself in these letters as a sharer of Stephen Dedalus' neo-Platonic ideal of chaste love and beauty. If Joyce's early poems are enough in themselves to suggest that he was drawn toward a worship of divinely innocent femininity, these letters expand considerably our awareness of his spiritual affinity with Stephen. In them he indicates that the mood of the poems was not a passing one: that the wading, dovelike girl was sacred to him as well as to his protagonist, and that the unpleasant realities which challenged her existence for Stephen also threatened idols of his own.

It is not necessary to take these letters as definitive Joycean pronouncements in order to admit their considerable value. The letters, it is true, were intended for a single reader and were written under particular circumstances. In this case, however, the fact that the intended reader was Joyce's wife is all the more reason for serious study of the letters. Joyce was ordinarily an extremely cautious correspondent, wary of confiding in others, reluctant to show his hand. Here we find him opening up to an extent unknown in other correspondence. It would be a mistake to lift isolated statements from the letters and to use them indiscriminately to plead a special case. Taken as a whole, however, the letters offer us a window on Joyce's mind.

A still more important reason for considering the correspondence lies in the fact that the sentiments and ideas, the ideals and fears, the hopes and shames which it displays—all these are quite clearly reflected in *Exiles*, in *Ulysses*, and in *Finnegans Wake*. Just as he embodied childhood experiences in the *Portrait*, Joyce appears to have fashioned his later characters partially out of aspects of himself. And perhaps more so than the *Portrait*, the later works display a Joycean fondness for self-satire, even for self-castigation and self-ridicule. The letters to Nora are a clue to Joyce's attitude toward himself and to the artistic use he made of himself.

· I ·

In December of 1909, Joyce wrote his wife about the Christmas gift which he had prepared for her. It was to be a manuscript copy of *Chamber Music*, his early romantic poems, leather-bound, with his own and Nora's initials intertwined on the cover. "Perhaps this book I send you now," he wrote to her, "will outlive both you and me. Perhaps the fingers of some young man or young girl (our children's children) may turn over its parchment leaves reverently when the two lovers whose initials are interlaced on the cover have long vanished from the earth. Nothing will remain then, dearest, of our poor human passion-driven bodies and who can say where the looks that looked on each other through their eyes will then be. I would pray that my soul be scattered in the wind if God would but let me blow softly forever about one strange lonely dark-blue rain-drenched flower in a wild hedge at Aughrim or Oranmore."[2] Joyce gave this copy of *Chamber Music* to his wife as a symbolic gesture. Although he had not yet met Nora when he composed *Chamber Music*, he came to see his wife as the embodiment of the spiritual, passionless love which those poems celebrate. In telling her of his Christmas gift, he distinguishes between physical passion and the beauty of his verses: "Our poor, human passion-driven bodies" will have vanished, while his poetry, a series of hymns in praise of an ethereal kind of love, endures. In another letter Joyce is more specific about the close relationship among Nora, his poetry, and his Stephen-like

[2] Letter to Nora Joyce, 22 December 1909, *Letters*, II, 277-78. Joyce's correspondence with Nora is part of the extensive Joyce Collection at the Cornell University Library. Most of the letters have been published by Richard Ellmann in *ibid.*, II, but my paraphrase, below, of the letter of 2 December 1909 is based directly on the manuscript.

⟨   37   ⟩

ideals of spiritual beauty: "I like to think of you reading my verses (though it took you five years to find them out). When I wrote them I was a strange lonely boy, walking about by myself at night and thinking that some day a girl would love me. But I never could speak to the girls I used to meet at houses. Their false manners checked me at once. Then you came to me. You were not in a sense the girl for whom I had dreamed and written the verses you now find so enchanting. She was perhaps (as I saw her in my imagination) a girl fashioned into a curious grave beauty by the culture of generations before her, the woman for whom I wrote poems like 'Gentle lady' or 'Thou leanest to the shell of night.' But then I saw that the beauty of your soul outshone that of my verses. There was something in you higher than anything I had put into them. And so for this reason the book of verses is for you. It holds the desire of my youth and you, darling, were the fulfillment of that desire."[3]

Again dissociating Nora and his verses from physical passion, Joyce begins this letter by contrasting what he regards as the falseness of prostitutes with the "higher" affection of spiritual love. The girl to whom the poetry is addressed—whose "curious grave beauty" certainly brings to mind Stephen's feminine images—is not Nora, but Nora becomes for Joyce the personification of an even more exalted virtue. To him she is a fragile, melancholy reminder of the evanescence of life, the transcendence of beauty. She becomes his "gentle lady," to whom even these verses seem inadequate:

> Gentle lady, do not sing
> Sad songs about the end of love;
> Lay aside sadness and sing
> How love that passes is enough. . . .[4]

[3] Letter to Nora, 21 August 1909, *ibid.*, II, 236-37.
[4] This is poem xxviii of *Chamber Music*.

Nora is the fulfillment of a passionless kind of desire, an intellectual and spiritual desire which, while devoid of erotic impulse, burns with a flame of its own—as in this passage from a letter to Nora: "Do you know what a pearl is and what an opal is? My soul when you came sauntering to me first through those sweet summer evenings was beautiful but with the pale passionless beauty of a pearl. Your love passed through me and now I feel my mind something like an opal, that is, full of strange uncertain lines and colors, of warm lights and quick shadows and broken music."[5] Nora's love adds the fire of an opal to the passionless beauty of a pearl. But this is not the language of erotic passion; it befits the passion of stained glass or the aesthetic passion which Walter Pater termed a "gemlike flame." The opal burns with light, not erotic fire; and it is Joyce's "mind," not a poetically less precious part of his anatomy, which glows like an opal.

Stephen Dedalus' worship of chaste femininity began with a special devotion to the Blessed Virgin, the Tower of Ivory, and House of Gold, and his cult of the virginal was quite similar in form and spirit to his earlier religious impulses. Joyce's own cult of the virginal here, with Nora as its devotional figure, also bears a strong resemblance to Roman Catholic veneration of the Virgin, and Joyce was no doubt examining his own psychology in creating this aspect of Stephen's idealism. A break from the authority of the Church did not mean a purging of characteristic Catholic habits of mind. At times Joyce relied on explicitly religious material to convey to Nora the spiritual nature of his regard for her, as in a letter of 11 December 1909, written just after a visit to her old room in Dublin: "Yes, I too have felt at moments the burning in my soul of that pure and sacred fire which burns forever on the altar of my love's heart. I could have knelt by that little bed and abandoned myself to a flood of tears. The tears were be-

5 Letter to Nora, 21 August 1909, *Letters*, II, 237.

sieging my eyes as I stood looking at it. I could have knelt and prayed there as the three kings from the east knelt and prayed before the manger in which Jesus lay. They had travelled over deserts and seas and brought their gifts and wisdom and royal trains to kneel before a little new-born child and I had brought my errors and follies and sins and wondering and longing to lay them at the little bed in which a young girl had dreamed of me."[6] Again this love-flame is not that of erotic desire, but a "sacred" one which burns upon an "altar," before which the lover "kneels." So similar to a religious fervor is Joyce's love for Nora that he permits himself the extravagance of comparing her to the Christ Child and himself to the worshipful kings. The emphasis placed upon his own "sins" is in keeping with this Christian analogy. And Joyce was quite conscious of the kinship between his abandoned formal religion and his succeeding spirituality. He knew himself as an apostate who was yet inclined toward Catholic predilections: he was able to say to his wife, "You have been to my young manhood what the idea of the Blessed Virgin was to my boyhood."[7]

The position of one who tries to protect his ideals from contamination by unpleasant reality is always precarious: reality eventually persuades the idealist either to modify his ideals or to lie to himself. Thus Stephen Dedalus, indulging in something close to self-deception, discourses upon aesthetics to the boorish Lynch, turns erotic dreams into religious hymns, and finally tries to elude the sordid tides of life by escaping from Ireland altogether. No doubt Joyce himself had tried similar tactics, but by 1909 he was attempting to come to terms with life directly, not to escape or to turn certain aspects of life into something he knew they were not. Joyce could never bestow his approval indiscriminately; he could never joyously embrace all hu-

[6] *Ibid.*, II, 272-73.
[7] Letter to Nora, 31 August 1909, *ibid.*, II, 242.

man existence. On the contrary, he remained an idealist. Idealism shaped his very nature; ideals influenced his every judgment. In *Stephen Hero* he has Cranly say to Stephen:

"–You idealize everything. . . . You imagine that people are capable of all these . . . all this beautiful imaginary business. They're not. Look at the girls you see every day. Do you think they would understand what you say about love?

"–I don't know, really, said Stephen. I do not idealize the girls I see every day. I regard them as marsupials. . . . But still I must express my nature" (*SH*176). If Stephen, particularly in the *Portrait*, carries his idealism to the extreme of ignoring ugly truths, Joyce himself nevertheless engaged in a constant quarrel with reality–accepting its existence while struggling to transcend it. He believed in what he termed a "higher" element within himself and in his love for Nora. He paid this element frequent homage and regarded it as a standard of spiritual excellence toward which others might do well to strive. He was cynical, however, about the spiritual qualities of his fellow man: "All men are brutes, dearest," he wrote Nora, "but at least in me there is also something higher at times."[8]

Joyce saw clearly that two forces threatened his values: one force came from within himself, the other from the society around him. He felt that Irish society itself was the antithesis of the better parts of his own nature. All his life the Continent represented to him if not a vale of innocence, then at least an escape from the peculiarly Irish forms of moral hypocrisy. Irish deceit was somehow more abhorrent to him than that of any other land. Returning to his native soil in 1909, Joyce was generous with his contempt for Ireland: "I am a shell of a man; my soul is in Trieste. You alone know me and love me. I have been at the theatre with my father and sister–a wretched play, a disgusting

8 Letter to Nora, 11 December 1909, *ibid.*, II, 273

⟨ 41 ⟩

audience. I felt (as I always feel) a stranger in my own country. Yet if you had been beside me I could have spoken into your ears the hatred and scorn I felt burning in my heart. Perhaps you would have rebuked me but you would have understood me. I felt proud to think that my son . . . will always be a foreigner in Ireland, a man speaking another language and bred in a different tradition."[9]

Joyce felt disgust, hatred, and scorn for Ireland because he knew that its moral corruption was a threat to himself. If only Nora were with him, he thought, perhaps her innocence could shield him. He refers to her as though her presence might have protected him from Ireland the way some devout Roman Catholics believe a medallion of the Blessed Virgin can ward off the powers of evil: "I loathe Ireland and the Irish. They themselves stare at me in the street though I was born among them. Perhaps they read my hatred of them in my eyes. I see nothing on every side of me but the image of the adulterous priest and his servant and of sly deceitful women. It is not good for me to come here or to be here. Perhaps if you were with me I would not suffer so much."[10]

Significantly Joyce often chooses to single out sexual offenses as his examples of Irish moral decrepitude. Hypocrisy, to be sure, is his main target when he speaks of adulterous priests and sly deceitful women. But these hypocrites attempt to conceal sexual acts. And in considering the second force which Joyce saw threatening his values—the personal force—one notes that this concern with sex as a moral weakness carries over into Joyce's criticism of himself. Contemptuous of the Irish for their moral paralysis, he did not spare himself the same contempt when he felt himself to be similarly culpable.

For all the strength of his devotion to an ideal of chaste feminine beauty, Joyce was convinced that his sexual

[9] Letter to Nora, 27 October 1909, *ibid.*, II, 255.
[10] Letter to Nora, 27 October 1909, *ibid.*, II, 255.

drives represented a challenge to this ideal. He saw his own nature as irreparably split between opposing impulses, one of beauty and the other of lust. He clearly did not think it possible for beauty and lust to be intermingled: the one represented an ideal, the other a debasing of that ideal. "Dublin is a detestable city and the people are most repulsive to me," he wrote Nora; but in the same letter he noted that a part of himself was similarly disgusting and repulsive to him: "Nora . . . you must really take me in hand. Why have you allowed me to get into this state? Will you, dearest, take me as I am with my sins and follies and shelter me from . . . misery? If you do not I feel my life will go to pieces. Tonight I have an idea madder than usual. I feel I would like to be flogged by you. I would like to see your eyes blazing with anger.

"I wonder is there some madness in me? Or is love madness? One moment I see you like a virgin or madonna and the next moment I see you shameless, insolent, half-naked and obscene. What do you think of me at all? Are you disgusted with me?"[11] Joyce was disgusted with himself. Was he no better than the vulgarians he had scorned in *Dubliners*? In one of those stories he had introduced a sexual pervert into the innocent world of boyhood, personifying moral corruption in this degenerate male figure, who masturbates in full view of two surprised youths. How could Joyce claim moral superiority if he too felt perverse masochistic longings stirring within him? Only Nora, to him the embodiment of innocence, could save him from himself. And yet she too seemed infected with lust: "I remember the first night in Pola when in the tumult of our embraces you used a certain word. It was a word of provocation, of irritation and I can see your face over me . . . as you murmured it. There was madness in *your* eyes too and as for me if hell had been waiting for me the moment after I could not have held back from you.

11 Letter to Nora, 2 September 1909, *ibid.*, II, 243.

"Are you too, then, like me, one moment high as the stars, the next lower than the lowest wretches?"[12] This last sentence conveys human nature and conduct as Joyce saw them. Man was capable of both sublimity and wretchedness. Polar forces drove him to alternate extremes. In Joyce's case, idealism beckoned him toward the sublime, but to his chagrin the embodiment of that idealism, Nora, was herself capable of what he termed wretchedness.

Some readers may find these conventional moral concepts curious in a writer often praised—or damned—for his experimentalism. Joyce is perhaps known best as an innovator, a stylistic and technical virtuoso, who displayed his debt to the past often by a remarkable fondness for parodying it. And as for Joyce's moral position, his most prominent critic has told us that "the initial and determining act of judgment in Joyce's work is the justification of the commonplace. . . . Yeats was aristocratic and demanded distinctions between men; Joyce was all for removing them. Joyce's discovery, so humanistic that he would have been embarrassed to disclose it out of context, was that the ordinary is extraordinary."[13] But when we find Joyce writing to Nora, "All men are brutes, dearest, but at least in me there is also something higher at times," he certainly does seem to be "demanding distinctions between men," as well as distinctions between noble and ignoble conduct in the same man. And one need not be labeled "aristocratic" to demand such distinctions. Joyce's concepts may be alien to our own post-Marxian and post-Freudian thinking; they may sound more like St. Paul than one would expect a twentieth-century writer to sound; but they are not therefore aristocratic, any more than any dualistic theory can be termed aristocratic. Joyce was simply anachronistic enough to believe that matter and spirit were forever separate and that man's higher nature, comprising reason and

[12] Letter to Nora, 2 September 1909, ibid., II, 243.
[13] Ellmann, James Joyce, p. 3.

spirit, was constantly in danger of debasement by the lower nature, comprising lust and moral weakness or paralysis. Joyce was in some ways judging mankind by traditional Christian standards: that man is strong who participates in the life of the spirit; that man is weak who participates in the life of the flesh. Hence in passing judgment on himself he could write to Nora, "I want you to say to yourself, Jim, the poor fellow I love, is coming back. He is a poor weak impulsive man and he prays to me to defend him and make him strong.

"I gave others my pride and joy. To you I give my sin, my folly, my weakness & sadness."[14]

The Irish have been called a race of celibates, and the sexual emphasis of Irish Catholic morality is greater than that of any other Catholic country. Only American Catholicism, which is after all predominantly Irish-American, rivals the Irish Church in the stress which it lays upon the seriousness of carnal sins. The reasons for this phenomenon are complex and obscure, and this is not the place for discussion of them, but one of the historical strengths of the Catholic Church seems to have been its ability to adapt ostensibly immutable doctrines to the peculiarities of national character. The carnal sinners receive relatively light punishment from Dante, who places them in only the second circle of his Italian hell. Few Irishmen would let them off that easily.

The origins of Joyce's moral tenets are therefore not difficult to trace. In the *Portrait* he represents Stephen's reverence for images of chaste femininity as an outgrowth of a youthful veneration of the Blessed Virgin; and though Stephen leaves the Church, he retains an Irish Catholic fear of lust which mirrors Joyce's own mistrust of the flesh. "It is a curious thing, do you know," says Cranly truthfully to Stephen, "how your mind is supersaturated with the religion in which you say you disbelieve" (P240). Years of

14 Letter to Nora, 2 September 1909, *Letters*, II, 243.

Jesuit training had not been without their effect upon Joyce as well, for his dualism was quite consistent with the theories he must have committed to memory and recited again and again from his catechism.[15] In *Stephen Hero* Joyce has Stephen say candidly, "At present I have a reluctance to commit a sacrilege. I am a product of Catholicism; I was sold to Rome before my birth. Now I have broken my slavery but I cannot in a moment destroy every feeling in my nature. That takes time" (*SH*139). Joyce too was a product of Catholicism; the "feelings in his nature" were evidently not erased, even by time. His apostasy was directed against the Church as an institution, but he does not seem to have had any quarrel with a Catholic view of the nature of man. "Catholicism is in your blood," a priest tells Stephen. "Living in an age which professes to have discovered evolution, can you be fatuous enough to think that simply by being wrong-headed you can recreate entirely your mind and temper or can clear your blood of what you may call the Catholic infection?" (*SH*206). As if to affirm that he himself had not been able or, perhaps, had not chosen to rid himself of that "infection," Joyce wrote in 1909 of ". . . the truth inherent in the soul of Catholicism: that man cannot reach the divine heart except through that sense of separation and loss called sin" (*CW*205). The experience of sin may be necessary for the perception of goodness, but to Joyce, the willing heir of a dualistic tradition, the distinction between sin and right conduct was clear.

Joyce was not simply a superficial puritan who ranted against sex merely because religion and society ranted against it. His puritanism ran deep enough for him to associate sex with bestiality and the loss of human will. The vehemence of his language is at times startling, for it testifies to the painfulness of the battle which he must con-

[15] For an illuminating study of Joyce's Jesuit education, see Kevin Sullivan, *Joyce Among the Jesuits* (New York, 1958).

stantly have been waging against himself, against the sensual urges which he could neither accept nor deny. Sex was weakness. To give in to libidinous yearnings was to become an animal. He could not write to Nora simply that he longed for her embrace; he had to say, "There is some star too near the earth for I am still in a fever-fit of animal desire."[16] He could not accept his sensuality as something normal and perfectly excusable, let alone desirable; instead he came to say, "It is wrong for you to live with a vile beast like me or to allow your children to be touched by my hands."[17] For him the act of love could not be beautiful: it was "brief, brutal, irresistible and devilish."[18] The letter to Nora of 2 December 1909 expresses with particular force and clarity Joyce's dualistic frame of mind, his intellectual aversion to sex, despite its power over him. Unfortunately, I have been unable to obtain permission to quote the unpublished portions of this letter in full, but because it is an extremely valuable document for the understanding of Joyce's attitudes and temperament, I shall paraphrase the deleted sections. If my own language here seems offensive, I apologize for it; but so much of the meaning of the letter is bound up with the extremely frank language which Joyce employs, that I have had to approximate his terminology in order to convey any of the spirit of the original. Clinical terms or euphemisms would be misleading.

"You thank me for the beautiful name I gave you," Joyce begins. "Yes, dear, it is a nice name 'My beautiful wild flower of the hedges! My dark-blue, rain-drenched flower!' You see I am a little of a poet still. . . . *But,* side by side and inside this spiritual love I have for you there is also a wild beast-like craving for every inch of your body, for every secret and shameful part of it, for every odour and

[16] Letter to Nora, 3 December 1909, *Letters,* II, 270.
[17] Letter to Nora, 18 November 1909, *ibid.,* II, 265.
[18] Letter to Nora, 2 December 1909, *ibid.,* II, 268.

⟨   47   ⟩

act of it. My love for you allows me to pray to the spirit of eternal beauty and tenderness mirrored in your eyes or to fling you down under me. . . ." And here Joyce begins a portrait of the sex act as he perceives it. Besides inspiring prayerful worship of Nora's spiritual beauty, his love enables him to fling her down on that pliant fleshy front of hers and to shove it up her from behind, like a gross pig atop its mate, fooling in the very stench and slime of her anus, reveling in the shameful spectacle of upturned skirts and underclothes and in the frenzy of a flushed face and wild hair. His love "allows me to burst into tears of pity and love at some slight word, to tremble with love for you at the sound of some chord or cadence of music . . ." or, he goes on, to feel her fingering his balls or his arse and to feel her hot mouth working on his prick while his own mouth sucks greedily at the gross red quim between her fat legs, his hands grasping at the soft round pillows of her butt. He has taught Nora almost to faint with sweet emotion at the sound of his voice hymning to her soul the strangeness, the sacred passionate mystery of life, but at the same time he has taught her to make obscene gestures to him with her mouth, to excite him by filthy motions and sounds, and even to perform before him the dirtiest, most shameful of bodily functions. Does she remember, he asks, the time she drew up her dress and let him lie down and look up at her while she did this act? Then she could not bear to look him in the eyes.

"You are mine, darling, mine! I love you. All I have written above is only a moment or two of brutal madness." The last drop of spunk has only just been shot up her quim before all this is done with and his real love for her, the love of *Chamber Music*, the love of his eyes for her mysterious alluring gaze comes drifting over his soul like a fresh wind from the East. His cock is still aching and trembling from the last animal thrust it has given her when a distant sacred chorus can be heard rising in soft sad praise of her from the shadowy sanctuary of his heart.

"Nora, my faithful darling, my sweet-eyed blackguard schoolgirl," Joyce exhorts her at last, she can be his mistress, his fuckstress as much as she likes. But "you are always my beautiful wild flower of the hedges, my dark-blue rain-drenched flower."[19]

If Joyce's hostility toward sexuality was ever in question, this letter should remove many doubts. It is a consciously literary performance: the two sides of love, one spiritual and the other bestial, are carefully contrasted by a series of juxtapositions which remind one of certain passages in the *Portrait*. In the *Portrait* Joyce contrasts the sordid with the beautiful, so as to indicate Stephen's attempt to forsake unpleasant reality in search of the ideal: moonlit pools upon the strand are juxtaposed with the pool of grease in a jar of dripping; Stephen, the ascetic aesthete, discourses upon Aquinas to a dung-consuming companion, who cares more about Venus' backside than her aesthetic harmony. Here in this letter to Nora, Joyce juxtaposes the physical and the spiritual sides of love, arguing for the incompatibility of the two, yet asserting the inevitability of their co-existence. He reserves for the spiritual unqualified homage, for the physical unqualified scorn. In his view these two aspects of love are perpetually at war with one another for the domination of his soul, a war which is the source of mental torture for Joyce. He cries out for a total victory for the spiritual side, and yet he has no real hope of such a victory. The mental anguish will endure. The spiritual love will continually be contested, and regularly overcome, by "a wild beast-like craving," a physical abandon which mocks the delicacy of that "beautiful name" Joyce gave Nora—"my beautiful wild flower of the hedges, my dark-blue rain-drenched flower."

In order to emphasize the irreconcilable nature of this division between physical and spiritual, Joyce employs dis-

[19] Letter to Nora, 2 December 1909, *ibid.*, II, 268-69.

tinctly contrasting imagery. Just as Nora has become symbolically the Blessed Virgin of his manhood, so too the spiritual side of his love for her is associated with religion and is therefore described through religious imagery. His spiritual love causes him to "pray to the spirit of eternal beauty" and to engage in a hymn-like singing or murmuring to Nora's soul; when the physical side of the act of love is over, he becomes overtly religious, as a faint hymn rises worshipfully from his heart. By contrast with this worshipful imagery, the language Joyce uses to convey his intellectual rejection of physical love is almost ingeniously repulsive. One can scarcely imagine any but the most ardent sodomite delighting, whatever the universal pleasantries of the female posterior, in the very stench and sweat of an arse. Here Joyce is being deliberately disgusting, as when he likens the union of a man and a woman to that of hogs and sows. He does not merely share the reservations of those who delight in pointing out that men and women look awkward or amusing when copulating. No, to him the act itself is shameful, bestial, and spiritually degrading. In his mind the sexual is linked with the excretive process—to him the most shameful and filthy act of the body—and like defecation, the sexual act rids one of fetid matter.

Joyce hasn't a single kind word for pure sexuality—here or anywhere else in his writings. His position seems to be a curious mixture of Irish Catholicism and, at times, sexual aberration, for masochism is obvious enough in his requests for flogging and in his peculiar fascination with excrement. His psychological stress was not lessened by his rejection of the sacrament of Penance as a road to absolution. For him there was no forgiveness waiting in the darkness of the confessional. Nor was he at all sympathetic to psychoanalysis. In some ways his writing must have been a means of expiation, of purgation, because he eventually made great sport of his sins and follies in *Ulysses* and in *Finnegans Wake*. But he seems to have writhed in perpetual guilt, pouring out his lust and shame to Nora, to whom he bemoaned that "this too is part of my love. Forgive me! Forgive me!"[20] Pigs might delight in sex; they were simply fulfilling their nature. But Joyce was devoted to an ideal of virginal beauty which bestiality could only taint.[21]

The manuscript of an autobiographical love story, *Giacomo Joyce*, recently discovered by Richard Ellmann and to be published in 1968, appears to extend our sense of Joyce's ideals. I have not yet seen the complete text, but the story, written in 1914, conveys Joyce's impassioned adoration of a young Italian girl, whose chaste beauty he celebrates in languid prose and whom, with characteristic reverence, he compares to Dante's Beatrice and to Beatrice Cenci, "stainless of blood and violation."

Attempting to escape Irish moral hypocrisy, Joyce exiled himself on the Continent for most of his life; but he could not escape what he considered bestial within himself. He continued, moreover, to brood upon Ireland as he brooded upon himself, attacking what he called immorality with the sharp sword-edges of his conscience and his pen. Joyce's art was born of the moral conflicts around him and within

---

[20] Letter to Nora, 3 December 1909, *ibid.*, II, 271.

[21] Mary T. Reynolds, "Joyce and Nora: The Indispensable Countersign," *Sewanee Review*, LXXII (Winter 1964), 29-64, interprets Joyce's correspondence with Nora in purely psychological terms, concluding that Joyce was simply trying to arouse Nora's attention and reduce his own nervous anxiety by writing to her in this way. While I see the letters as an important indication of Joyce's moral bent, Mrs. Reynolds goes so far as to state that Joyce was sometimes insincere in his use of "sentimental" language as contrasted with franker, sexual language. She sees the correspondence as a way for Joyce to have "reduced his anxiety level" and states that the letters show his "ego distress" and "a line of progression toward greater insight, adjustment of tensions, and a consequent lowering of the level of diffuse anxiety in both Nora and James." Mrs. Reynolds insists that "in these erotic letters there is no intellectualizing" and that the letters somehow show that Joyce was headed toward an "integration of polar traits in his personality." My own interpretation of the correspondence is obviously quite different: Mrs. Reynolds may indeed be correct in seeing psychological stress and strain in the letters, but the letters also show Joyce's distaste for and disgust with his "bestial" side and his *inability* to integrate polar traits in his personality.

him. Even his poetry, which early in his life was devoted exclusively to a celebration of purely spiritual love, came eventually to mirror his mistrust of sensuality. One of the *Pomes Penyeach* speaks of "itch and quailing, nude greed of the flesh," of "greasy lips" and "Love's breath . . . / As sour as cat's breath, / Harsh of tongue."[22] Another reflects Joyce's view of love as a mixture of the virtuous and the sinful: "And all my soul is a delight, / A swoon of shame."[23] Joyce devoted one entire poem to a commentary on the double nature of love:

A PRAYER

Again!
Come, give, yield all your strength to me!
From far a low word breathes on the breaking brain
Its cruel calm, submission's misery,
Gentling her awe to a soul predestined.
Cease, silent love! My doom!

Blind me with your dark nearness, O have mercy,
    beloved enemy of my will!
I dare not withstand the cold touch that I dread.
Draw from me still
My slow life! Bend deeper on me, threatening head,
Proud by my downfall, remembering, pitying
Him who is, him who was!

Again!
Together, folded by the night, they lay on earth.
    I hear
From far her low word breathe on my breaking brain.
Come! I yield. Bend deeper upon me! I am here.
Subduer, do not leave me! Only joy, only anguish,
Take me, save me, soothe me, O spare me!

The poem conveys a distinctly cheerless view of sexual

[22] From "A Memory of the Players in a Mirror at Midnight" (1917).
[23] From "Alone" (1916).

⟨   52   ⟩

intercourse. This much is apparent in the dramatic situation alone: a lover laments, while inviting, the painful pleasure of sex. Presumably the italicized words represent the commands of an aggressive partner, while the rest of the poem constitutes a paradoxical prayer to this aggressor, a prayer setting forth the mingled desire and scorn which Joyce himself felt for sex. Opposites contend unceasingly in the poem, and no resolution occurs, because no such resolution was possible in Joyce's view of human nature. To introduce this notion quickly into the poem, Joyce employs an oxymoron in line four: submission will bring tranquility, a balm for the libidinous itch, but this tranquility will be a "cruel calm," cruel because it entails the surrendering of human will. From the first the aggressive lover has made clear the exacting price of pleasure, for she demands, "Come, give, yield all your strength to me!" And the submissive lover addresses his prayer to the "beloved enemy of my will!" who would soon be "Proud by my downfall. . . ." The speaker cries out, "I dare not withstand the cold touch that I dread" because the pain of resistance seems greater than the pain of submission. To yield to lust is to invite a "joy" followed by "anguish," a momentary ecstasy compromised by the "misery" of the conscious loss of will. Joyce ends the poem with the futile exhortation "O spare me!"—a final note of agony and helplessness.

"A Prayer" is a dramatic exploration of the ideas Joyce expressed to Nora in his letters of 1909, though the poem was not written until 1924, when Joyce was forty-two, a lapse of time which testifies to the continuity of his thought: *Ulysses* had been completed three years earlier. The brutal language of the letters is absent, but the ideas are the same. The sexual act is the most obvious triumph of instinct over rationality, and in Joyce's view there seems to be no hope of any sustained victory of the will. Lust is too strong. The grace of God, that tranquilizer of Christian doctrine, is absent. The moral man puts up a valiant struggle at best, yielding when he must, regaining self-control when he can. And the ordinary man offers little resistance to his lower, brutal self. Joyce is perhaps closer to hopelessness and despair than official Catholic teaching would countenance, but one can see much truth in Mary M. Colum's judgment, when she wrote: "Actually, I have never known a mind so fundamentally Catholic in structure as Joyce's own, nor one on which the Church's ceremonies, symbols, and theological declarations had made such an impression. After he left Dublin I do not think he ever entered a church except for the music or some great traditional ceremony. And yet the structure was there: his whole mind showed the mental and moral training of the Church, and his esteem for many of its doctors and philosophers was greater than he expressed for other outstanding mentalities."[24]

If Joyce was able to reject the Church as an institution, why did he continue to accept a conception of morality plainly derived from his Irish Catholic upbringing? Why did he allow his conscience to plague him with demands impossible to fulfill and certain to cast over him a shadow of perpetual shame? The answer to these questions lies in that habit of mind common to Joyce and his self-projection, Stephen Dedalus—a persistent idealism; a preference for the ideal, not the actual; for the exemplary, not the common. When Joyce writes to Nora, "You are to my young manhood what the idea of the Blessed Virgin was to my boyhood," he displays his belief in a supernal innocence, before which he was always reverent and from which he felt the moral man ought to shape thought and action. Unlike Stephen, Joyce does not allow this belief to obscure harsh realities; he does not try to ignore public squalor, nor to immerse himself in aesthetics, nor to create hymns out of erotic dreams. Burdened with his stringent morality, he turns the eye of his conscience upon his en-

[24] Mary and Padraic Colum, *Our Friend James Joyce* (New York, 1958), pp. 134-35.

vironment and upon himself and looks upon both with equal dissatisfaction, finding himself "one moment high as the stars, the next lower than the lowest wretches," and finding Ireland "the sow that eats her young."[25] He shuns any art which obscures truth for the sake of beauty, believing instead that the beautiful—for him the image of moral innocence—is better served by that art which reveals man as he is—at worst morally loathsome, a two-sided creature at best.

· 2 ·

In 1916 Joyce completed a play in which the implications of his moral judgments upon himself and upon his fellow man were explored. The play is of particular interest as a prelude to *Ulysses*: *Exiles* is a dramatization of the moral vision with which Joyce gave thematic shape to the odyssey of Leopold Bloom. Ideas provide dramatic conflict within the play, as within its central character. Richard Rowan vacillates between two opposing concepts of morality, the one based on freedom and the other based on the spiritual bondage of love. He appears unable to choose between the two, unable to determine whether he should grant his wife sexual liberty and the chance to share love with others, or whether he should yield to his own love for his wife—and her pleadings—and confine both himself and her to a monogamous existence. Richard's dilemma is the chief dramatic conflict in *Exiles* in that it governs the play's main action; but this conflict is greatly complicated by the multiplicity of motives behind Richard's indecisiveness. On the surface Richard is simply torn between his love for Bertha and his intellectual commitment to absolute freedom: love moves him to a desire for perfect union with Bertha, while his principles counsel that

---

[25] This phrase is entered in an alphabetically arranged notebook of Joyce's, under "Ireland" (Cornell Collection). Later the phrase was changed slightly for Stephen in the *Portrait*: "Do you know what Ireland is? asked Stephen with cold violence. Ireland is the old sow that eats her farrow" (P203).

he has no right to restrict, even by suggestion, her freedom, whatever the traditional ignominy of cuckoldry. Richard's desire to give his wife absolute liberty thus seems to be an example of noble and rational selflessness. But Joyce throws the nobility of Richard's liberal position into serious doubt, for while Richard's motives are in part rational, they also consist partly of masochistic and possibly homosexual urges, of a sexual delight in the idea of Bertha's promiscuity, and, least nobly of all, in a desire to involve the innocent Bertha in guilt, thereby humbling her and degrading her. To examine the ways in which Joyce reveals Richard's complex motivations is to discover *Exiles* as a mirror of Joyce's moral vision.

Beatrice Justice is the least developed of the central characters in the play, but she plays an important role in the unmasking of Richard's motivations. For her conversation with Richard at the start of Act I provides the first hint that Richard's outward carelessness about his wife's fidelity conceals inner doubts and scruples. Beatrice and Richard have been exchanging letters for eight years, ostensibly as part of a purely intellectual friendship. But when Beatrice admits that she comes now to visit Richard simply because "Otherwise I could not see you," she implies a physical attraction for him as well. Richard has been writing about Beatrice in his fiction. He suggests to her that perhaps his writing reveals something about her which she cannot admit to herself—"On account of others or for want of courage—which?" "Courage," Beatrice replies softly. Timidity has prevented her from expressing her physical desire for Richard. At first he taunts her with her lack of courage. "You cannot give yourself freely and wholly," he says to her. Richard feels he speaks from an intellectually superior position. He has recognized no conventions. He lives with his wife and child, but unmarried, unbowed by convention; and Beatrice, he implies, wants the courage to defy convention, to give herself freely and wholly to him or to anyone.

⟨   56   ⟩

But Beatrice's reply to Richard's taunt is worth noting: "It is a terribly hard thing to do, Mr. Rowan—to give yourself freely and wholly—and be happy" (*E22*). Evidently something more than a lack of courage lies behind her inability openly to declare her passion. She senses that such freedom might not bring happiness; and although Richard counters her remark with a gibe at happiness as an ideal—"But do you feel that happiness is the best, the highest we can know?"—he is moved by her statement to a sudden confession: "O, if you knew how I am suffering at this moment! For your case, too. But suffering most of all for my own." With this admission Richard casts doubt upon his own position. When, as the play develops, he begins to act with increasing uncertainty—a man torn by conflicting emotional and intellectual impulses, not at all sure of his devotion to a principle of sexual *laissez faire*— we can recall this brief outburst as the first hint of Richard's complex motivation. Having chided Beatrice for her timorousness, Richard acknowledges that he suffers both for her case and for his own, affirming, in effect, that her reluctance might be justly founded.

Joyce does not allow us to see at once into the nature of Beatrice's scruples. At first we know only that she chooses to distinguish between freedom and happiness. With the entrance of Robert Hand, however, Beatrice's ideas become more lucid, if only by implication. Robert is the utter sensualist, who does not believe in conscience, who acts upon impulse without reflection. To Robert, right conduct consists in the satisfying of one's appetites. Of Beatrice's scrupulous devotion to her duties as a tutor to Richard Rowan's son, Robert remarks with mild contempt, "You see what it is to have a conscience" (*E29*). He in fact does not see, because a conscience is what he lacks. He speaks of the "protestant strain" in Beatrice—"gloom, seriousness, righteousness"—and in so doing he helps to define those doubts which Beatrice has about an affair with Richard: her doubts are evidently moral ones.

Robert now confronts Bertha, with whom he finds himself alone, and attempts to get her to agree to a secret meeting. From the start he is aggressive, she reluctantly acquiescent at most. Joyce's stage directions tell us that Bertha is unsure of herself—"a little confused, tries to withdraw her hand . . . repelling his embrace, confused." She seems curiously detached. She kisses him, but "quickly," and follows this gesture with a flippant, "Why don't you say: thanks?" (E35). Her attitude contrasts with that of her lover, whose ardor moves him to a series of fervent clichés: "I am afraid. . . . At last I hold you in my arms. . . . Let me feel your lips touch mine. . . . My life is finished—over. . . . To end it all—death. . . . Listening to music and in the arms of the woman I love" (E35).

Robert is the crude sensualist who is intent upon giving vent to his passions, though their object is the wife of a supposedly dear friend. When Richard enters again, Robert "rises, with nervous friendliness," and soon offers Richard his services as a journalist "for the sake of . . . our friendship, our lifelong friendship," on the condition that Richard allow him to imply to the public that the Rowans are legally married. "I understand your pride and your sense of liberty. I understand their point of view also," says Robert (E39). The word "liberty" takes on certain ambiguous connotations here, since it comes from the mouth of a man who intends to take certain liberties with Richard's wife. The ambiguity is deliberate on Joyce's part, for *Exiles* may be thought of as a dramatic attempt to define "liberty." To Richard, liberty means freedom from conventions: he has refused to marry Bertha in a legal ceremony because he regards such a convention as an infringement by the state on his personal liberty. As for sexual liberty, he is less certain: he taunts Beatrice for her timidity, but confesses to his own doubts in the matter. Robert, of course, parades his dedication to complete sexual freedom: "Lord, when I think of our wild nights long ago—talks by the hour, plans, carouses, revelry. . . ." Richard again reveals his personal doubts, this time more directly:

RICHARD: It was not only a house of revelry; it was to be the hearth of a new life. (*Musing.*) And in that name all our sins were committed.

ROBERT: Sins! Drinking and blasphemy (*he points*) by me. And drinking and heresy, much worse (*he points again*) by you—are those the sins you mean?

RICHARD: And some others.

ROBERT (*lightly, uneasily*): You mean the women. I have no remorse of conscience. (*E41*)

"No remorse of conscience"—the basic difference between Robert and Richard, whose remorse of conscience causes him to suffer, because, in Joyce's eyes, it causes him to consider the moral implications of his actions and consequently to reflect upon the meaning of the word liberty. Richard tries to arouse Robert's conscience by asking him if lust can rightly be termed an homage to beauty, but Robert replies with characteristic insensitivity, "You will give me a headache if you make me think today. I cannot think today. I feel too natural, too common." And thus he indulges in a bit of unconscious self-irony, this hedonist, who cautions Richard, "I think you look too deeply into life. . . . Be gay. Life is not worth it" (*E44*).

Richard continues, however, to look deeply into life, continues to be plagued by his conscience, which seems to advise that liberty is at once necessary and dangerous, or even sinful. When Richard and Bertha discuss Robert's advances, moreover, the question of liberty becomes increasingly complicated. He has decided to do nothing to prevent Bertha from having an affair with Robert, presumably because he does not wish to interfere with her own liberty. Yet we have already noted her lack of enthusiasm for Robert, her confusion before his blunt advances, her apparent reluctance to take him altogether

seriously. Her enthusiasm cools even further when she discovers—"shocked"—that the cottage where Robert has proposed to meet her was the scene of his former revels with
Richard: her delicate nature is evidently bruised by this
revelation. Far more than a liaison with Robert she desires
some indication, some affirmation of love from Richard:
"Tell me not to go and I will not," she begs him, and "Am
I to go to this place? . . . Am I to go? . . . Do you tell me to
go? . . . Do you forbid me to go?" (E55-56). A word from
Richard would obviously be far more welcome to her than
Robert's embraces, but Richard refuses her pleadings. His
commitment to a principle of liberty begins to look foolish,
for in his love of principle he is ignoring another kind of
love, as well as a principle known to all men, namely, that
a woman likes and needs to be told what is expected of her.
And in addition Richard, though he tries to conceal it, is
quite jealous—that is to say, he is a human being as well
as an intellectual devoted to liberty. He rants against Robert: "A liar, a thief, and a fool! Quite clear! A common
thief!" Yet he will not favor Bertha with the single word
which could render Robert a liar, a fool, and an unsuc-
cessful thief. There is something in Richard which wants
to be betrayed. Joyce writes in his notes for *Exiles*, "Richard's Masochism needs no example."

A commitment to liberty, a masochistic tendency—Rich-
ard's inaction can be attributed to at least two motives.
But there is a third, ferreted out by Bertha when she asks,
"Which of us two is the deceiver?"

RICHARD: Of us? You and me?
BERTHA (*in a calm decided tone*): I know why you
have allowed me what you call complete liberty.
RICHARD: Why?
BERTHA: To have complete liberty with—that girl (*E53*).

If Bertha's accusation is just, and certain succeeding
events testify that it is, then Richard begins to look less
like a principled libertarian and more like a man driven

by an unpleasant alliance of principle, perversity, and lust. This last element, lust, has two aspects: Richard's attraction to Beatrice, whom he accuses of being too timid to declare her passion; and Richard's sexual delight in the idea of Bertha's promiscuity. The first aspect of Richard's lust leads him to encourage Bertha's liaison with Robert so that he, Richard, may be free to pursue Beatrice—"that girl," as Bertha terms her. On the most practical level, Bertha's transgression would then give Richard something to point to, were his intrigue with Beatrice discovered; on a psychological and moral level, Richard's own sense of guilt would be assuaged if he could effect, through inaction, an end to Bertha's innocence. The second aspect of Richard's lust—sexual delight in the idea of Bertha's promiscuity—is exposed through the series of questions Richard asks Bertha about her meeting with Robert. In his excessive curiosity about the encounter between his wife and her hopeful lover, Richard betrays his own excitement:

RICHARD: . . . What else went on?
BERTHA: He asked me to give him my hand. . . .
RICHARD: Did you?
BERTHA: Yes. . . . Then he caressed my hand and asked would I let him kiss it. I let him.
RICHARD: Well?
BERTHA: Then he asked could he embrace me—even once? . . . And then . . .
RICHARD: And then?
BERTHA: He put his arm round me.
RICHARD: . . . And then?
BERTHA: He said I had beautiful eyes. And asked could he kiss them. . . . I said: "Do so."
RICHARD: And he did?
BERTHA: Yes. First one and then the other . . .
RICHARD: And then?
BERTHA: He asked for a kiss. I said: "Take it."

⟨ 61 ⟩

RICHARD: And then?
BERTHA: . . . He kissed me.
RICHARD: Your mouth?
BERTHA: Once or twice.
RICHARD: Long kisses? . . . With his lips? Or . . . the
other way? . . . Did he ask you to kiss him? . . . What
way? . . . Were you excited? . . . (E47-49)

And so on. Richard derives obvious sexual pleasure from
these descriptions, a fact which Bertha confirms in Act II
when she tells Robert, "It excited him. More than usual"
(E81). Perhaps one could term this excitement a further
manifestation of Richard's masochism, but his masochism
appears to function quite independently of any specifically
sexual delight in Bertha's promiscuous experiment. Masochism causes him simply to long for betrayal, and his inaction is thus a form of self-laceration for its own sake.
His sexual pleasure in Bertha's detailed descriptions is less
masochism than a kind of voyeurism, which when combined with his masochism, his lust for Beatrice, and his
devotion to liberty as a principle, makes Richard's motivation highly complex.

As the complications of Exiles unfold, one recognizes
Joyce's characteristic obsessions emerging: the Madonna-
like figure of the innocent female; questions of guilt, sin,
moral weakness and strength. The assault on Bertha's innocence—pursued actively by Robert, abetted by Richard—
is of a piece with Stephen Dedalus' concern with his own
ideals of innocent beauty and with his own lust: that is,
the assault pits the highest and the lowest elements in
human nature against one another, and as such it becomes
a battle symbolic of the moral element in Joyce's earlier
writing. In a broader sense the assault is symbolic of
Joyce's conscience itself, for it is an action chosen by Joyce
as representative of the problems central to his own moral
vision. In his letters to Nora of 1909, Joyce articulated his

worship of an ideal of innocence, his disgust for and mistrust of sexuality, and his belief that morality consists in the attempt at least to balance the sordidness in one's nature with a spiritual "something higher." *Exiles* has as its central figure a man concerned directly with these moral questions: Richard, though an advocate of absolute liberty, has confessed his suffering doubts about his "case" and that of his potential mistress. His decision not to raise a finger to prevent his wife's infidelity stems jointly from libertarianism, masochism, and lust—and is thus a decision powerfully motivated.[26] Yet his conscience urges him against this decision. ". . . How I am suffering . . . !" he says, uncovering the moral doubts hammering away at him. His masochism, his desire to be free to pursue Beatrice, and his voyeurism—these are obviously reprehensible motivations for desiring Bertha's freedom, reprehensible by moral standards far less rigid than Joyce's. But as for the principle of sexual liberty, its particular deficiencies can be seen only in the perspective of Joyce's moral vision, only in the light of Joyce's own combination of idealism and lingering Irish Catholicism. To Joyce, sexual fidelity was an affirmation of the highest capabilities of human nature. To give in to random sexual impulses was to admit the dominance of one's bestial side; to confine sex within the limits of a spiritually vital relationship was to behave morally and to foster the most admirable elements in one's nature. We have already seen this Joycean brand of puritanism, this apostate Irish Catholicism, expounded in Joyce's own words. Now in *Exiles* it becomes the moral structure of a dramatic situation. And in Joyce's notes for *Exiles*, we can examine his own words again: "The soul like the body may have a virginity. For the woman to yield

---

[26] Joyce indicated Richard's perverse way of provoking his own betrayal when he discussed the play with Frank Budgen, drawing an analogy between Richard and Leopold Bloom. See Frank Budgen, *James Joyce and the Making of Ulysses* (Bloomington, 1960), pp. 314-15.

it or for the man to take it is the act of love. Love (understood as the desire of good for another) is in fact so unnatural a phenomenon that it can scarcely repeat itself, the soul being unable to become virgin again and not having energy enough to cast itself out again into the ocean of another's soul. It is the repressed consciousness of this inability and lack of spiritual energy which explains Bertha's mental paralysis" (E113).

Love to Joyce is "so unnatural a phenomenon" because it runs against bestiality—that powerful current in human nature. To give love or to receive it is to give or to receive the soul's virginity—a mystical concept, perhaps surprising in a writer who has left the Church, but by now not surprising in Joyce. Virginity becomes a sacred word, a symbol of innocence: Bertha has bestowed that innocence upon Richard in an act of spiritual love. He has become the guardian of that innocence. His libertarianism, therefore, works against the phenomenon of love as Joyce sees it; he pretends indifference to a mystical symbol of union between himself and Bertha, and thus he comes near to abandoning Bertha's precious gift to him. To Joyce, the principle of sexual liberty ignored these vital spiritual facts of love.

Any attempt to defend or to attack Joyce's position on logical grounds is, of course, hopeless and beside the point. Joyce was more mystic than logician. He felt comfortable in his morality and was not conscious of its logical inconsistencies—or at least did not care about them. His remarks on "the virginity of the soul," for example, are evidence that the mystical appeal of a concept mattered more to him than its logicality: for no reason at all he implies that virginity belongs only to the woman, never the man. The woman "yields" it or the man "takes" it; the man never yields, the woman never takes. A woman could be, like Nora, a symbol of innocence, a secular Madonna to Joyce, and hence it is she who bestows her soul's virginity in love, that unnatural phenomenon which occurs but once.

In Act II Richard shows that his conscience encompasses more than the domain of logic: he demonstrates his awareness of these Joycean spiritual facts of love. To begin with, he violates his libertarian code by confronting Robert directly. Although he justifies this action to Bertha, and probably to himself, as proceeding simply from a desire to let Robert know that Bertha might be unfaithful but never deceitful to him, Richard goes much further than that. He goes so far, in fact, as to define explicitly for Robert's benefit the Joycean distinction between love and lust—that same distinction which led Joyce to write to Nora, "Ah not lust, dearest, not . . . wild brutal madness . . . , not the wild beast-like desire for your body, dearest, is what drew me to you then and holds me to you now. No, dearest, not that at all but a most tender, adoring, pitiful love for your youth and girlhood and weakness."[27] For when Robert declares, "Those are moments of sheer madness when we feel an intense passion for a woman. We see nothing. We think of nothing. Only to possess her. Call it brutal, bestial, what you will"—Richard counters: "I am afraid that longing to possess a woman is not love." Robert is incapable of drawing the essential Joycean distinction between love and lust, incapable moreover of discerning that distinction even when Richard spells it out for him. Richard goes on to confess his own feeling of guilt at having betrayed Bertha: "I remember the first time. I came home. It was night. My house was silent. My little son was sleeping in his cot. She, too, was asleep. I wakened her from her sleep and told her. I cried beside her bed; and I pierced her heart. . . . And I was feeding the flame of her innocence with my guilt."

Richard completes his exposition of the Joycean conscience by depicting Bertha as the divinely innocent Madonna, whom he has offended with his sinful bestiality.

Robert protests against Richard's self-castigations: "O, don't talk of guilt and innocence. You have made her all that she is. . . ."

RICHARD (*darkly*): Or I have killed her.
ROBERT: Killed her?
RICHARD: The virginity of her soul.
ROBERT (*impatiently*): Well lost! What would she be without you? . . .
RICHARD: Is it worth what I have taken from her—her girlhood, her laughter, her young beauty, the hopes in her young heart?
ROBERT: . . . Yes. Well worth it.   (E66-67)

In his letter to Nora quoted above, Joyce had contrasted his love for her "youth and girlhood" to his "wild beast-like desire" for her body, and here he contrasts the insensitivity of a sensualist to the perceptions of Richard, who, like Joyce, speaks of the soul's virginity as a verifiable entity. Liberty and love are incompatible: this is Richard's position at the moment of his dialogue with Robert. Richard shares with Stephen Dedalus and Joyce himself a cult of the virginal, but as Joyce writes in his notes to *Exiles*, "Robert is convinced of the nonexistence, of the unreality of the spiritual facts which exist and are real for Richard" (E116).

Though in Act II Richard does reveal the causes of his "suffering," though he does indicate his belief in mystical innocence and spirituality, he cannot bring himself to abandon his libertarian principles altogether. He describes to Robert his fear "that I stand between her and any moments of life that should be hers, between her and you, between her and anyone, between her and anything. I will not do it. I cannot and I will not. I dare not" (E69). Were it not for our knowledge of Richard's masochism and voyeurism and lust for Beatrice, we might applaud his persistent adherence to this declaration of freedom for all. But in a moment Richard confesses that he "longed to be be-trayed by you and by her. . . . I longed for that passionately and ignobly, to be dishonoured forever in love and in lust" (*E*70). In Act I his motives could only be deduced, tenta-tively, from action and speech, but now they are upon his own lips, even his desire to humble Bertha because of her innocence and his guilt: "From pride and from ignoble longing. And from a deeper motive still." That deeper mo-tive, of course, is his desire to be free to follow his own lust. Richard is highly critical of this deeper motive and of all his ignoble longings. When Robert preaches the supremacy of passion—"free, unashamed, irresistible"—Richard dismisses the argument with disdain: "It is the language of my youth" (*E*71). He harbors no illusions about the morality of passion, for he despises the bestiality within himself and reveres Bertha's innocence. But he will not interfere with her actions, even when she pleads with him, "Dick, my God, tell me what you wish me to do?" (*E*75).

The final act of *Exiles* brings no resolution of the con-flicts which divide Richard Rowan against himself and against his wife. He has confessed his own mingling of noble and ignoble motives, and we have witnessed his in-ability to make the single gesture of love which might re-unite him with Bertha. He does not make this gesture, because he cannot. "I did not make myself," Richard says. "I am what I am." And that is a mixture of strength and weakness, of conscience and ignobility, in short, a Joycean man.

Richard's conflicting longings prevent his ever accept-ing Robert's assurance that "She is yours, as she was nine years ago, when you met her first." Richard sees too deeply into himself to be able to embrace the reality of Bertha's love as a panacea for all his moral and psycho-logical woes. Instead he will continue to live in a state of doubt and confusion about himself and about Bertha, still conscious of the ambiguity of his own nature, still masochistically torturing himself, still committed to a principle of liberty, but wearied from the struggle: "I do not wish to know or to believe. . . . It is not in the darkness of belief that I desire you. But in restless living wounding doubt. To hold you by no bonds, even of love, to be united with you in body and soul in utter nakedness—for this I longed. And now I am tired for a while, Bertha. My wound tires me."

"O, my strange wild lover, come back to me again!"—this is Bertha's cry, ending the play, calling upon Richard to surrender himself to the complexities of the human soul, and from the throes of a love both sacred and profane perhaps to partake in that spiritual "something higher." There is a mystical, Joycean kind of reason in her plea. It seems the only escape for this troubled exile.

Exiles is a battle of ideas, in which two abstractions—liberty and love—are set against one another by the author. On no other occasion, before or after, did Joyce confine himself so fixedly to the domain of ideas. We may be thankful for that: Joyce's genius was best exercised upon more concrete grounds, and for all its intricacy of design, *Exiles* alone would not have merited its creator immortality. As noted above, however, the play is of interest as a prelude to *Ulysses*. It reminds us of Joyce's moral concerns; it expands our comprehension of Joyce's moral vision, his conception of the human soul as divided between noble and ignoble longings. Joyce must have written the play as a public airing of his conscience. In the past and in the future he concealed that conscience behind multiple layers of artistic indirection: yet the conscience persisted, infusing his writings with moral significance. Like Stephen Dedalus, he threw off religious orthodoxy only to assume a more personal kind of faith; always an idealist, he allowed the unearthly Madonna of his youth to be superseded by a flesh and blood madonna, to whom he prayed, "Guide me, my saint, my angel, Lead me forward. *Everything* that is noble and exalted and deep and true and moving in what I write comes, I believe, from you. O take me into your soul of souls and then I will become indeed the poet of my race."[28] From *Chamber Music* to *Finnegans Wake* Joyce continued to shape his writing according to ideals which he considered "noble and exalted and deep and true." He continued to think of his artistic role as a moral one, and this declaration of artistic purpose—"I am one of the writers of this generation who are perhaps creating at last a conscience in the soul of this wretched race"—is no less true for *Ulysses* and *Finnegans Wake* than for the *Portrait, Dubliners,* and *Exiles.*[29]

[28] Letter to Nora, 5 September 1909, *ibid.,* II, 248.

[29] This declaration of artistic purpose is taken from a letter to Nora, 22 August 1912, *ibid.,* II, 311. Note that this moralistic purpose (and accompanying violent negativity toward the "race" that was to be his subject matter) is declared only two years before Joyce started working full time on *Ulysses.*

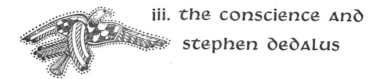

iii. the conscience and stephen dedalus

In his notes for *Exiles*, Joyce reminds himself that "the doubt which clouds the end of the play must be conveyed to the audience" (*E*125). Similarly my concern has been to convey the doubts which clouded Joyce's own mind—doubts about his own nature and hence about human nature. Joyce says of Richard Rowan that he "has fallen from a higher world and is indignant when he discovers baseness in men and women" (*E*116). The remark describes Joyce's own moral indignation. Doubt, confusion, indignation: these are characteristics of Joyce's mind, of Richard's mind, and, particularly in *Ulysses*, of Stephen's mind. Stephen's thoughts and words in *Ulysses* reveal him as the sad bearer of Joyce's own indignant moral conscience. He too has discovered baseness in life, in men and women, and by now he can no longer pull the cowl of self-deception over himself, metamorphosing baseness into beauty.

But Joyce, ever the critic of himself as well as of the life around him, never created a protagonist with whom he wholly sympathized: there was always scrutiny enough to reveal the inevitable human flaws. In the *Portrait*, Stephen accomplishes a great deal by freeing himself from his environment; and as the letters to Nora and *Exiles* show, Joyce's own polarized view of human nature was quite close to Stephen's. Despite these factors, Joyce manages to criticize certain of Stephen's self-deceiving, escapist actions—and in *Ulysses* Joyce is no less critical of him, if for different reasons. Stephen ambles slowly through *Ulysses*, thinking many of Joyce's own thoughts, emitting Joycean phrases by the hundreds—but he is just a bit too Joycean even for Joyce. That is to say, Stephen indulges himself.

Hints of impending disillusion for Stephen, hints of a failure of optimism and self-confidence, were scattered throughout the *Portrait*: no faith is secure which is sheltered by evasion and self-deception. That the scales have at last fallen from Stephen's eyes is apparent in the first three episodes of *Ulysses*. Melancholy suffuses these three prose-poems of frustration and despair. If one were to shut *Ulysses* permanently after the third episode—it has been done—one would probably conclude that Joyce had lost all joy or laughter or hope. But once Joyce momentarily abandons the morose Stephen, once Leopold Bloom becomes the novel's cynosure, the tone of *Ulysses* changes radically from gloomy to jocular—even from tragic to comic. The effect of this change is to underline the difference between Joyce and Stephen. That difference is similar to the contrast between *Tristram Shandy* and *Gulliver's Travels*: both books mirror the folly of humankind, but Sterne guffaws whilst Swift gnashes his teeth. *Ulysses*, another book about folly, has its share of gnashing, but once Joyce leaves Stephen brooding on the strand in "Proteus," *Ulysses* then assumes a far gayer, far lighter air, an air maintained with a fair degree of consistency all the way through to the end—and on into *Finnegans Wake*. Life apparently became not so cheerless to Joyce as to Stephen. In the *Portrait* Joyce shared Stephen's youthful idealism, even his cult of the virginal and exaltation of beauty; but at the same time he made the reader aware of the deficiencies in Stephen's vision. In *Ulysses* Joyce likewise sympathizes with Stephen's pessimism and subscribes to his concern with sin and guilt. But as in the *Portrait*, Joyce calls atten-

⟨   71   ⟩

tion to the limitations of Stephen's perspective, this time questioning not the substance but the tone of Stephen's thoughts.

Here again is the familiar Joycean distance or irony or detachment—three hackneyed critical terms which nonetheless are useful ways of describing the coolness of Joyce toward his protagonists. Though each looks at the world through Joycean eyes, neither Stephen nor Richard Rowan enjoys Joyce's full approval. After all, Joyce himself did not merit anything near Joyce's full approval. The measure of his distance from Stephen cannot be gauged until the appearance of Leopold Bloom, because then the explosive mirth with which Joyce handles Bloom prevents one from taking Stephen's tragic stance entirely seriously. The comic figure of Bloom himself acts ultimately as an antidote for any world view quite so bleak as Stephen's, for while we laugh, we hold despair at bay.

· I ·

Long before Bloom appears, Joyce's comic muse makes a tentative first entrance in the form of "stately, plump Buck Mulligan," who begins *Ulysses* with a mockery of the mass, intoning *introibo ad altare Dei* while holding aloft a shaving bowl and complaining of "a little trouble about those white corpuscles" in changing his shaving water into the blood of the Savior. This blunt ridicule of the Catholic liturgy is new in Joyce, as is the derisive tone of Mulligan's "Ballad of Joking Jesus":

If anyone thinks that I amn't divine
He'll get no free drinks when I'm making the wine
But have to drink water and wish it were plain
That I make when the wine becomes water again.

There may be some significance in the fact that Joyce himself did not compose the "Ballad of Joking Jesus"; it is the work of Oliver St. John Gogarty, upon whom the character of Mulligan is largely based.[1] One could easily make too much of this fact: perhaps Joyce simply wanted to stress the connection between Mulligan and Gogarty by putting the latter's verses into the former's mouth. But it is interesting that Joyce relies on someone else's invention to supply Mulligan with his most extravagant piece of irreverence—interesting as evidence of Joyce's personal dissociation from Mulligan's kind of wit. Joyce made many a joke against the Church and against its potentates and plenipotentiaries, but there is no record of his ever having mocked Christ in the style of Mulligan. And indeed one would not expect a man with so puritanical a conscience to be quite so cheerfully blasphemous—a different thing from anticlericalism.[2]

Surely we are meant to laugh at Mulligan's jokes; and we do laugh, unless inhibited by an excessive degree of religious gravity. Yet there is something vaguely unsatisfying in Mulligan's humor something a bit tinny, something abruptly amusing, but wearisome, perhaps, in large doses. As Joyce himself once remarked of Mulligan, "He should begin to pall on the reader as the day goes on."[3] Though he does not begin to pall in "Telemachus," his wit when scrutinized is shallow. It is mockery merely, not mockery infused with moral vision or conscience, and as

[1] For the background to this fact, see Richard Ellmann, *James Joyce* (New York, 1959), pp. 213 and 286. Of Gogarty, Joyce wrote: "Heaven and earth shall pass away but his false spirit shall not pass away." (Notebook, Cornell University Library.)

[2] A. M. Klein, in "The Black Panther (A Study in Technique)," *Accent*, x (Spring 1950), 139-55, sees a simple "equation" between Stephen and Christ, Mulligan and St. John, and Haines and Satan. Mr. Klein's use of the word "equation" is ill-chosen, for it rules out the irony which riddles the episode. These "equations" are not serious but mocking.

[3] Quoted by Frank Budgen in his *James Joyce and the Making of Ulysses* (Bloomington, 1960), p. 116. Budgen himself thought Buck Mulligan consistently amusing, throughout *Ulysses*, as have many readers, including myself. There remains a great difference between mere mockery and Joyce's moral vision.

⟨   73   ⟩

such it is not Joyce's own kind of mockery.[4] Beside the effusive Buck, Stephen appears sullen and self-obsessed: he is the ideal target for Mulligan's barbs because he takes himself so dreadfully seriously—to the point of tedium. And when Mulligan dubs him a "jejune jesuit," we cannot but agree and applaud the accuracy of Mulligan's thrust. But for all his moroseness, Stephen is at least seriously concerned with moral issues and has a conscience, while Mulligan has none. The reader's sympathies are thus divided between the welcome but shallow laughter of Mulligan and the honest but self-indulgent moral anguish of Stephen.[5] One might speculate that were only Stephen's moral sense mixed with Mulligan's wit, a satisfactory comic perspective might emerge. Joyce might have speculated similarly, for such is the nature of his achievement in *Ulysses*, a book just as moral as it is funny.

Mulligan's humor ripples through the opening of *Ulysses*, but the limitations of that humor reveal themselves in the context of Stephen's predicament. Consider that at the end of the *Portrait* Stephen enjoyed an optimistic frame of mind. He had presumably escaped the nets of his environment; he had formulated a supposedly viable aesthetic theory; and his career as an artist of the beautiful evidently lay splendorously before him. Such optimism, as we learn at the outset of *Ulysses*, has given way to a melancholy which makes Stephen a rather somniferous companion for the ebullient Mulligan, but a melancholy indicative of the broadening and sharpening of Stephen's perspectives. For Stephen has abandoned his aesthetic theory as a falsification of reality, has fallen prey to serious doubts about his artistic future, and, perhaps most discouraging

---

[4] See note 3, above.
[5] See S. L. Goldberg, *The Classical Temper* (London, 1961), pp. 114-16, for an excellent analysis of the ways in which Joyce's irony cuts both Stephen and Mulligan. Mr. Goldberg points out that Mulligan will never be more than a Dublin wit, while Stephen has at least the potential of something greater within him.

of all, has found himself once again entrapped by environmental nets. All of the major elements of this predicament are introduced in "Telemachus" and are then expanded and clarified in "Nestor" and "Proteus."

Like his Homeric counterpart, Telemachus, Stephen fears the loss of his heirdom.[6] For Telemachus, heirdom was a physical entity, the inheritance due him as the son of Ulysses. For Stephen, the heirdom is spiritual or symbolic, the artistic monarchy of his race. Stephen first indicates his concern with heirdom when he calls upon Daedalus in the *Portrait*: "Old father, old artificer, stand me now and ever in good stead." These last words of the *Portrait* hover like a motto over "Telemachus," where Stephen fears that artistic inheritance—in the form of his own artistic paternity—is to be denied him. Daedalus, his spiritual or symbolic or artistic father, has apparently not stood him in good stead but has failed him, just as Ulysses had apparently failed Telemachus by allowing Ithaca to fall within the grasp of usurpers. Mulligan's keeping of the key to the tower, though Stephen pays the rent, hints at the idea of usurpation. Indeed the last word of "Telemachus" is "Usurper"; it refers in Stephen's mind to Mulligan and to Haines, the Englishman, whom Stephen fears will fall heir unjustly to his own artistic kingdom. Haines, as an Englishman, is of course physically a usurper of Ireland; but in a different sense Stephen's proudly independent art is threatened with debasement by Haines's fatuous interest in it as a bit of quaint Irish folklore; meanwhile the conscienceless Mulligan accepts Haines as a useful evil, willing to profit by the Englishman's interest. Stephen rightfully, if self-righteously, resents these potential usurpers.

Yet because he has nothing but dreams and ambitions to show, Stephen feels powerless before Mulligan's hollow

---

[6] Stephen is, of course, in this respect a Hamlet-like figure, too. For a discussion of this aspect of the Telemachiad, see William M. Schutto, *Joyce and Shakespeare* (New Haven, 1957), pp. 17-28, 46-47, 98-103.

Irish mockery and Haines's acquisitive English interest. He thinks of "the subtle African heresiarch Sabellius who held that the Father was Himself His own Son": this anti-Trinitarian doctrine symbolizes for him his own artistic ambition to become his own father, to give birth to himself through the paternity of his art.[7] He does not wish to be subservient to his environment, as a son is supposed to be subservient to his father, but to create himself anew, "to press in my arms," in the words of the *Portrait*, "the loveliness which has not yet come into the world." His melancholia in "Telemachus" stems from the frustration of this design. Stephen fears he has not escaped childhood: Joyce first suggests this fear by allowing Buck Mulligan to refer to the tower in which he and Stephen live as an *omphalos*. Stephen has escaped his childhood environment only to return to it once again, only to be held in thrall by Ireland as a child is joined to its mother at the omphalos or navel. His ambitions thwarted, he has not become his own artistic father but remains still a child, beset with all of the self-doubts and confusions of childhood. No longer spiritually invigorated by the blossoming of artistic sensitivity, Stephen has retreated from his future back into a dreary Irish past.

[7] There is no reason to assume, as some readers and critics have assumed, that this paternal ambition of Stephen is condemned by Joyce. Here is a pertinent example of the dangers of an excessively "Catholic" interpretation of Joyce. As my Chapter II argues, Joyce certainly did retain a puritanical, Irish Catholic habit of mind in regard to morality, especially sexual morality. But the conclusion does not therefore follow that Joyce remained a believer in Canon Law or in the myriad doctrines of the Church: it is precisely these doctrines which he threw off, while consciously or unconsciously retaining his puritanism. Father William T. Noon, S.J., in his *Joyce and Aquinas* (New Haven, 1963), goes too far when he in effect damns Stephen for violating orthodox Aquinian Trinitarianism (p. 95). When Stephen says that he wants to give birth to himself through art, he is speaking acceptable Joycean doctrine, whether or not St. Thomas would agree with him. The irony of Stephen's statement lies not in his anti-Trinitarianism but in the dearth of his artistic production. Sabellius, the "subtle African heresiarch," was closer to Joyce, the subtle Irish heresiarch, than Father Noon admits.

Stephen retreats because reality has overwhelmed his dreams and theories, has rendered his self-willed obsession with beauty impossible. The "Proteus" episode demonstrates this fact most clearly, but "Telemachus" states it poetically by means of Joyce's technical skill in manipulating certain liquid images. Through these liquid images Joyce establishes the similarity between Stephen's present predicament and that of his childhood; conversely, this water imagery enables Joyce to contrast Stephen's position at the outset of *Ulysses* with his position at the moment of his artistic nativity and during the latter part of the *Portrait*. Dedalus, "Telemachus" implies, has become Icarus. The waxen wings on which he soared artistically toward the music of the spheres have melted and Stephen-Icarus is adrift and paralyzed by fear of drowning. Inundated by the tides of reality, he feels a failure. Buck Mulligan is vicious but to the point: "—The bard's noserag. A new art colour for our Irish poets: snotgreen. . . .

"—God, he said quietly. Isn't the sea what Algy calls it: a grey sweet mother? The snotgreen sea. . . . She is our great sweet mother" (*U*5). Some months before, Stephen had run down to the sea and had seen there a young girl, standing before him in the tide like a strange seabird, delicate and pure, the symbol of his embryonic art. Now the sea fades into the vile color of mucous, snotgreen. Green too was the sluggish bile vomited forth from the rotten liver of his poor dying mother (*U*5). Stephen had not knelt down to pray for his mother; he had denied the last request of her who had given him life, and thus he is plagued by guilt, "agenbite of inwit," remorse of conscience for his willful inaction. Like this ugly deathroom memory, the sea threatens metaphorically to engulf him, "a dull green mass of liquid" (*U*5) and Stephen fears he will drown: "The man that was drowned. A sail veering about the blank bay waiting for a swollen bundle to bob up, roll over to the sun a puffy face, salt white. Here I am" (*U*21). Perhaps

Stephen thinks "Here I am," the words of the drowning man, as if to reassure himself that it is not he who has drowned, who has sunk beneath the surface of the sea. Homer's Telemachus feared his father's "white bones . . . lie wasting in the rain upon the mainland or the billow rolls them in the brine,"[8] while Joyce's Telemachus, longing to become his own father through artistic creation, thinks of a similar end to fatherhood.

Broadly, the snotgreen sea may be said to represent those aspects of reality which have been the bane of Stephen's old optimism. And Joyce extends the significance of this water imagery—through the figure of a bowl—to encompass sordid aspects of reality both past and present. Mrs. Dedalus' sluggish bile was held by a "bowl of white china"; the sea is depicted as a "bowl of bitter waters"; and Buck Mulligan carries a shaving bowl which reminds Stephen of his dark days of servitude at Clongowes: "So I carried the boat of incense then at Clongowes. I am another now and yet the same. A servant too. A server of a servant" ($U7$, 11, 13). Through the symbol of a bowl Joyce ties together the unpleasant realities of a distant past (Clongowes), the immediate past (Stephen's mother's death), and the present (the surrounding Irish sea). As a young boy, always an outsider, Stephen had listened to the noise of other boys at their games: "through the quiet air the sound of the cricket bat . . . like drops of water in a fountain falling softly in the brimming bowl" ($P59$). He is another now—and yet the same. Once again he writhes uncomfortably in bondage to his surroundings, immersed in a "bowl of bitter waters," a server at the altar of environmental tyranny. As in the first three chapters of the *Portrait*, he is afflicted with a symbolic hydrophobia: here he

---

[8] *Odyssey*, I, 5. This and all subsequent quotations from the *Odyssey* are taken from the translation of S. H. Butcher and Andrew Lang (London, 1930), since Frank Budgen tells us that "As a work of reference for his *Ulysses* [Joyce] used the Butcher-Lang translation of the *Odyssey*." *James Joyce and the Making of Ulysses*, p. 323.

fears the snotgreen Irish sea, while as a child he feared the memory of that slimy, rat-infested ditch. The two water-images convey the same Joycean hostility to sordid aspects of existence.[9] "Telemachus" shows Stephen held again by the omphalos, the old bonds of his childhood, unable to escape simply because there is no escape from reality.

Wearied at last of his efforts to dam up the tides of reality, Stephen has given himself up to despair, a despair which Buck Mulligan's kind of wit does nothing to dispel. Mulligan's humor does place the reader at a certain distance from Stephen, however; for while one sympathizes with Stephen's predicament, Mulligan's lightheartedness makes this would-be artist seem somewhat self-indulgent. Stephen lacks Mulligan's sense of humor, while Mulligan lacks Stephen's conscience. Fortunately, Joyce does not ask the reader to choose between shallow witticisms and lugubrious self-laceration: *Ulysses* has just begun, and the dominant tone of the book will not be set until the entrance of Leopold Bloom.

• 2 •

In the first episode of *Ulysses* Joyce establishes certain parallels with the *Odyssey*, the central parallel being the similar positions of Stephen and Telemachus, each of whom feels deprived of his rightful inheritance. In the second episode a new pattern emerges in these parallels: a pattern of comic inversion, by which certain Homeric characters appear in twentieth century Dublin amusingly transformed. One might argue that Joyce's pattern of comic inversion has begun already, since Stephen's rather boring, self-pitying narcissism does seem to contrast with the vigor of Telemachus in books I-IV, XV-XVII, XIX, and XXIV of the *Odyssey*. But for all his self pity, Stephen's perceptions are

[9] Cf. Maurice Beebe, "Barnacle Goose and Lapwing," *PMLA*, LXXI (June 1956), 308-309.

acute, and even if some contrast with Telemachus is evident, this contrast is not nearly so extreme nor so comic as that between several other Homeric figures and their Joycean analogues.

The correspondence between Mr. Deasy and Nestor is the first overtly comic Joycean inversion of Homeric dignity. A rather close analysis of this inversion may be useful here, because so much disagreement exists over the question of Joyce's use of Homer. The Deasy-Nestor parallel serves as at least one indisputable example of at least one function of the *Odyssey* in *Ulysses*. Surely there can be no question of Joyce's satiric purpose in this instance. We need not yet conclude whether satire is simply one of many Joycean uses of the *Odyssey* in *Ulysses*; but as for Mr. Deasy, the Homeric parallel is used to mock him.[10] In the *Odyssey* Nestor appears as a wise old man who informs Telemachus about the outcome of the Trojan War, and who sagely advises Telemachus to seek further news of Ulysses in Sparta. Athene, herself the fount of all wisdom, has instructed Telemachus to "go straight to Nestor, tamer of horses: let us learn what counsel he hath in the secret of his heart. And beseech him thyself that he may give unerring answer; and he will not lie to thee, for he is very wise."[11] Nestor lives up to Athene's praise of him: he is the most dignified of mortals, the "great glory of the Achaeans," the beloved father of many sons. He is also extremely generous: he provides Telemachus with swift horses for the journey to Sparta, as well as with one of his sons as guide. And he is humble: he bows before the wisdom of the gods and is always ready with sacrifices for them. Mr. Deasy, Nestor's Irish counterpart in *Ulysses*, exhibits precisely opposite characteristics, and the result is an amusing con-

[10] Critics who dislike Stephen intensely must perforce try to palliate the gross offensiveness of Mr. Deasy, since the two characters are played off against one another in this episode. For such an attempt, see William York Tindall, *A Reader's Guide to James Joyce* (New York, 1959), pp. 141-43.

[11] *Odyssey*, III, 23.

trast in which Mr. Deasy, who impresses one immediately as a fool, appears even more fatuous in the shadow of sagacious old Nestor. Where Nestor is wise, Mr. Deasy displays the narrowness of a provincial bourgeois; where Nestor is generous, Mr. Deasy is uncommonly niggardly; and where Nestor is humble, Mr. Deasy is arrogant.

"—You think me an old fogey and an old tory," Mr. Deasy says to Stephen, and we nod in agreement. Mr. Deasy is obsessed with saving money and with saving England and Ireland from the Jews. He regards "I never borrowed a shilling in my life" as the proudest boast of any man, and of the Jews he comments, "—They sinned against the light. And you can see the darkness in their eyes. And that is why they are wanderers on the earth to this day" (*U*34). Stephen, of course, thinks Mr. Deasy vacuous and offensive: "Is this old wisdom?" he asks himself (*U*34), reminding us of Nestor's old and veritable wisdom. Mr. Deasy's Polonius-like insistence upon the immoral nature of borrowing is particularly irritating to Stephen, who lists ten creditors, as such an insistence must also have been annoying to Joyce, who once wrote to his brother, "There are some people in Ireland who would call my moral nature oblique, people who think that the whole duty of man consists in paying one's debts: but in this case Irish opinion is certainly only the caricature of the opinion of any European tribunal."[12] Thus where Homer's Telemachus was able to benefit from the sage advice of Nestor, Joyce's Telemachus must listen in aggrieved silence to the platitudes of Mr. Deasy, whose moral sense is remote from Joyce's own. Joyce's inversion of the *Odyssey* has a distinct effect: the figures in Joyce's world are ludicrous by the classical standards evoked through Joyce's

[12] Letter to Stanislaus Joyce, 19 July 1905, *Letters*, II, 99-100. In this same letter Joyce speaks of his "struggle against conventions . . . with the intention of living in conformity with my moral nature." Stephen is engaged in a similar struggle and—for all his self-indulgence—as such contrasts sharply with the compromising Mulligan.

allusions. These allusions expand our conception of Stephen's position. His melancholy stems from his own sense of moral isolation. He feels alone with his conscience: his artistic heirdom is threatened by usurpers, and his pride is further compromised by virtue of his inferior rank to Mr. Deasy. Though supposedly a teacher now, he might as well be entrapped as a student at Clongowes once again.

A final mythic inversion renders the ignominy of Stephen's predicament complete. Homer's Nestor is humbly conscious of his indebtedness to the beneficence of the gods; and in order to express this humility in a traditional way, he frequently sacrifices bullocks with proper ceremony. There are five references to such sacrifices in the "Nestor" episode of the *Odyssey*, and the climactic action of that episode is taken up with the ritualistic slaughter of a heifer in honor of Athene. Similarly yet conversely, the climactic action of Joyce's "Nestor" episode also involves cattle. Mr. Deasy has written a platitudinous letter on the hoof and mouth disease and asks Stephen to try to get the letter inserted in a Dublin newspaper.[13] Unenthusiastic about having to perform such a menial service for this garrulous old fool, Stephen nevertheless agrees to try. Again Joyce's comic inversion of material in the *Odyssey* underlines the absurdity of Stephen's position. This absurdity is evident without reference to the *Odyssey*, but in the context of Homer, Joyce's comic-satiric intentions stand out in bolder relief. In a second mythical context, that of Daedalus, Stephen's ridiculous situation is further amplified: Stephen's mythical namesake had designed a labyrinth to contain and therefore to conquer that bullish monster, the Minotaur. But Stephen Dedalus finds himself

[13] Joyce himself wrote a newspaper article on the hoof and mouth disease (*CW* 238-41), so there is probably an element of self-satire in having Stephen serve the same cause. Notably, Joyce's article warned of "mischief-makers" like Mr. Deasy, who were trying to exclude Irish cattle from English markets. This may seem a petty point, but it does serve to underline the ignominy of Stephen's having to serve Deasy—that old tory and old fogey.

the lackey of an old man who wants to gain publicity for himself as a friend of cattle. The ludicrousness of this development is apparent to Stephen, for he thinks to himself, "Mulligan will dub me a new name: the bullockbefriending bard" (*U*36). To Stephen, ever conscious of his proud surname, this is an additional ignominy. Joyce manages to squeeze every possible comic ramification out of Homeric and Daedalian mythic analogies. As true as it is that the essential elements of *Ulysses* are quite perceptible without reference to any mythic counterparts, conflicts in interpretation can be reduced if we approximate the care with which Joyce established these analogies by our own care in observing them. Any reader may choose to ignore the analogies or to regard them as mere "scaffolding"; but he sacrifices a great deal of Joyce's comedy in so doing.

"Telemachus" establishes the general basis of Stephen's melancholy: he feels his artistic heirdom threatened by usurpers and recognizes that he may be drowning in the snotgreen sea of Irish paralysis. "Nestor" provides the reader with a more specific sense of Stephen's predicament not only through mythic analogies but also through several brief glimpses into his personal moral vision. In "Nestor" one recognizes a Joycean conscience in Stephen Dedalus. Stephen is first of all ridden with a sense of personal guilt: his recurrent thoughts about his inaction beside his mother's deathbed are a sign of this conscience.[14] Second, Stephen views history as the bloodstained record of man's inhumanity to man: life to him is a series of "jousts, slush and uproar of battles, the frozen deathspew of the slain, a shout of spear spikes baited with men's bloodied guts" (*U*32). The history book itself is to him "gorescarred." Thus Stephen condemns the bloody course of human history. Third, he suspects this bloody pattern to be inescapable. A familiar prayer runs through his mind in this episode, a prayer which asserts in absolute terms

14 See note 17 below

the ineluctable nature of existence: "As it was in the beginning, is now. . . . and ever shall be. . . . world without end" (*U*29). And as a further meditation upon the inevitable, Stephen wonders, "Was that only possible which came to pass?" (*U*25). Thus he asserts to Mr. Deasy, "History is a nightmare from which I am trying to awake" (*U*34).

In the *Portrait* Stephen might have considered history as a bloody nightmare, but he had small doubt of his own ability to awake from it. His awakening was to take place through beauty; but in *Ulysses* this aesthetic confidence has vanished: Stephen has come closer to the Joycean view. A sense of guilt, personal and historical, now blots out former optimism, and he can think only that he has no more been able to change the course of his own life than mankind has been able to change the gory course of history. The sight of a scrawny, bespectacled student causes Stephen to muse, "Like him was I, these sloping shoulders, this gracelessness. My childhood bends beside me. . . . Secrets, silent, stony sit in the dark palaces of both our hearts: secrets weary of their tyranny: tyrants willing to be dethroned" (*U*28). Stephen's childhood bends beside him as an apparition of his own failures; for he has not been able to escape servitude to the triple tyranny of his environment, his own moral failures, and history itself. "I am another now and yet the same," he says to himself in "Telemachus." These are his secrets, tyrannical secrets, "tyrants willing to be dethroned"—if only Stephen has the will to break them. For the moment he does not have sufficient will. For the moment he cannot awake from the nightmare, cannot dethrone the usurpers of his heirdom, cannot escape Mulligan nor Haines nor this inverted Nestor nor his own guilt. Burdened with the exactitude of Joyce's own moral conscience, he has not yet discovered Joyce's own final stance toward the world, the essence of which is comedy.

⟨   84   ⟩

· 3 ·

In "Proteus" Joyce expands the themes and techniques of "Telemachus" and "Nestor," placing still further emphasis upon the weight of conscience which Stephen bears. By sounding again and again these moral chords at the beginning of *Ulysses*, Joyce influences our reading of the more whimsical episodes which follow, encouraging the reader to perceive a relationship between the humorous actions of Leopold Bloom and Stephen's gloomy broodings upon blood, guilt, and shame. A close examination of "Proteus" is therefore worthwhile not only as another glimpse into Stephen's mind but as a thematic prelude to ensuing action.

That a protean process has taken place in Stephen is evident well before the "Proteus" episode. His aesthetic cult of the virginal, which had been the basis of his theory of art, has given way to a persistent dwelling upon less pleasing facets of life and of humanity. During the year which has elapsed since his departure for Paris, Stephen has come round to a more Joycean position. Confronted with the "realities of experience" he so longed to encounter at the end of the *Portrait*, Stephen has begun to see the world in a different light. Hitherto he had turned erotic dreams into hymns, had thought of delicate verse amid the slums of dirty Dublin, and had declaimed Aristotle and Aquinas to the reptilian Lynch. Hitherto he had walked along the strand beneath "dappled seaborne clouds," had felt the "wild air," and had turned a smiling eye upon "brackish waters and the seaharvest of shells and tangle and veiled grey sunlight and gayclad lightclad figures of children and girls and voices childish and girlish in the air" (P171). Now, a year later, in the "Proteus" episode, Stephen sees scattered across the beach the "Ineluctable modality of the visible . . . seaspawn and seawrack, the nearing tide, that rusty boot. Snotgreen, bluesilver, rust:

coloured signs. . . . His boots trod again a damp crackling mast, razorshells, squeaking pebbles . . . wood sieved by the shipworm, lost Armada. Unwholesome sandflats waited to suck his treading soles, breathing upward sewage breath" (*U*37, 40-41). The contrast between Stephen's vision in the *Portrait* and his vision here in "Proteus" is extreme. The ethereal scene of his artistic awakening is now strewn with the rubble of centuries, the open graves of vain hopes —Stephen's artistic hopes among them. The dovelike girl he had seen wading in the water as a virginal symbol of his art has been washed over by the bitter waters of reality, sunk like Lycidas beneath the watery floor, just as Stephen fears he himself is sinking beneath the snotgreen Irish sea of paralysis. Here in the strand-setting of "Proteus," Joyce in effect reverses the paramount scene of the *Portrait*: the sordid tides of life have banished beauty.

With characteristic thoroughness Joyce completes this reversal of the *Portrait* by replacing the dovelike girl with a creature commensurate with the rubble which now litters Stephen's vision of reality. In place of the girl an unwholesome little dog appears on the beach—sniffing carrion and making his own brief but frequent contributions to the waters washing Ireland's shores. "Did you see the point of that bit about the dog?" Joyce once asked Frank Budgen. "He is a mummer among beasts—the Protean animal. . . . This [passage] certainly wasn't done by a dog-lover," Joyce continued. "I don't like them. I am afraid of them."[15] The dog thus acts in a role of double-reversal: Joyce substitutes him not only for the virginal girl of the *Portrait* but for that sea-god of Greek mythology, Proteus, who appears in the *Odyssey* as the elusive knower of Ulysses' whereabouts. Through Menelaus, Telemachus learns the secret knowledge of Proteus; as Joyce's Telemachus, Stephen is in search of analogous truths. But just as Mr.

[15] Budgen, *James Joyce and the Making of Ulysses*, pp. 53-54.

Deasy was the comic counterpart of Nestor, this faintly disgusting little dog is the comic counterpart of Proteus. Menelaus informs Telemachus of the remarkable feats of the magic arts of Proteus: "First he turned into a bearded lion, and thereafter into a snake, and a pard, and a huge boar; then he took the shape of running water, and of a tall and flowering tree."[16] Joyce's dog performs similar feats, though unconsciously and with significant differences, differences which point up Joyce's distinctly un-Homeric purpose: "The carcass lay on |the dog's| path. He stopped, sniffed, stalked round it, brother, nosing closer, went round it, sniffing rapidly like a dog all over the dead dog's bedraggled fell. . . . Along by the edge of the mole he lolloped, dawdled, smelt a rock and from under a cocked hindleg pissed against it. He trotted forward and, lifting his hindleg, pissed quick short at an unsmelt rock. The simple pleasures of the poor. His hindpaws then scattered sand: then his forepaws dabbled and delved. Something he buried there, his grandmother. He rooted in the sand, dabbling, delving and stopped to listen to the air, scraped up the sand again with a fury of his claws, soon ceasing, a pard, a panther, got in spouse-breach, vulturing the dead" (U46-47). Unconsciously skillful in mimicry, the dog assumes like Proteus the animated shapes of many animals; unlike Proteus, however, and very much in keeping with Joyce's comic-satiric purpose here, the dog performs a series of unsavory actions. In Homer Proteus is beautiful to watch, as a versatile dancer is beautiful: he neither sniffs at carcasses, nor pisses quick short, nor claws the earth above a hypothetically buried grandmother. Nor is a vulture among the creatures he imitates. This little canine bastard ("got in spouse-breach") thus serves Joyce well as the central figure in his inversion of Odyssean grandeur, and he serves equally well as the repellent counterpart of the dovelike wading girl.

16 *Odyssey*, IV, 45.

Through these implied allusions to the *Portrait* and direct allusions to the *Odyssey*, Joyce elucidates the changes in Stephen's outlook. For Stephen, the beauty which once held a dominant position in reality has become engulfed by sordid tides. In his searches after truth he cannot hope to encounter, like Telemachus, tales of heroic nobility, enchantingly unfolded by sea-god narrators. Instead he must look for truth among the old boots and worm-eaten masts and broken shells along the strand, find truth embodied in the unlikely protean figure of a dog.

Just as the now-absent dovelike girl of the *Portrait* heralded Stephen's aesthetic awakening, so this protean dog becomes the emblem of Stephen's new moral and aesthetic vision. "Signatures of all things I am here to read," Stephen declares to himself on the first page of "Proteus": this sentence represents a revolution in his aesthetic thinking. Heretofore the end of art was for him strictly the apprehension of the beautiful; now the artist must read "signatures of *all* things," including "that rusty boot," "snotgreen bluesilver rust," all visible things, be they beautiful or loathsome. The domain of art must be, as Stephen phrases it, the "Ineluctable modality of the visible: at least that if no more, thought through my eyes" (*U*37). In the *Portrait* Stephen approvingly quoted Plato's aphorism, "Beauty is the splendour of truth," and explained, "I don't think that it has a meaning but the true and the beautiful are akin" (*P*208). By the time we see him again in *Ulysses*, Stephen has decided that not only the beautiful is akin to truth. He now sees truth as a protean entity, multifaceted, symbolized both by a virginal girl and a nasty little mongrel. As an artist he must not try to ignore either but instead must read the signatures of both.

In dramatizing Stephen's artistic and moral position in "Proteus," Joyce does not always rely upon the poetic indirections of allusion but provides us with Stephen's direct commentaries as well. As in "Nestor," Stephen meditates upon the bloodstained history of mankind and upon his own participation in human guilt. The interrelated themes of historical and personal guilt were but furtively mentioned in "Telemachus" and "Nestor," but they dominate "Proteus." On the first page of that episode, when Stephen concerns himself with no less pervasive a question than the nature of reality ("modality of the visible"), he tries a familiar little experiment: after viewing the litter on the beach which signifies to him the incoherent flotsam and jetsam of life, he closes his eyes—playfully wondering whether the mess might disappear by the time he reopens them. Eyes closed, he quickly discovers that even blindness brings no escape, for the "Ineluctable modality of the visible" is replaced by the "ineluctable modality of the audible," as his boots crush and crackle the wreckage beneath them, sound conveying the same meanings as sight. "Open your eyes now," he thinks. "Has all vanished since? . . . I will see if I can see. See now. There all the time without you: and ever shall be, world without end" (U37). Stephen's facetious experiment substantiates his assertion that the modality of the visible is indeed ineluctable, is there forever with or without him.

Stephen connects the disheartening rubble of the strand with a bleak view of mankind's development, or lack of it. His fancy pushes his mind back toward Eden and a vision of Eve which coincides with his conviction that the moral blemishes of man are inherent. Eve herself, he speculates, was without blemish; but her womb generated an unending succession of morally flawed creatures: "[Eve] had no navel. Gaze. Belly without blemish, bulging big, a buckler of taut vellum, no, whiteheaped corn, orient and immortal, standing from everlasting to everlasting. Womb of sin" (U38). This Edenic fantasy constitutes Stephen's personal version of the doctrine of original sin. Because of his inherent flaws, man has expended thousands of years of energy in bloodthirsty conquest. Bloodlust punctuates Ireland's own history. The very strand upon which Stephen walks has trembled beneath the weight of countless invasions: "Galleys of the Lochlanns ran here to beach, in quest of prey, their bloodbeaked prows riding low on a molten pewter surf. . . . Then from the starving cagework city a horde of jerkined dwarfs, my people, with flayers' knives, running, scaling, hacking in green blubbery whalemeat. Famine, plague and slaughters. Their blood is in me, their lusts my waves" (U45).

While thinking of the bloodlusts of the past, Stephen significantly and characteristically involves himself in the errors of his forefathers, because as a believer in original sin he cannot exempt himself from guilt. Their lusts are his. The modality of history is ineluctable. Still more pointedly Stephen reminds himself, "Wombed in sin darkness I was too, made not begotten. By them, the man with my voice and my eyes and a ghostwoman with ashes on her breath. They clasped and sundered, did the coupler's will" (U38). His existence has sprung from a lustful clasp in darkness: he was not euphemistically "begotten" but bluntly, bestially "made." In making him his parents renewed the inevitable pattern of sin, the God-ordained pattern which Stephen cannot escape: "From before the ages He willed me and now may not will me away or ever" (U38).

The conscience which Stephen brings to bear upon himself, his surroundings, and human history strongly resembles Joyce's own. Like Joyce, Stephen now acknowledges to himself the belief that a lower force in man rivals and often overcomes his higher nature. In typically Joycean—and typically Irish—fashion, Stephen fixes upon sexuality as an important, perhaps the most important, moral issue. In Ireland only the names of Jameson and Guinness rival that of the Virgin Mary in the national pantheon: and when Stephen laments that he was "wombed in sin darkness," he indicates his adherence to the puritanical, Irish,

Joycean conviction that the sexual act is itself sinful, is itself perhaps the origin of man's moral weakness. "Darkness is in our souls," Stephen silently muses. And to express his sense of that moral darkness he chooses—or Joyce chooses for him—sexuality as a metaphor. "Our souls, shame-wounded by our sins, cling to us yet more, a woman to her lover clinging, the more the more" (U48). Eternally lovers will clasp in darkness, eternally bloodlusting armies will clash; intervals of innocence and peace will follow, but inevitably the shameful pattern will resume.

Stephen is trying to rise above this flux to some degree, though he knows he cannot escape it altogether. He seems to doubt that he can escape it at all. Certainly an obsession with the beautiful was no answer but led to self-deception and an art remote from life. As we see him in "Proteus" he wanders aimlessly, brooding upon the protean nature of truth, upon history and sin, and fearing that the Irish earth is sucking him into its paralyzing self: "Unwholesome sandflats waited to suck his treading soles, . . . He stood suddenly, his feet beginning to sink slowly in the quaking soil. Turn back. . . . he scanned the shore south, his feet sinking again slowly in new sockets" (U41, 44). And just as in the *Portrait* and "Telemachus," Joyce employs water imagery to epitomize Stephen's fears: "The man that was drowned nine days ago off Maiden's rock. . . . I am not a strong swimmer. Water cold soft. When I put my face into it in the basin at Clongowes. Can't see! Who's behind me? Out quickly, quickly! Do you see the tide flowing quickly in on all sides, sheeting the lows of sands quickly . . . ? If I had land under my feet. I want his life still to be his, mine to be mine. A drowning man. His human eyes scream to me out of horror of his death. I . . . With him together down . . . I could not save her. Waters: bitter death: lost" (U45-46). A terror of drowning in the waters of his environment besets him; he wonders if he is strong enough to stay afloat, thinks of his analogous terrors at Clongowes, feels the sordid tides of life drawing him out to sea and has a vision of the horrors of sea-death—spiritual death, in the context of the episode and its imagery. This watery reverie culminates in an "agenbite of inwit," a bite of conscience, as he again recalls his inaction at his mother's bedside: "I could not save her."[17]

Stephen's persistent idealism makes him want to save himself, despite his disillusionment with the nature of things. At the close of the *Portrait* he had entertained a view of himself as an artist which was incompatible with the sea of reality. Now, disheartened, fearing the disappearance of his soul into the depths of that sea, he still hopes somehow to transcend reality through art. But his art must confront life directly, must immerse itself in bitter waters. Stephen watches "the writhing weeds lift languidly and sway reluctant arms, hising up their petticoats, in whispering water swaying and upturning coy silver fronds. Day by day: night by night: lifted, flooded and let fall. Lord, they are weary: and, whispered to, they sigh. . . . To no end gathered: vainly then released, forth flowing, wending back: loom of the moon. Weary too in sight of lovers, lascivious men, a naked woman shining in her courts, she draws a toil of waters" (*U*49-50). He sees in this movement of weeds and waters a metaphor of his own view of life, history, human nature: the Joycean view, the Joycean conscience. Sexuality pervades the metaphor,

---

[17] Like Stephen, Joyce himself felt guilty about his mother's death, though not necessarily because of any failure to pray at her deathbed. Joyce confessed to Nora that "My mother was slowly killed, I think, by my father's ill-treatment, by years of trouble, and by my cynical frankness of conduct. When I looked on her face as she lay in her coffin—a face grey and wasted with cancer—I understood that I was looking on the face of a victim and I cursed the system which had made her a victim." 29 August 1904, *Letters*, II, 48. This quotation aids our understanding of Stephen's predicament: like Joyce, he is both guilt-ridden and filled with hatred of and rebellion against the Irish "system." The self-indulgence which Joyce attributes to him should not obscure all sympathy and authorial empathy.

as the weeds lift their petticoats to the waters, time and time again, turning their fronds like women their skirts, weaving the pattern of the moon. And in the goddess of the moon, the virginal Diana, Stephen sees his familiar ideal of virginal innocence. The moon, that most feminine of symbols, weary of lasciviousness, yet herself the magnetic source of lasciviousness, her nature like a toil, or net, drawing her wearisome yet inevitable lovers: This ineluctable pattern must become the subject of Stephen's new art, as it has become the subject of Joyce's. Even if spiritual innocence—"the virginity of the soul" as Joyce called it— is to be his spiritual standard, he can no longer ignore the baseness in life, nor the moral weakness that has marred the history of mankind. He can no longer ignore that sniffing, clawing, urinating little dog as a protean symbol of truth. He can, however, continue to harbor his ideal of innocence, even as Gretta Conroy in "The Dead" harbored her ideal of Michael Furey, or as Joyce himself harbored such an ideal: the conscience of *Ulysses*.

iv. the conscience and Leopold Bloom

The first three chapters of *Ulysses* show Stephen the prisoner of despondency, despairing of the universe, history, mankind, himself. He has become a misanthrope. In similar moods and circumstances Joyce may have been able to take solace in the "something higher" he felt to be an elevating part of his own nature, but like Stephen he was in his earlier writings predominantly misanthropic. The indictment of Ireland in *Dubliners*, the confusion and despair of *Exiles*—all find their reflections in the first three chapters of *Ulysses*, where the quality of Stephen's anguish resembles, even in its self-pity, that of Joyce's letters to his wife. Hints of a brighter mood show up in Mulligan's wit and in the portrait of old Deasy, but they are as two poppies in a field of weeds.

And yet *Ulysses* is a laugh, a cheering, purging laugh; and Stephen's mood is no more Joyce's than Jaques's mood is Shakespeare's in *As You Like It*. This Joycean laughter, which dominates and controls *Ulysses*, is not that of celebration or affirmation, for Joyce's essential ideas and opinions have not altered. He is still no indiscriminate lover of mankind, no celebrant of human folly. But while shunning the sentimental, he has mellowed. Depending upon how sympathetic one is with Joyce's moral position, one might say either that the Joycean frown has given way to an indulgent laugh, or that the Joycean snarl has been succeeded by a smirk. Whichever, humor has won out. Rage and rancor are controlled by elaborate jokes. In *Ulysses* most of the jokes are on Leopold Bloom and his fellow citizens; in *Finnegans Wake* the joke assumes cosmic proportions. But in both books laughter tempers Joyce's scorn.

Joyce evidently was impelled to leaven his burdensome moral conscience, and laughter became his chosen ingredient. Laughter provided him with an escape from despair, without necessitating the abandonment of his moral principles. Men might still be beasts, history a nightmare, and beauty an elusive ideal. But now the frustrations and vexations and illusions of life were found amusing as well as enraging.

Laughter renders Joyce's morality more palatable to the reader, especially to that reader who may not share Joyce's conscience. Joyce's artistic design, as he wrote Nora, was to create "at last a conscience in the soul of this wretched race": in *Ulysses* he created a conscience so jovial that it can be enjoyed even by readers unwilling to accept its moral premises. The rigorous Joycean conscience remained, unsurprisingly, unchanged: Joyce began full-time work on *Ulysses* in 1914, only five years after he had written Nora that revealing series of letters and a year before *Exiles* had been finished. It would be misleading to interpret the light tone of *Ulysses* as a total break with the Joycean past, for Joyce's puritanism was no more eradicated than the Irish Jesuits from whom he acquired it. But by avoiding the offensive cant of sermon or tract, and by keeping to a comic tone throughout, Joyce made *Ulysses* a readable morality.

Stylistically, the change to comedy came naturally to Joyce, for he had already mastered the art of treating his characters with detachment. All he needed to add to this detachment was an element of the ridiculous—and *Ulysses* was born. Joyce's two chief protagonists before *Ulysses*, Stephen Dedalus and Richard Rowan, are criticized by

⟨   95   ⟩

means of the inevitable Joycean ironic distance, but they share enough of the author's own convictions to merit a large amount of authorial sympathy. Both Stephen and Richard are Joycean enough to be "shocked by the baseness in men and women" and to believe in "the virginity of the soul." Leopold Bloom is an entirely different sort of protagonist—one who does not share Joyce's stringent morality, one whose humorous foibles all but obscure what virtues are his. But Joyce's comic treatment of Bloom is stylistically and technically only an extension or exaggeration of his detached treatment of Richard and Stephen.

Comedy brought Joyce certain artistic complications along with benefits. For while few readers can mistake the scorn of, say, *Dubliners* for praise, entirely contradictory interpretations of *Ulysses* are possible. Attitudes toward Leopold Bloom, for example, vary from admiration to ridicule: to some readers he is a pacifistic hero (or anti-hero), patient and forbearing throughout the trials of his life; to others he is a symbol of the degeneration of industrial society; to still others he is simply an amiable boob. The origin of this disagreement among the readers of *Ulysses* lies to a certain extent in the regrettable if universal tendency to see in a book what one wishes to see, particularly if one has been assured beforehand that the work in question is a masterpiece. For if a book be excellent, the reader tells himself unconsciously, it must therefore contain something of my own excellent philosophy. But the interpretive chaos surrounding *Ulysses* lies further and more particularly in the nature of humor itself. Few jokes are thought funny by everyone, and on a more exalted plane, what comic literary masterpiece is thought to be comic for the same reasons by every reader? That *Don Quixote* is a comic masterpiece all readers agree, and yet to some the Knight of the Mournful Countenance is a fool, while to others he is a hero, and to still others he is both.

Yet amid this confused subjectivity a hope does exist

for extrication—a hope in the form of hint, placed in *Ulysses* by Joyce as a clue to his own intentions. That hint or clue is the exhaustive parallel which Joyce drew between his own comic epic and Homer's *Odyssey*, and especially between the Greek Ulysses and Leopold Bloom. No aspect of *Ulysses* has aroused more comment or more disagreement than the Homeric parallel, and a score of explanations has been proposed for its existence. Essentially, such explanations fall into three groups: those finding that the parallel *equates* Joyce's characters with the heroic figures of the *Odyssey*, thereby coloring Dubliners with some sort of heroic grandeur; those finding that the parallel is a mock-heroic device which points up the absurdities of Dubliners as compared with their Homeric counterparts; and finally those finding the parallels useless as keys to Joyce's meaning.[1] Propounding this last view, which lately has gained wide acceptance, Ezra Pound wrote in 1922, "These correspondences are part of Joyce's medievalism and are chiefly his own affair, a scaffold, a means of construction. . . ."[2] Mr. Pound's view has since been echoed

[1] Most prominent among those critics who equate Joyce's characters with Homer's, especially Leopold Bloom with Ulysses, is Richard Ellmann, throughout the analytical portions of his biography of Joyce, *James Joyce* (New York, 1959); but as an extreme instance of this approach, see Joseph Prescott, "Homer's *Odyssey* and Joyce's *Ulysses*," *Modern Language Quarterly*, III (September 1942), 427-44. Perhaps the most convincing argument for a mock-heroic approach to the Homeric parallels is Lawrance Thompson, *A Comic Principle in Stern—Meredith—Joyce* (Ann Arbor, 1967), pp. 44-64. Others arguing effectively for this view have been Vivienne Koch, "An Approach to the Homeric Context of Joyce's Ulysses," *Maryland Quarterly*, I (1944), 119-30; and Rudolph Von Abele, "*Ulysses*: the Myth of Myth," *PMLA*, LXIX (June 1954), 358-64. Harry Levin gave impetus to a now widespread dismissal of the thematic importance of the parallels when he wrote in his *James Joyce* (New York, 1941) that the effect of the parallels is both mock-heroic and heroic, both ironic and magnifying, and therefore probably of greater importance to Joyce as scaffolding than to the reader as a thematic key. And David Daiches, *The Novel and the Modern World* (Chicago, 1960), argues that Joyce provides no distinctions between heroic and unheroic: that both are reduced or leveled-out to the same plane, contrary values thus being indistinguishable (pp. 113ff.).

[2] *Literary Essays of Ezra Pound*, ed. T. S. Eliot (London, 1954), p. 406.

countless times. Yet one wonders why Joyce labored so scrupulously to establish these parallels if his readers were not really intended to bother with them. And one wonders further why Joyce gave his novel the title he did give it— calling immediate attention to the Homeric parallel—if he expected his readers to ignore Homeric parallels. It is all very well for a recent critic to advise us that "it would be a grave mistake to found any interpretation of *Ulysses* on Joyce's [Homeric] *schema*, rather than on the human actions of Stephen, and Molly, and Mr. Leopold Bloom."[3] That sounds sensible enough—but a glance backward at my Preface should suggest that when you try to evaluate "human actions" you get very human, and therefore very subjective, criticism: that is to say, you get the chaos of Joyce criticism. The Homeric parallel provides an escape from that subjectivity.

Since Joyce abandoned in *Ulysses* his previously outright moral indignation in favor of a gentler irony and comedy, he needed a sturdy objective standard, a standard which would give voice to the Joycean conscience and which would help his readers to assess the characters and events within *Ulysses*. And since nearly every action of Leopold Bloom parallels some action of Homer's Ulysses, Joyce invites his readers to draw an analogy between the two figures, invites them to compare Bloom with Ulysses, to employ the classical hero as a measuring stick for this modern hero or anti-hero.

Many readers and critics have responded to Joyce's invitation. But subjectivity again prevents any kind of consensus, for as many have found Bloom to be a noble embodiment of Ulyssean virtues as have found him to be a comic reversal of those virtues. "Bloom *is* Ulysses . . . ,"[4] writes Richard Ellmann. "Mr. Bloom is the opposite of the

[3] A. Walton Litz, *The Art of James Joyce* (New York, 1961), p. 40.
[4] Ellmann, *James Joyce*, p. 371.

crafty, conquering warrior-king,"[5] writes Edwin Burgum. And just to confuse matters thoroughly, Hugh Kenner insists that Bloom *is* Ulysses alright, but that we are burdened with a complete misunderstanding of Ulysses himself, who is not really a hero at all but rather the protagonist of a rollicking comedy—the *Odyssey*. Mr. Kenner further insists that this view of the *Odyssey*, peculiar though it may seem to us, is not only his own but Joyce's as well: Joyce saw the *Odyssey* as a comedy and therefore made his own *Ulysses* equally ridiculous by paralleling it with Homer. Admitting the novelty of this approach, Mr. Kenner concedes that "The immediate source of [Joyce's] Homeric insight is a mystery. He didn't know much classical Greek. . . ."[6] Mr. Kenner does not suggest how Joyce expected his readers to attain comparable "Homeric insight" when nearly all of them undoubtedly think of Ulysses as a crafty, resourceful, brave hero, and think of Penelope as synonymous with marital fidelity.

I have entered these critical jungles only to suggest that in the matter of the Homeric parallel one must tread carefully, because one is bound to tread on critical toes. What must be evident from this brief excursion is that one question must be answered first, before any single theory of Joyce's use of the *Odyssey* is settled upon: What exactly was Joyce's idea of Ulysses as a hero? Was Ulysses a strong hero in Joyce's mind, or a comic figure? Was it Ulysses' famous craftiness which most impressed Joyce? Or was Joyce thinking of a figure unfamiliar to most of us, when he drew so many careful parallels between the Homeric hero and Bloom? Before this matter is determined, before

[5] Edwin Berry Burgum, *The Novel and the World's Dilemma* (New York, 1947), p. 99.
[6] Hugh Kenner, *Dublin's Joyce* (London, 1955), pp. 192-93. Mr. Kenner's argument is based upon the comic approach of the Rouse translation of the *Odyssey*. Significantly, the Rouse translation was not completed until 1937, fifteen years after Joyce finished *Ulysses*.

Joyce's idea of Ulysses as a hero is ascertained, no one can be sure whether Leopold Bloom is being mocked or flattered when Joyce compares him to his mythical counterpart.

· I ·

Like Christian doctrine, Ulysses has represented many things to all men. He has proved himself an extremely versatile hero throughout the centuries. In fact he has proved himself a villain on occasion. Hero to Homer, he was villain to Sophocles in his *Philoctetes* and to Euripides in his *Hecuba*: in these two plays the Ulyssean guile which is a heroic quality in the *Odyssey* becomes the weapon of an unscrupulous schemer. Dante, like any good Italian a Trojan sympathizer, placed Ulysses with the evil counselors in the eighth circle of Hell. During the English Renaissance, contradictory attitudes toward Ulysses abounded. An epitome of honor, bravery, and wisdom, a seeker of just fame—Ulysses was regarded by some of Shakespeare's contemporaries as the embodiment of virtues then held in highest repute. Thus Samuel Daniel, in his "Ulysses and the Siren" (1605), depicted the Greek hero as honorably and chastely impervious to the siren's allure:

> Delicious nymph, suppose there were
> Nor honor nor report,
> Yet manliness would scorn to wear
> The time in idle sport.

Shakespeare's *Troilus and Cressida*, however, shows that even in the same decade in England there was little agreement as to the essence of Ulysses' character; for Shakespeare's Ulysses resembles the schemer of Sophocles, Euripides, and Dante more than the honorable gentleman of Samuel Daniel. Two hundred years later the author of the *Adventures of Ulysses* (1808), Charles Lamb, endowed Ulysses with the daring and immunity to harm of a fully romantic hero. In our day, among certain scholars, Ulysses has become the quintessential confidence-man, the classical trickster, perhaps the original anti-hero: but this is a minority view, so far as I have been able to determine.[7] Most modern classical scholars regard Ulysses as the embodiment of the Greek heroic ideal. C. M. Bowra describes that heroic ideal as "an outlook which regarded action as the main end of life and attached to it an ideal which demanded that a man must make the utmost of his body and his mind." Furthermore, writes Mr. Bowra, "The essence of the heroic outlook is the pursuit of honour through action. The great man is he who, being endowed with superior qualities of body and mind, uses them to the utmost and wins the applause of his fellows because he spares no effort and shirks no risk in his desire to make the most of his gifts and to surpass other men in his exercise of them. His honour is the centre of his being, and any affront to it calls for immediate amends. He courts danger gladly because it gives him the best opportunity of showing of what stuff he is made." Ulysses is such a man: he "is indeed brave to the point of recklessness but is renowned preeminently for counsel and resource."[8] Another eminent classicist of our day, Richmond Lattimore, concurs in Mr. Bowra's description of Ulysses as a hero: "Essentially, he can be described by the Greek word *sophron.* . . . It means, not necessarily that you have superior brains, but that you make maximum use of whatever brains you have got. Odysseus is the antithesis of Achilleus. Achilleus has a fine intelligence, but passion clouds it; Odysseus has strong passions, but his intelligence keeps them under control."[9]

Thus Ulysses has been both scoundrel and hero to those

7 W. B. Stanford, *The Ulysses Theme: A Study in the Adaptability of a Traditional Hero* (Oxford, 1954), documents Ulysses' protean qualities throughout literary history.

8 C. M. Bowra, *The Greek Experience* (New York, 1957), pp. 27, 20-21, 31.

9 *The Iliad of Homer,* trans. with an introduction by Richmond Lattimore (Chicago, 1951), pp. 50-51.

who have read of him in the 2,500-odd years of his existence. It may be that time will yet consign him to hell, but as we shall see forthwith, Ulysses was a hero to James Joyce—and much the same kind of hero as he was to Homer. Joyce was something of a hero-worshipper throughout his life. Many of us have youthful idols whom we later abandon, but Joyce clung tenaciously to his heroes. Charles Stewart Parnell was such a one, the Greek Ulysses another. As a child and later as a man, Joyce admired Parnell in life and Ulysses in literature; long before he broke with the Catholic Church, a protestant and a pagan had captured his imagination, both of them by virtue of bravery, of heroism. One notes with surprise, in view of the monolithic qualities of his Jesuit education, that young Joyce, when asked to write an essay on the topic "My Favorite Hero," named Ulysses as his subject. Joyce's was the only pagan hero among all the essays submitted on that topic, and we are told that the choice irritated his teacher.[10] At the age of thirteen the rebelliousness within him was already in evidence: it must have taken some courage to pass over such likely candidates as Loyola or perhaps St. Patrick.

Although Joyce's essay on Ulysses is lost to us, it is possible to ascertain just what it was that fascinated him about Homer's hero. At this time Joyce had not read a translation of the *Odyssey* itself; he got his first impressions from Charles Lamb's *Adventures of Ulysses*.[11] Romanticist that he was, Lamb was not inclined to emphasize the guile of Homer's hero; in fact, Lamb's Ulysses is a thoroughly idealized figure, a paragon of moral and physical strength

[10] See Ellmann, *James Joyce*, p. 47; Herbert Gorman, *James Joyce* (New York, 1939), p. 45; and Valéry Larbaud, "James Joyce," *Criterion*, I (October 1922), 99.

[11] For an interesting discussion of the position of Lamb's *Ulysses* in the history of Homeric translations, including an analysis of Lamb's reliance upon the moralistic translation of Chapman, see W. B. Stanford, "The Mysticism That Pleased Him," *Envoy*, v (April 1951), 63-69.

and courage—exactly the kind of hero which would en-
thrall the imagination of a thirteen-year-old. Lamb describes his particular treatment of the *Odyssey* in the preface to his *Adventures of Ulysses*: "The picture which it
exhibits is that of a brave man struggling with adversity;
by a wise use of events, and with an inimitable presence
of mind under difficulties, forcing a way out for himself
through the severest trials to which human life can be
exposed; with enemies natural and preternatural surrounding him on all sides."[12] Lamb was struck, as was the young
Joyce, with the relevance of the adventures of Ulysses to
life. He felt that the Greek hero manifested the indom-
itable courage essential to heroism in any day; and as for
the prevarication sometimes singled out as Ulysses' salient
characteristic, to Lamb this was simply "an inimitable
presence of mind." Lamb generally ignores or palliates
Ulysses' guile, presenting craftiness as simply another
means of combating an evil foe. The reader who, like
Joyce, first encounters Homer through the eyes of Charles
Lamb would easily be led toward a romantic conception
of Ulysses. For Joyce this first impression was a lasting
one. In his earliest known work of fiction, the draft of the
Portrait known as *Stephen Hero*, he employs Homeric
imagery in a manner suggesting his continued hero-wor-
ship of Ulysses, long after the writing of that schoolboy
essay. Joyce's attitude toward his protagonist in *Stephen
Hero* is a matter of some critical controversy, but there is
no doubt that he is strongly sympathetic at least to the predicament of Stephen as a nascent artist, trammelled by a
parochial environment. And in one of *Stephen Hero*'s most
effective passages, Joyce looks to the *Odyssey* for his controlling metaphor, drawing a distinct analogy between the
adventures of Ulysses and the plight of young Stephen,
thus: "The deadly chill of the atmosphere of the college

[12] Lamb, *Adventures of Ulysses* (London, 1827), p. iii.

⟨   103   ⟩

paralyzed Stephen's heart. In a stupor of powerlessness he reviewed the plague of Catholicism. . . . The spectacle of the world in thrall filled him with courage. He, at least, though living at the farthest remove from the centre of European culture, marooned on an island in the ocean, though inheriting a will broken by doubt and a soul the steadfastness of whose hate became as weak as water in siren-arms, would live his own life according to what he recognized as the voice of a new humanity, active, unafraid and unashamed" (SH194).

One recalls that Book V of the *Odyssey*, which first introduces Ulysses into the narrative, places the Greek warrior upon the island of a sea-siren, Calypso. Despite Ulysses' protestations, Calypso refuses to allow him to return to his native Ithaca. Ulysses fears he is bound forever to the goddess, who will not yield to his supplications, even when he protests to her that he cannot return her vigorous love. The imagery of the above-quoted passage from *Stephen Hero* implies that the enthrallment of the artist in Ireland is analogous to Ulysses' imprisonment by Calypso. The artist is spoken of as "marooned on an island in the ocean" and "weak as water in siren-arms"—strong overtones of Ulysses' imprisonment. Here the island is, of course, Ireland; and Calypso may be thought of as Mother Church, "the plague of Catholicism" which Joyce regarded as a prominent element in Irish moral paralysis. The task of the artist was to free himself from the Calypso-arms of his island and, once safe in the Ithaca of a liberated spirit, to mirror forsaken tyranny in his art. In this instance our sense of Stephen as hero is reinforced by the flattering comparison with Ulysses.

Joyce's attitude toward Ulysses did not change with the passage of time, as Frank Budgen's reminiscences confirm. Mr. Budgen was one of the few people with whom Joyce talked freely about his work. He had his first discussion about *Ulysses* with Joyce in 1918, when the book was just beginning to take shape. Joyce raised the question, Mr. Budgen tells us, of whether there existed any "complete" man in literature. He rejected suggestions ranging from Hamlet to Faust and finally insisted that the only complete man in literature was Homer's Ulysses. "Ulysses," said Joyce, "is son to Laertes, but he is father to Telemachus, husband to Penelope, lover of Calypso, companion in arms of the Greek warriors around Troy and King of Ithaca. He was subjected to many trials, but with wisdom and courage came through them all."[13]

Evidently the Joyce of 1918 was the same hero-worshipper who had chosen Ulysses as his favorite childhood hero. His terming Ulysses a complete man, who "was subjected to many trials, but with wisdom and courage came through them all," sounds much like a paraphrase of Charles Lamb's estimation of Ulysses. It also resembles C. M. Bowra's characterization of the Greek heroic outlook.

Joyce was not unduly modest, and one is not surprised to learn that he was capable of identifying himself with his favorite hero. In 1921 Joyce wrote Harriet Weaver about what he regarded as erroneous opinions concerning himself: "There is a further opinion that I am a crafty simulating and dissimulating Ulysses-like type, a 'jejune Jesuit,' selfish and cynical. There is some truth in this, I suppose; but it is by no means all of me (nor was it of Ulysses) and it has been my habit to apply this alleged quality to safeguard my poor creations."[14] This bit of self-analysis is doubly revealing: it shows that Joyce not only identified himself with Ulysses but also that he considered Ulyssean craftiness a virtue, employed in his case "to safeguard my poor creations" and in Ulysses' case to safeguard his life. These remarks also elucidate Joyce's conception of Ulysses as a "complete" man: one who was willing to employ all

13 Budgen, *James Joyce and the Making of Ulysses* (Bloomington, 1960), p. 16.
14 Letter to Harriet Shaw Weaver, 24 June 1921, *Letters*, I, 166.

his resources for a noble purpose. Such a man was bound to be misunderstood and oversimplified (by certain Homeric commentators), but Joyce warns us that Ulysses to him was heroic: craftiness was but one of his capacities.

If further proof of the consistency of Joyce's idealization of Ulysses is desired, one can turn to a letter written by Joyce in 1922, after the completion of the odyssey of Leopold Bloom. Joyce's aunt, Mrs. William Murray, had expressed perplexity over the meaning of *Ulysses*: like many readers after her, she was exasperated and discouraged by the surface complexity of the book. Unlike other readers, however, she had the advantage of friendship with the author, from whom she requested aid. Joyce advised her, "You say there is a lot of [*Ulysses*] you don't understand. I told you to read the *Odyssey* first. As you have not done so I asked my publisher to send you an article which will throw a little light on it. Then buy at once the *Adventures of Ulysses* (which is Homer's story told in simple English much abbreviated) by Charles Lamb. . . . Then have a try at *Ulysses* again."[15] One notes that Joyce does not term Lamb's *Adventures of Ulysses* a romanticization or idealization of Homer, but only an abbreviation of the epic in simple English. At the age of forty Joyce remained faithful to his youthful admiration for Ulysses as a hero, suggesting Charles Lamb as the best introduction to the world of Leopold Bloom. As a warning to those who would like to dismiss the importance of the *Odyssey* to *Ulysses*, as an antidote to the theory that Joyce established his intricate correspondences with Homer only for the sake of "scaffolding," Joyce's own admonition might be placed on the first and last pages of every volume of *Ulysses*: "I told you to read the *Odyssey* first."

If Joyce looked to Homer for standards of heroic conduct, and if he took great pains to cause the actions of

---

[15] Letter to Mrs. William Murray, 10 November 1922, *ibid.*, I, 193.

Leopold Bloom to parallel the actions of Homer's Ulysses, a comparison between Bloom and Ulysses is not merely invited: it is demanded. We can learn a great deal about Joyce's moral convictions from his earlier works and from his letters; but as helpful as these insights may be, they do remain outside *Ulysses* itself. The Homeric parallel operates within *Ulysses*; it is Joyce's continuous hint to his readers, his most sustained and significant attempt to counteract the obscurity for which he has so often been damned. What we know of Joyce's idea of Ulysses as a hero helps to explain the intended use of the Homeric parallel: Ulysses was to Joyce a wise and courageous son, father, husband, lover, and warrior. He was, in short, the natural hero to a man who viewed human nature as irreparably split between the opposing forces of spirit and flesh, idealism and bestiality. If virginal beauty was Joyce's feminine ideal, a wise and courageous Ulysses was his masculine ideal. Leopold Bloom must thus be measured against Joyce's conception of Ulysses. If such a procedure seems unfair to Bloom, one must remember that Joyce was ever an idealist, ever a man bitten by the most stringent of moral consciences. In *Ulysses* moral fervor is fortunately mellowed by comedy, but the Homeric parallels remind us constantly of the moralist who wrote this comic epic.

The episode by episode analysis of the relation of Joyce's conscience to Leopold Bloom which takes up the remainder of this chapter is not founded upon the Homeric parallel in *Ulysses*: it is founded upon a close look at the text. But in the discussion of each episode, the Homeric parallel will be invoked—discreetly I trust—to aid our understanding of Joyce's own conception of Bloom, to help us keep our subjective reactions to Bloom as a man under control, so that we may treat him as a literary character, the fictional device of the author. The Homeric parallel is a part of Joyce's technique of comic and moral judgment; it reminds us that *Ulysses* is art—carefully constructed to reveal the author's peculiar meanings, personal world-view, and, in the case of Joyce, moral conscience.

· 2 ·

A comic spirit permeates nearly every description of Bloom. Joyce's introduction of his hero is but the first instance: "Mr Leopold Bloom ate with relish the inner organs of beasts and fowls. He liked thick giblet soup, nutty gizzards, a stuffed roast heart, liver slices fried with crustcrumbs, fried hencod's roes. Most of all he liked grilled mutton kidneys which gave to his palate a fine tang of faintly scented urine" (*U*55). A comically curious way to introduce one's protagonist: the description sounds a bit like an extract from the case history of some poor fellow gone sexually astray. The last line in particular, with its suggestion of Bloom's desire to smell and taste urine, alerts the reader immediately to certain psychological peculiarities.[16] The passage is amusing chiefly because of the impression one gets of Mr. Bloom eating inner organs with relish: perversions aside, he emerges from the start as a highly sensual sort of man, a man to whom smell and taste and touch mean a great deal. This initial sensual image of Bloom devouring giblets, gizzards, hearts, roes, and kidneys is amplified with every passing page of the "Calypso" episode. After deciding that today is not a good day for mutton kidney at one butcher shop, Bloom trots off to a pork butcher, arrives at the shop window, and instead of proceeding inside directly, pauses in affectionate reverence before the display of raw pork. Again, Joyce unveils Bloom's unusual manifestations of sensuality, causing Bloom first to stare at the meaty display and then in-

---

[16] See Magnus Hirschfield, *Sexual Anomalies* (New York, 1955), pp. 36off., for a discussion of the connection between "urolagnia" and masochism. Hirschfield's entire discussion of masochism is extremely relevant to Bloom: see Chapters XIX and XX.

forming us, to our discomfort, that Bloom "breathed in tranquilly the lukewarm breath of cooked spicy pig's blood" (*U*59). By now even the casual reader is aware of Bloom's peculiar love of inner organs, his relishing of the faint taste and scent of urine, his delight in the smell of cooked blood. But one cannot be sure of what this odd sort of sensuality adds up to until Bloom spies at the counter a young neighbor of his, a girl whom he has watched whacking carpets on a clothesline: his reaction to the girl resembles his reaction to the nice pork kidney which "oozed bloodgouts on the willow-patterned dish" (*U*59). He wants the girl in the same way, in the same terms, as he wants the kidney, thinking of her as though she were another hunk of meat hanging in the butcher shop: "Sound meat there like a stallfed heifer" (*U*59). He remembers her whacking a carpet, recalls "the way her crooked skirt swings at each whack," and having imagined her as a stallfed heifer, thinks associatively of beasts in their pens and of "breeders in hobnailed boots . . . slapping a palm on a ripemeated hindquarter . . . unpeeled switches in their hands" (*U*59). Girl whacking, hobnailed boots, heifers being slapped and whacked: the pattern is clear. Bloom is indulging himself in the perverse, pleasurable pain of a sado-masochistic fantasy. Once we know that Bloom enjoys the taste and scent of urine and blood; once we see him excited by the thought of a vigorous young woman whacking away at a carpet; and once we watch his mind flit from this image to one of hobnailed boots, unpeeled switches, and slapping, whacking breeders—we should recognize the avid masochist. If any doubt remains, it is erased when Bloom makes his way into the street to follow the girl, finds she has vanished, and Joyce informs us significantly that "The sting of disregard glowed to weak pleasure within his breast. For another: a constable off duty cuddled her in Eccles Lane" (*U*59-60). Bloom is ultimately pleased by the girl's disregard of him; he takes masochistic pleasure in watching her being cuddled by another.

It is far from sufficient, of course, to label Bloom a masochist and to leave it at that. Masochism is only a prominent manifestation of his extreme sensuality; masochism is a pattern into which many of his sensual acts fall, but his sensuality overflows the boundaries of any single pattern. Bloom is no fiend. He is mild—one might even say harmless—in every respect. His forays into sexual abandon take place mostly in his own mind, and they are provided an outlet through his peculiar eating habits and through other means elaborated in later episodes. But Bloom's sensuality has had a tangible effect upon his daily life. It has placed him, for example, in an awkward and undignified position in his own household. We encounter him for the first time just as he sets about making breakfast: nothing unusual, except that meanwhile Mrs. Bloom lolls in opulent slumber upstairs. Bloom not only gets his own breakfast but her breakfast as well—a tender gesture, perhaps, if received and appreciated with tenderness. But such is not the case.

Mrs. Bloom treats her dutiful husband with less tenderness than one would normally accord a household pet, snapping at him, "Hurry up with that tea." Bloom obeys, clearing first his wife's petticoat and soiled linen from a chair. Later she merely points her finger imperiously, and he carries out the silent command: "Following the pointing of her finger he took up a leg of her soiled drawers from the bed. No? Then a twisted grey garter looped round a stocking: rumpled, shiny sole.

"—No: that book.
"Other stocking. Her petticoat.
"—It must have fell down, she said.
"He felt here and there. . . .
"—Show here, she said" (U63-64).

Bloom utters not a word of protest but scurries about in silent obedience, willing slave to an imperious mistress, his own wife. His behavior is understandable and explicable only in terms of his obsessive sensuality: the flesh of Molly Bloom is his true monarch, and when he cannot be near that, he substitutes the inner organs of beast and fowl. In the street he had thought of the combination of tea, kidney, and Molly—"To smell the gentle smoke of tea, fume of the pan, sizzling butter. Be near her ample bed-warmed flesh. Yes, yes"—and had hurried home. Serving Molly in bed, he does not care if she treats him disdainfully. He is near her. Only the smell of his precious kidney burning in the pan draws him away from Molly: he races to it and rescues it with paternal solicitude.

Bloom is paternally solicitous about his daughter as well as about his kidney. He worries about the possibility of her losing her virginity—a natural qualm of the bourgeois father. But even in thinking about his own daughter, Bloom allows his sex-obsession to get the better of him. For he cannot simply fret over the chance that she may no longer be a maid: he imagines the very act of deflowering, gives himself up, in fact, to the contemplation of it: "Will happen, yes. Prevent. Useless: can't move. Girl's sweet light lips. Will happen too. He felt the flowing qualm spread over him. Useless to move now. Lips kissed, kissing kissed. Full gluey woman's lips" (U67).

This first glimpse afforded us of Bloom, the "Calypso" episode, both amuses and alarms. His love of innards; his masochism; his highly active, if thwarted, sexual drive; his subservience to his wife—these things contribute to a comic portrait, and they indicate as well a man not in control of his life or of himself. We may laugh at the way Bloom does his wife's bidding, but we would not wish to change places with him: we shudder at the suggestion. These reactions are, of course, instinctive and perhaps subjective. Sex and marriage are always difficult to handle objectively. But fortunately Joyce has placed at the disposal of the reader an objective hint of the author's own attitude toward Bloom and his predicament: the Homeric parallel. Without this aid one could never be reasonably sure of Joyce's point of view. What we know of his moral position—his fear and mistrust of sex; his belief in spiritual ideals—would strongly suggest that Joyce is holding up Bloom as an example of comic weakness, as an image of the ridiculous posture a man assumes who allows his sensual nature to dominate. But only the Homeric parallel, that ineradicable clue within the narrative of *Ulysses*, can reliably refute or substantiate these suppositions.

Joyce originally titled this episode "Calypso," indicating an analogy between the plight of Ulysses on Calypso's island and the plight of Leopold Bloom.[17] Homer depicts Ulysses as the restless prisoner of Calypso: "Howsoever by night he would sleep by her, as needs he must, . . . unwilling lover by a willing lady. And in the day-time he would sit on the rocks and on the beach, straining his soul with tears, and groans, and griefs, and through his tears he would look wistfully over the unharvested deep."[18] Ulysses laments his enslaved position; he longs for his native shore and for the faithful Penelope who awaits him. So entranced is Calypso with him, however, that she is enraged at the gods' command to set Ulysses free; and she is gravely disappointed when Ulysses assures her that though she is more beautiful than Penelope, and immortal to boot, he longs to return to his wife and home. When one compares Bloom's position in "Calypso" to its Homeric counterpart, one finds that Joyce has established a complete inversion or comic reversal. Bloom like Ulysses is the prisoner of a woman. But unlike Ulysses, Bloom is the prisoner of his own wife—and not by reason of his own

[17] The chapter headings were probably removed as a part of the delight Joyce took in encouraging conflicting and confused interpretations of his work; they are as relevant to each chapter as the title *Ulysses* is to the book: that is, quite relevant.

[18] *Odyssey*, trans. Butcher-Lang (London, 1930), v, 58.

charms, but solely because of his infatuation with Mrs. Bloom's effulgent fleshliness. And in contrast to the dignified protestations of Ulysses, Bloom meekly acquiesces to a succession of feminine whims and commands. Ulysses longs for the embrace of his Penelope, but Bloom is the lackey of his Molly. And while Ulysses finds himself not only happily wed but the love-object of such delicious nymphs as Calypso, Bloom is both the man-servant of his wife and the scorned admirer of other women.

Considered in terms of Joyce's idealization of Ulysses, as discussed above, the Homeric parallel supplies the reader with an objective authorial position. The parallel acts as Joyce's technique of judgment, establishing an ideal action in contrast to the facts of Bloom's existence. Thus this comic inversion of the *Odyssey* permits the reader to discern Joyce's moral vision within the "Calypso" episode, permits, in Lawrance Thompson's words, "the collaborative reader to measure these Dublin characters against the generally accepted moral values represented by Ulysses, Penelope, and Telemachus; permits the reader to recognize the discrepancy between ideal and actual moral values. . . ."[19] Ulysses is Calypso's restless prisoner, while Bloom is his own wife's contented prisoner and ultimately the prisoner of himself. He has enslaved himself to his passions, to the extent that personal dignity apparently means little to him. As long as he can be near Molly's flesh, and as long as he can chew thoughtfully on a kidney, he doesn't care if he is a servant in his own house. In fact he seems rather to like it.

· 3 ·

In "Calypso" Joyce touches on the theme of escapism

19 *William Faulkner, An Introduction and Interpretation* (New York, 1963), p. 24. Mr. Thompson suggests that Faulkner learned to use myths as meaningful points of reference by reading Joyce; and in the course of that suggestion, Mr. Thompson gives what is probably the clearest and most convincing statement of the mock-heroic effects of the Homeric parallels in *Ulysses*.

briefly when he makes Bloom daydream of a trip to far-off places: ". . . strange land, come to a city gate, . . . Wander through awned streets. Turbaned faces going by. Dark caves of carpet shops, . . . Cries of sellers in the streets. Drink water scented with fennel, sherbet. Wander along all day. . . . The shadows of the mosques along the pillars: priest with a scroll rolled up. . . . Night sky moon, violet, colour of Molly's new garters. Strings. Listen. A girl playing one of these instruments what do you call them: dulcimers" (U57). Bloom's is a universal day-dream: everyone longs for the mysterious East, the lure of bazaar, harem, hasheesh. But in the "Lotus-eaters" episode Joyce expands this theme of escapism into a more general critique of Bloom's psychology. Joyce's implications are reminiscent of his treatment of escapism in *Dubliners*. In that book many of the "helpless animals" about whom Joyce wrote dreamed constantly of escaping the depressions of dear, dirty Dublin—but none left. They continued on in the same old patterns, lingering wistfully at quayside or bar or committee room or cathedral, unable to rouse themselves. So it is with Bloom, spiritual kin to those Dubliners. Joyce originally planned *Ulysses* as but another story in *Dubliners*, and Bloom is in many ways a compendium of those earlier Joycean characters. Like them he longs for escape but does not move toward it, taking refuge, as "Lotus-eaters" demonstrates, in narcotic substitutes for action.

The brunt of Joyce's irony cannot be felt without reference to the *Odyssey*. That "Lotus-eaters" is figuratively strewn with flowers of all kinds strikes even the quick skimmer of pages, but that these flower images contribute cumulatively to Joyce's critique of escapism becomes clear only in the light of Homeric parallels. Edmund Wilson once complained, "What is the value of all the references to flowers in the Lotos-Eaters chapter . . . ? They do not create in the Dublin streets an atmosphere of lotos-eating—we are merely puzzled . . . as to why Joyce has chosen to have Bloom think and see certain things, of which the final explanation is that they are pretexts for mentioning flowers."[20] The value of all the references to flowers is that they supply us with the author's value judgment: they indicate Joyce's second major comic reversal of the *Odyssey*, the first being the "Calypso" episode. They remind us of the island of the lotus-eaters which Ulysses visited with his men. As Ulysses himself narrates: "Now whosoever of [my men] did eat the honey-sweet fruit of the lotus, had no more wish to bring tidings nor to come back, but there chose to abide with the lotus-eating men, ever feeding on the lotus, and forgetful of their homeward way. Therefore I led them back to the ships weeping, and sore against their will, and dragged them beneath the benches, and bound them in the hollow barques."[21] Ulysses himself does not partake of the lotus-flowers: he remains immune to the temptation of the honey-sweet fruit. He saves his men and himself by his strength of will. Now if one were to construct a comic reversal of this incident, the natural course would be to allow one's comic Ulysses to eat the lotus, to enjoy the lotus, and to succumb to its pleasing narcotic effect, abandoning heroics in favor of a life of forgetful ease. Such is Joyce's stratagem with Bloom, and the value of the countless flowers in the episode is that they make Joyce's technique and meaning clear.

Joyce's most obvious reversal of the *Odyssey* occurs on the first page of this episode, as Bloom stands wistfully before the window of a tea shop; for here the flower imagery is equated directly with a lotus-like narcotic effect which Bloom craves: "His right hand once more slowly went over again: choice blend, made of the finest Ceylon brands. The far east. Lovely spot it must be: the garden of the world, big lazy leaves to float about on, cactuses, flowery meads, snaky lianas they call them. . . . Not

20 *Axel's Castle* (New York, 1931), p. 214.
21 *Odyssey*, XI, 99.

doing a hand's turn all day. Sleep six months out of twelve. Too hot to quarrel. Influence of the climate. Lethargy. Flowers of idleness. . . . Hothouse in Botanic gardens. Sensitive plants. Waterlilies" (*U*71). The references to flowers of idleness and waterlilies reflect back upon the *Odyssey*, whose hero had no desire to sleep six months out of twelve. Such a yearning is typical of Bloom, and given the circumstances of his daily life—a surly, dominating, unfaithful wife; a dull job as an advertising canvasser; his home in Dublin—one can understand why. Less easy to understand is Bloom's inertia.

Since he cannot, or does not, set sail for the lethargic East, Bloom substitutes various more transient narcotics for the "big lazy leaves to float about on" of Ceylon. He escapes into a world of fantasy, adopting the *nom de plume* "Henry Flower" and engaging in a titillating little correspondence with someone named Martha Clifford—his pen pal sweetheart, upon whom he has never laid eyes or hands. The very existence of this correspondence is a poignant example of Bloom's dissimilarity to the Greek Ulysses: unable to sustain a satisfactory relationship with his wife, Bloom takes refuge in a sweetheart whom he will never have to encounter physically. There is no risk involved: this is strictly a postal affair, an adventure of the imagination. As with the Ceylonese tea shop, flowers serve Joyce again as emblems of the narcotic sensuality which Bloom does not resist, for Martha encloses a flower with her letter, thereby transforming the letter itself into another one of Joyce's effective flower images. Joyce's Ulysses is thus symbolically a lotus-eater, engaged in the sensuality his Homeric counterpart rejects.

Bloom's curious relationship with Martha Clifford seems innocent and amusing enough, though it does make Bloom out to be something of a buffoon. But the letter writing has its more unsavory side. Consider these lines from Martha's letter: "I am awfully angry with you. I do wish I could punish you. . . . Please write me a long letter and tell me more. Remember if you do not I will punish you. So now you know what I will do to you, you naughty boy, if you do not write" (U77-78). These lines mean more to Bloom than any others in the letter, for these are the ones he repeats to himself: "Angry tulips with you darling man-flower punish your cactus if you don't please poor forget-menot how I long violets to dear roses when we soon anemone meet all naughty nightstalk wife Martha's perfume" (U78). The interweaving of flowers with Martha's words underlines Joyce's use of the letter as another symbol of narcotic sensuality; but beyond this general significance, the words have a specifically unhealthy ring to them. This is the language of a sadist, however mild. The statement of anger, the threat of punishment, the appellation "naughty boy"—these are characteristically sadistic approaches and terms.[22] Martha Clifford's gentle admonitions are a pale version of the commands the truly sadistic mistress utters to her masochistic slave, often in written form. The most famous prototype of such a woman is probably Wanda von Dunajew, the first wife of Leopold Baron von Sacher-Masoch, who once wrote to her husband, "Should you at any time feel that you can bear my dominion no longer, that my chains are too heavy for you, then *you* must kill yourself; I shall never liberate you."[23] Martha Clifford's threats fall quite short of Wanda von Dunajew's, but they proceed from a similar psychology. And Bloom's masochism, already exposed in the "Calypso" episode, is the perfect complement to such threats. Bloom revels in them. "Go further next time," he thinks. "Naughty boy: punish: afraid of words, of course. Brutal, why not? Try it anyhow. A bit at a time" (U78). It is the sadism which he cherishes most in the letter. We must wait for the "Circe" episode to discover the true extent of Bloom's masochistic tendencies, but for

[22] See Hirschfield, *Sexual Anomalies*, Chapters XVII-XX.
[23] Quoted in *ibid.*, p. 281.

now they serve as a part of this flowery, sensual episode—
another aspect of Bloom's weakness for narcotic escapism,
another example of Bloom's comic distance from the self-
denying Greek Ulysses.

Always prone to self-mockery in his writings, Joyce is
probably parodying both his letters to Nora, often sprin-
kled with requests for punishment and other sado-masochistic details, and his letters of 1918-19 to Martha Fleishmann, a young Swiss for whom he conceived a romantic
passion at first sight. When Bloom sits down later at the
Ormond Hotel to write a letter to Martha Clifford, he dis-
guises his handwriting with Greek ϵ's, and Joyce did the
same when writing clandestinely to Martha Fleishmann.
Again like Bloom, Joyce adopted a posture of weakness
and surrender to his Martha, although Joyce's letters are
a good deal more lyrical than anything the prosaic Bloom
might conjure up.[24] Joyce did actually meet his Martha,
but their affair was never consummated, perhaps because
of Joyce's loyalty to Nora and his abhorrence of infidelity.

"Varieties of Escape": Joyce might have given that title
to this chapter had he not eschewed chapter titles of any
sort, erasing even the helpful Homeric headings from
Ulysses before publication. Lotus-eating serves as a symbol embracing all the varieties of escape described in this
episode—the several varieties in which Bloom indulges.
After dreaming of obliviousness in tropical Ceylon, of a
mildly perverse encounter with his unseen sweetheart, and
then of an Irish version of the Great Flood, in which the
land is inundated with "a lazy pooling swirl of liquor bearing along wideleaved flowers of its froth" (*U*79), Bloom
falls into still another variety of escape—a church. Joyce's
flower imagery conveys Bloom's reason for entering the
church: "The cold smell of sacred stone called him"
(*U*80). That mysterious mixture of incense, burning wax,
and flowers lures Bloom on this hot June morning, holding

24 See *Letters*, II, 426-36.

⟨   118   ⟩

out to him a promise of cool darkness and repose. Entering softly, he sees a priest giving out communion to the inevitable *habitués* of weekday mass—a group of women, most of them old. He watches, curious, capable of several trenchant observations: "Good idea the Latin. Stupefies them first. . . . Rum idea: eating bits of a corpse why the cannibals cotton to it. . . . Old fellow asleep near that confession box. Hence those snores. Blind faith. Safe in the arms of kingdom come. Lulls all pain. Wake this time next year. . . . English. Throw them the bone. . . . Confession. Everyone wants to. Then I will tell you all. Penance. Punish me, please. Great weapon in their hands. More than doctor or solicitor" (U80, 81, 82-83). Though we discover in a later episode that Bloom has been baptized no fewer than three times, his detached attitude here demonstrates a lack of anything like "blind faith" in Christianity: he has probably been baptized for social reasons, as another variety of escape—this time from his Jewishness. His presence in the church this morning stems simply from a desire for isolated tranquility. His satiric observations on the mass testify to a potential liveliness of intellect, but he dreams on through the morning, floating languidly from one Dublin avenue of escape to another.

The final such avenue in this episode is a Turkish bath. Within it Bloom hopes to achieve a state of mindless euphoria close to his far-eastern fantasies: even the bath house itself reminds him of a mosque and is thus associated with his Ceylonese dreams and with the house of worship which he has just left. Each of the flower images of the episode has conveyed Bloom's preoccupation with escape through sensual gratification: the last of these images supplies the underlying psychological cause of this preoccupation—narcissism. It is not without significance that Bloom, as we learn in the "Ithaca" episode, displays a statue of Narcissus in his home. As this modern Ulysses foresees himself sinking into the liquid comfort of his

Turkish bathwater, Joyce establishes imagistically Bloom's fixation on that flower of flowers, Bloom himself: "He foresaw his pale body reclined in it at full, naked, in a womb of warmth, oiled by scented melting soap, softly laved. He saw his trunk and limbs riprippled over and sustained, buoyed lightly upward, lemonyellow: his navel, bud of flesh: and saw the dark tangled curls of his bush floating, floating hair of the stream around the limp father of thousands, a languid floating flower" (U86).

Bloom is entranced by his own body and by the bloom of Bloom, the sensual center, the fatal bush and flower of that plump body, his genitals. He is addicted to that primeval narcotic, narcissism. As we learn in the "Nausicaa" episode, Bloom considers masturbating as he lolls, staring at himself in the bathwater: "Damned glad I didn't do it in the bath this morning over her silly I will punish you letter" (U368). Here is the final link in the concatenation of flowers which binds the "Lotus-eaters" episode together: Narcissus drowning in his own image. Bloom the paralyzed Dubliner, gazing contentedly at his genitals: the synthesizing Joycean epiphany, in which Joyce's distrust of sex is manifest. Sex was to Joyce the narcissistic self-indulgence which threatened constantly the "something higher" within himself, the passion which could metamorphose spiritual love into bestial craving. The sexual itch in Bloom leads him to debase himself in servitude to his wife, whose very "orangeflower scent" makes him weak at the knees; it leads him as well into an amusing but faintly perverse correspondence with the invisible Martha Clifford; and before Bloomsday is through it will lead him into further frustrations of what heroic, Ulyssean potential might be his. Such is the peculiarly Irish Catholic authorial viewpoint of a self-proclaimed rebel from the Church.

No one was more conscious than Joyce of the human, ordinary nature of Bloom's foibles. As the letters to Nora attest, many of Bloom's characteristics, notably his masochism, were Joyce's own. No doubt Joyce exaggerated certain of his own weaknesses to comic proportions, thus fashioning in Bloom his humorous image of common humanity: kindly, well-intentioned, but more dreamer than doer, more clown than hero. Joyce could salve his own conscience with the writing of what he knew were masterpieces; and as Bloom laves himself blissfully in the bath, Joyce demonstrates an admirable capacity to laugh at himself, however privately.

· 4 ·

Fortunately Joyce's portrait of Bloom is not all passion, narcissism, masochism, and general moral spinelessness. If it were, Bloom would be merely a type, not a character; and considering the rigidity of Joyce's attitude toward the passions, one can easily imagine his creating types. But Joyce gives us instead a portrait in depth and in the round, a portrait of a man morally weak in Joyce's terms, and therefore human in Joyce's terms, but of a man often meriting sympathy. The "Hades" episode allows Bloom to exhibit certain more praiseworthy aspects of his nature. He has already shown a capacity for a blunt kind of wit in "Lotus-eaters," during his visit to a church. In "Hades" he silently makes macabre jokes to himself, as he stands watching the coffin of Paddy Dignam being lowered beneath the sod: "We are praying now for the repose of his soul. Hoping you're well and not in hell. . . . And if he was alive all the time? Whew! By Jingo, that would be awful! . . . They ought to have some law to pierce the heart and make sure or an electric clock or a telephone in the coffin and some kind of a canvas airhole. Flag of distress" (U111). Bloom's irreverent humor is ingratiating: it dispels the hypocritical solemnity of the occasion. We are likewise ingratiated by Bloom's thoughts of his dead son, Rudy, and of his father, who we learn committed suicide. Joyce draws the reader skillfully toward Bloom out of pity and embarrassment when Mr. Power says crassly that suicide is "the greatest disgrace to have in the family," and Mr. Dedalus adds, "They say a man who does it is a coward" (U96). In "Hades" Bloom is both capable of a good joke and deserving of pity.

The line between pity and contempt, however, is easily crossed. Bloom has had his misfortunes, and only the heartless would sneer at them; but Joyce certainly tempts one to contempt when he permits Bloom to make a fool of himself among men. We have already seen him make a fool of himself before a woman; and when Blazes Boylan, Mrs. Bloom's current paramour, passes by the carriage in which Bloom sits with three companions, Bloom's humiliating domestic situation is again touched upon. While Boylan is in sight, Bloom can only stare nervously at his nails (U92). There follows an amusing series of questions directed at Bloom about the concert tour which Boylan is organizing.

"—Have you good artists? Bloom is asked.

"—Louis Werner is touring her, Mr Bloom said. O yes, we'll have all topnobbers. J. C. Doyle and John MacCormack I hope and. The best in fact.

"—And *Madame*, Mr Power said, smiling. Last but not least" (U93). This courteous "And *Madame*" can only remind poor Bloom of the distinctly uncourteous actions of Blazes Boylan who, Bloom knows too well, will that very afternoon bring copies of songs to Mrs. Bloom, and with them melodies of a different sort. How many of the men present know that Bloom is the passive servant and cuckold of his wife? Joyce doesn't say, but that kind of information has a way of getting about. Yet Bloom does nothing to alter the situation, and thus he is the unprotesting victim of remarks like this one: "—In God's name, . . . what did [Mrs. Bloom] marry a coon like that for? She had plenty of game in her" (U106). One might be sorry for Bloom when John Henry Menton takes so nasty a swipe at

him behind his back, but when Bloom, who is quite conscious of Menton's dislike for him, deliberately tries to woo
Menton's favor by sniveling, "Excuse me, sir . . . your hat
is a little crushed," one is repelled by such sycophancy.
Menton seizes the opportunity to be curtly rude to Bloom,
who in return only draws back a few paces, "chapfallen"
(U115). If a helpless little dog is kicked, one pities it;
but if a man makes of himself a helpless little dog and gets
kicked, one can only scorn him. "Be sorry perhaps when
it dawns on him," Bloom hopes silently. "Get the pull over
him that way." Thus Bloom imagines a petty kind of revenge, unconsciously parodying Christian morality.

Similarly, Bloom compromises what pity one might have
for him as a bereaved father. We are with him, we are
compassionate toward him, when he thinks, "If little Rudy
had lived. See him grow up. Hear his voice in the house.
Walking beside Molly in an Eton suit. My son. Me in his
eyes. Strange feeling it would be. From me. Just a chance"
(U89). Here is the tragic lament of any father deprived of
his only son. If only Bloom would keep to this tragic level,
he might win our sympathies utterly. Instead he descends
to the more familiar Bloomian level of sensual desire; his
mind does not rest upon the loss of Rudy but moves on to
the conception of Rudy—the very moment of conception:
"Must have been that morning in Raymond terrace she
was at the window, watching the two dogs at it by the
wall of the cease to do evil. And the sergeant grinning up.
She had that cream gown on with the rip she never stitched.
Give us a touch, Poldy. God, I'm dying for it. How life
begins" (U89). Bloom has engaged in an unconsciously
self-deprecating recollection: not his own sexual allure,
nor any love Molly might have had for him, brought about
the conception of Rudy. Two dogs "at it" and the grin of a
sergeant set Marion Bloom in motion and caused her to
murmur, "Give us a touch, Poldy." The incident is a typically Joycean view of the sexual act: bestial (the dogs)

and obscene (the sergeant's grin and Molly's exhortation). It also adumbrates the Joycean view of poor Bloom as flaccid and ineffectual, for two dogs and a leering sergeant were as much responsible for Rudy as Bloom himself. And Bloom's dwelling with evident pleasure on Rudy's bizarre conception compromises the pity one feels for him as a grieving father.

Our attention focuses naturally on Bloom in "Hades," for the bulk of the chapter consists of his own stream of consciousness, and the action of the chapter is seen through his eyes. But "Hades" represents a broadening of the perspective in *Ulysses*. The episode takes in more than just Bloom, for its chief action consists of a favorite Irish pastime, attendance at funerals, and Joyce burlesques the triviality and false piety of the occasion. In "Hades" as in every episode, the Homeric parallel supplies a useful measuring device for the action. Although the Homeric analogy is perhaps not as essential an aid to the reader here as it is in other less explicit episodes—in "Lotus-eaters" for example—it does serve well as a means of verifying any possible interpretation of "Hades." As Lawrance Thompson has written, "The arrangements of traditional analogies . . . may provide one way of implying meanings or of assigning evaluation";[25] and in "Hades" these mythic analogies do provide an additional way of assigning a satiric evaluation to the episode. On a general level there is an obvious disproportion between Ulysses' dramatic trip to the underworld and Bloom's trivial trip to the cemetery. Ulysses seeks out the ghosts of fallen warriors, while Bloom tries to tell a joke, watches a toadish priest mumble Latin, spies an obese rat toddling along the side of a crypt, and finally attempts to ingratiate himself with John Henry Menton. There is a specific parallel with the *Odyssey* in this last-mentioned action: just as Bloom meets an old foe

[25] *William Faulkner*, p. 28.

in Menton, Ulysses meets an old foe in Ajax. But Ulysses does not try sycophantically to win a smile from Ajax, who still is angry because Ulysses took the armor of Achilles at Troy; he does not say to Ajax, "Excuse me, sir. . . ." He speaks boldly to him, blames the incident of the armor on the gods, and says finally, "Master thy wrath and thy proud spirit."[26] Joyce was once quoted as having said of Ulysses, "Don't forget the trait of generosity at the interview with Ajax in the nether world. . . ."[27] Ulysses is generously willing to make peace with Ajax, but unlike Bloom, he does not debase himself in trying to win Ajax over; and unlike Bloom he does not imagine some petty future revenge when Ajax might "be sorry after perhaps when it dawns on him. Get the pull over him that way" (U115).

Ulysses' most extensive encounter in the underworld is with Agamemnon, who warns Ulysses to be wary of a treacherous wife. For Agamemnon himself was slain by his Clytaemnestra. But in a moment Agamemnon retracts his warning: "Yet shalt not thou, Odysseus, find death at the hand of thy wife, for she is very discreet and prudent in all her ways, the wise Penelope, daughter of Icarius."[28] No parallel for this encounter exists in Joyce's *Ulysses*. How could it exist? Poor Bloom knows Agamemnon's speech too well; Bloom is comically his own Agamemnon, for Molly is planning to frolic that very afternoon with her own Aegisthus, Blazes Boylan—the "worst man in Dublin," as Bloom sadly and silently dubs him (U92). The Ulyssean meeting with Agamemnon adds an extra bit of comedy to "Hades" by virtue of its absence.

But as is usual with Joyce's Homeric parallel, these specific touches are less significant than the general contrast of character and action between *Ulysses* and the *Odyssey*. The importance of the parallel in "Hades" lies in the comic disparity between the tragic grandeur of the Greek under-

26 *Odyssey*, XI, 137.
27 Ellmann, *James Joyce*, p. 430.
28 *Odyssey*, XI, 134.

world, where fallen heroes glide in and out with ghostly solemnity, and this Dublin cemetery, where Joyce makes sport of Irish funereal rhetoric and ritual. The only fallen hero in sight is the besotted Paddy Dignam. The grave of a true hero, Parnell, is visited out of respect by several of the gentlemen present. In relation to Parnell, Joyce once wrote of his countrymen: "They have given proof of their altruism only in 1891, when they sold their leader, Parnell, to the pharisaical conscience of the English Dissenters without exacting the thirty pieces of silver" (CW196). Why, if Joyce felt so bitter about the Irish betrayal of Parnell, did he choose to place several pious Irishmen at Parnell's grave in the "Hades" episode? And why did he permit so ostensibly reverent and sincere and touching a visitation to take place in an otherwise satiric chapter? "Because," Joyce once wrote pointedly, "the Irish, even though they break the hearts of those who sacrifice their lives for their native land, never fail to show great respect for the dead" (CW192).

· 5 ·

WE SEE THE CANVASSER AT WORK

This headline refers with comically inappropriate drama to the humble labors of Mr. Bloom, as he tries to arrange an advertisement for Alexander Keyes, tea, wine, and spirit merchant. Not Bloom, however, but the windy rhetoric of the Irish press and pressmen is Joyce's main satiric target in this episode. Here in the offices of a "GREAT DAILY ORGAN," "IN THE HEART OF THE HIBERNIAN METROPOLIS," the Greek god of winds has his mock-heroic equivalent in the editor of the *Freeman's Journal and National Press* and his cohorts. Bloom is a part of this journalistic world, as he suggests the format of his ad to the business manager, worrying to himself, "Better not teach him his own business" (U120). Bloom's self-effacement persists even in his job. He endures the mild contempt of his editor—"—Begone! . . . The world is before you" (U129)—and the mockery of newsboys, who caper behind him as he walks off. This short glimpse of Bloom at his work fills in further the picture we are getting of him as a timid, ineffectual, inward-looking little man, whose chief interest appears to lie in not offending anyone and in obtaining what sensual gratification he can from his secret reveries. But "Aeolus," even more than "Hades," represents the outer fringes of Joyce's moral purpose in *Ulysses*: by not centering on Bloom here, Joyce manages to encompass an additional area of Irish life which he finds distasteful.

Newspapers often boast of being the voice of their readership. In fact these journalists do seem to speak with the authentic voice of Dublin: an indefatigable and interminable voice; a voice carefully modulated, punctuated, lifted and let fall; a voice more in love with words than with their meaning. As Stuart Gilbert meticulously demonstrates,[29] Joyce places countless rhetorical devices in the mouths of these journalists—chiasmus, solecism, synaeresis, the lot—so that one might the more easily perceive that they talk and write only for effect.

Joyce runs the risk, of course, of being himself thought to write only for effect in this episode. Are the journalists and their hangers-on really worth all the rhetorical energy expended on this episode, or is Joyce merely holding his own rhetorical skills up for admiration? Subsequent episodes provoke similarly irreverent questions, but whatever the fair and proper answer to them, Joyce does succeed in vindicating "Aeolus" in one important thematic respect: he manages to contrast Stephen Dedalus with these Aeolian hacks. In "Proteus" the threats to Stephen's idealism were presented in chiefly symbolic terms: the sea and its jetsam, the taut belly of Eve, the whispering weeds, and so on. Here

[29] *James Joyce's Ulysses* (New York, 1959), pp. 177-90.

in "Aeolus," however, and throughout the remainder of *Ulysses*, Joyce depicts these threats in more concrete terms, as Stephen appears in the very midst of several eloquent representatives of Irish paralysis. When Stephen enters the newspaper office, the vacuity of the journalists becomes all the more obvious and still more amusing.

· 6 ·

"—He's not too bad," Nosey Flynn says of Bloom in the "Lestrygonians" episode. "He has been known to put his hand down too to help a fellow. Give the devil his due. O, Bloom has his good points" (*U*178).

True enough, Bloom does often "put his hand down to help a fellow": there is much evidence of this kindly trait in "Lestrygonians," an episode inspired by the inhuman habits of the cannibals who destroyed eleven of Ulysses' ships, their men with them. In considering the number of generous acts committed by Bloom in this chapter, one might conclude that Joyce was setting up the humanitarianism of Bloom against the inhumanity of his fellow Dubliners. Bloom is certainly disgusted by the "cannibalistic" eating habits of the citizens he sees around him, repelled by the nauseating diners as symbols of life's viciousness: "Eat or be eaten. Kill! Kill!" (*U*170). He steps round to Davy Byrne's instead for a modest gorgonzola sandwich and a glass of burgundy. One admires this sensitivity in Bloom, and one is ready also to admire other instances of his humanitarian feelings—such as his pity for a little Dedalus girl, of whom he comments, "Good Lord, that poor child's dress is in flitters. Underfed she looks too" (*U*152). Out of the same compassionate spirit he spends a penny on cakes for the gulls: "Those poor birds" (*U*153). He later shows great sympathy for the incessantly child-bearing Mrs. Purefoy: "Poor thing! Three days! That's terrible for her" (*U*159). And he takes a moment to lend assistance to a blind stripling: "Poor fellow! Quite a boy. Terrible. Really terrible" (U182). Bloom evidently spends a great deal of his time feeling sorry for others, and even lending them a hand. What tenderness is here displayed! one thinks. Mr. Bloom seems to have room in his heart for every sort of suffering, human or animal, though he himself certainly has had his share of misfortune.

Before one interprets *Ulysses* as a tearful appeal to the emotions, however, a closer inspection of Bloom's penchant for pity casts certain doubts upon its nature. Gathered together, his compassionate ejaculations have a curious, almost formulaic ring to them: "Poor thing . . . poor birds . . . poor fellow . . . poor child's dress . . . terrible . . . really terrible. . . ." His pity for Mrs. Purefoy, moreover, is surely somewhat excessive, seemingly of infinite magnitude: "His heavy pitying gaze absorbed her news. His tongue clacked in compassion. Dth! Dth! . . . Sss. Dth, dth, dth! Three days imagine groaning on a bed with a vinegared handkerchief round her forehead, her belly swollen out! Phew! Dreadful simply! Child's head too big: forceps. Doubled up inside her trying to butt its way out blindly, groping for the way out. . . . Mina Purefoy swollen belly on a bed groaning to have a child tugged out of her" (U159, 161, 164). This kind of obsessive pity carries well beyond the limits of the "Lestrygonians" episode and culminates finally in a visit by Mr. Bloom to the maternity hospital where Mina Purefoy lies. The difference between noble sentiment and sentimentality is delicate and difficult to define. Bloom may seem sensitive to one reader and merely mawkish to another. A possible clue to Joyce's own attitude on the matter, however, may be couched with typically Joycean indirectness in the episode following "Lestrygonians." Toward the end of "Scylla and Charybdis," Buck Mulligan reads aloud a telegram sent to him by Stephen Dedalus: "—*The sentimentalist is he who would en-*

joy without incurring the immense debtorship for a thing done" (U199).[30] Stephen's message is a quotation from George Meredith's fictional study of sentimentality, *The Ordeal of Richard Feverel,* and while it has particular relevance to the episode in which it appears, it is useful in relation to Bloom as well. Bloom does in fact seem to "enjoy" the suffering toward which he manifests so much pity; and since he in no way must bear the brunt of this suffering, he can afford to enjoy it vicariously for as long as it continues to give him pleasure. That Bloom should linger sentimentally over the suffering of others, his tongue clacking "dth, dth, dth" in compassion, deepens one's understanding of the masochistic tendencies he has already displayed in earlier episodes. He seemed to enjoy being ordered about by Molly; "the sting of disregard glowed to weak pleasure within his breast" when a girl in the butcher shop ignored him; he craves the tang of urine; he daydreams of cattle being slapped and birched; he rehearses with pleasure the punishment threatened him by his playfully angry pen pal. Now he dallies over the suffering of others since he can commiserate with them without actually having to suffer himself, *"without incurring the immense debtorship for a thing done."* The enjoyment costs him nothing, save perhaps a penny for bird food or the time spent in a trip to the maternity hospital. Feeling himself the victim of life's cruelties, Bloom coddles and nurses his emotions through a sentimental participation in the misfortunes of others, putting himself in their place with masochistic pleasure.

Sentimentality is certainly no heinous crime, and no one can criticize the very sensitivity in Bloom which makes his lapses into mawkishness possible. But sentimentality is nevertheless a further example of the narcissistic self-indulgence of this Irish Ulysses, and while Bloom's actions in "Lestrygonians" should not be damned as criminal, neither

[30] Italics Joyce's.

should they be labeled noble. In Joycean terms they are simply human. Equally human in this sense is Bloom's play for the sympathy of Mrs. Breen. Meeting her in the street, he says to himself, "May as well get her sympathy," and proceeds to describe the recently deceased Paddy Dignam as "An old friend of mine," thereby wringing melancholy condolences from Mrs. Breen. Bloom thus gives further play to his sentimentality and self-pity. When he feeds the gulls, he again manages to achieve both sentimentality and self-pity: first he pities the "poor birds," buys them a penny's worth of cake, and feeds them, feeling sentimental all the while. Then he reverses himself nicely when he sees the gulls fighting over the cake and attains a satisfying state of self-pity: "I'm not going to throw any more. Penny quite enough. Lot of thanks I get. Not even a caw. They spread foot and mouth disease too" (U_{153}).

When we think of Bloom in this episode, we think of a man feeding upon himself. I do not choose the image at random: "Lestrygonians" is an episode about cannibalism, a comic reversal of that Homeric narrative in which eleven-twelfths of Ulysses' men were destroyed by cannibals. In the Dublin restaurants of Joyce's novel one encounters savages who devour their meat and guzzle their beer with cannibalistic relish—an apparently unreversed reflection of the Homeric Lestrygonians. But in the Ulysses of Joyce's novel one encounters not a hero who manages to elude cannibals but a sentimental, self-pitying, sensually oriented man who is a cannibal in a more subtle sense—he feeds upon himself.

It is in his sensual self-indulgence particularly that Bloom becomes a metaphorical cannibal. Just as he permits kindly instincts to lapse into sentimentality and self-pity, so he has allowed his love for Molly to degenerate into an unbalanced union of servant and mistress. Throughout "Lestrygonians" Bloom reminisces about the happier days of his marriage: "Sitting there after till near two, taking out her hairpins. Milly tucked up in beddyhouse. Happy. Happy. That was the night . . . I was happier then. Or was that I? Or am I now I? Twentyeight I was. She twenty-three when we left Lombard Street west something changed. . . . Are you not happy in your home, you poor little naughty boy?" (*U*156, 168). That final fleeting reference to Martha Clifford's language ("naughty boy") reminds the reader of the way in which Bloom has tried to allay his marital unhappiness through an illusory escape, the vaguely sado-masochistic correspondence with Martha Clifford. But Bloom's unhappiness is rooted within himself: he would rather drift on aimlessly, would rather let his painful home-life remain unaltered, because his devotion to Molly's flesh is more powerful than any other force within him—more powerful even than an urge to assert his own dignity. As he passes the windows of a silk merchant, the sway his senses hold over him becomes quite evident: "Sunwarm silk. Jingling harnesses. All for a woman, home and houses, silk webs, silver, rich fruits, spicy from Jaffa. . . .

"A warm human plumpness settled down on his brain. His brain yielded. Perfume of embraces all him assailed. With hungered flesh obscurely, he mutely craved to adore" (*U*168).

Bloom's "brain yielded" as it yields constantly to his senses, and to Joyce such acquiescence endangers the "something higher" within man. Bloom's happy love becomes unhappy lust, frustrated lust, omnivorous lust, inviting the self-indulgent, rather comical sort of cannibalism in which he engages. That he craves "with hungered flesh" suggests a metaphorical equation of lust with cannibalism; and soon Joyce makes this equation more explicit, as Bloom thinks frantically, "Duke street. Here we are. Must eat. The Burton. Feel better then" (*U*168). Cuckold and servant in his own house, denied normal sexual outlets, Bloom must calm hungered flesh by eating—deadening one

⟨   132   ⟩

appetite with another. His animal needs rage within: "Hot fresh blood they prescribe for decline. Blood always needed. Insidious. Lick it up, smoking hot, thick sugary. Famished ghosts.

"Ah, I'm hungry" (U171). Finally he enters a quiet pub—repelled, to his credit, by the more bestial Dublin eating places—and begins sipping a glass of burgundy. The elixir inspires a Bacchanalian reverie: "Glowing wine on his palate lingered swallowed. Crushing in the winepress grapes of Burgundy. . . . Touched his sense moistened remembered. Hidden under wild ferns on Howth. . . . Pillowed on my coat she had her hair, earwigs in the heather scrub my hand under her nape, you'll toss me all. O wonder! Coolsoft with ointments her hand touched me, caressed: her eyes upon me did not turn away. Ravished over her I lay, full lips full open, kissed her mouth. Yum. Softly she gave me in my mouth the seedcake warm and chewed. Mawkish pulp her mouth had mumbled sweet and sour with spittle. Joy: I ate it: Joy. Young life, her lips that gave me pouting. . . . Hot I tongued her. She kissed me. I was kissed. All yielding she tossed my hair. Kissed, she kissed me.

Me. And me now" (U175-76).

The central figure of the passage is the "seedcake" which, at the moment of greatest sensual intensity, passes from Molly's mouth into Bloom's. The very essence of the sexual act is thereby implicated with another instinctive act, the consumption of food, and thus is subtly associated with the theme of "Lestrygonians," cannibalism. As always Joyce is thorough in his imagery, since the word "seedcake" itself compounds the sexual and the edible. The reverie evokes the distant past, the happy past of Mr. and Mrs. Bloom, for Molly's lips are "young," and Bloom speaks of "young life." When Bloom thinks, "Me. And me now," moreover, he is sadly comparing his present self to his past self, contrasting the ignominious situation of his pres-

ent life with the happiness of the past. While once he frol-
icked in love-play with Molly, now he stands sipping wine
at a bar, munching on gorgonzola cheese as a substitute
for the flesh he craves to adore. He drinks old memories
with his wine. As a sad, sentimental, sensual little man,
he allows his brain to yield and feeds cannibalistically
upon himself.

The state to which Bloom's self-indulgence has reduced
him is dramatically epitomized in his chance encounter
with Blazes Boylan, just at the end of the "Lestrygonians"
episode. As Bloom runs in panic, lest he be forced to speak
to Boylan, one recognizes a classically comic portrait of
the cuckold. The timid, frightened Bloom strides quickly
toward the museum and pretends to be busy searching in
his pockets and gazing at the "cream curves" of the
statues: "Hurry. Walk quietly. Moment more. My heart.
. . . Yes. Gate.

Safe!" (U183).

Bloom is safe from Blazes Boylan, yes; safe from the
humiliating gaze of the man who will make love with his
wife that afternoon. But poor, funny Mr. Bloom cannot be
safe from that cannibalistic enemy of his happiness, his
own sensual self-indulgence. To maintain that Bloom's
acceptance of cuckoldry represents a commitment on his
part to rational pacificism is to belie the facts of Joyce's
narrative.[31] Bloom is not calm and rational about sex at
all: he walks about sexually agitated and is calmed comically only by a nice slice of gorgonzola; he runs in irrational terror from his wife's seducer. Bloom has simply let
sensuality get the better of him. Rather than risk giving
up what sexual pleasure Molly allows him, such as the
mere nearness of her orangeflower-scented flesh, he permits her promiscuity, perhaps deriving some weak masochistic joy from her tyranny over him.

[31] This interpretation seems to have gained widespread acceptance,
possibly in part because of Richard Ellmann's advocacy of it in his
biography.

"The brain," Joyce once said to Frank Budgen, "is the organ presiding over 'Scylla and Charybdis.' The Aristotelian and Platonic philosophies are the monsters that lie in wait in the narrows for the thinker."[32] By citing the Aristotelian and Platonic philosophies as separate entities, Joyce emphasized their differences, which might be stated as the differences between science and faith, or between materialism and idealism. Aristotelian materialism and Platonic idealism: Joyce evidently considered both extremes to be monstrous traps which the wise thinker ought to avoid. Stephen Dedalus assumes the role of the thinker in this episode: momentarily he takes over Bloom's position as the counterpart of Ulysses, who managed to steer his ship safely between Scylla and Charybdis. In the *Portrait* Stephen adhered to an idealism which caused him to ignore the base, materialistic aspects of existence: for a time he was ensnared by an otherworldly, Platonic Charybdis. Here in *Ulysses*, as "Telemachus," "Nestor," and "Proteus" also suggest, Stephen has become disillusioned with his former idealism and is now obsessed with the frankly physical, materialistic stuff of life: he is gripped by an Aristotelian Scylla. Joyce's statement to Budgen implies that Stephen should attempt to steer clear of either Aristotelianism or Platonism, that he should recognize life's physical basis, while still not losing sight of his spiritual ideals. In the "Scylla and Charybdis" episode, one finds Stephen confused and torn between materialistic and idealistic poles. One is not ultimately sure whether he will get past the two philosophical monsters or not.

Stephen's Ulyssean dilemma is illustrated on two levels in this episode. On an immediate plane he must decide whether or not to compromise his idealism by writing an article for *Dana*, an organ of the Irish literary renaissance:

[32] Budgen, *James Joyce and the Making of Ulysses*, p. 107.

to do so would be to lend his name and talent to a cause which he considers fatuous. On a more theoretical plane, his dilemma is illustrated by the arguments themselves of his proposed article, arguments which betray the extent to which Stephen is caught in the toils of an Aristotelian Scylla.

Joyce's own attitude toward the Irish literary renaissance is set forth in "The Holy Office," an amusing broadside which he delivered in 1904. The poem contains personal jibes at most of Joyce's contemporary Irish literati, including those who appear in the "Scylla and Charybdis" episode. W. K. Magee (or "John Eglinton"), for example, becomes:

> . . . him who will his hat unfix
> Neither to malt nor crucifix
> But show to all that poor-dressed be
> His high Castilian courtesy . . . .

And George Russell (AE) becomes:

> . . . him who once when snug abed
> Saw Jesus Christ without his head
> And tried so hard to win for us
> The long-lost works of Eschylus.
>
> (CW151)

Joyce embodies his general attitude toward the nationalistic literati in the final couplet, which runs, "And though they spurn me from their door / My soul shall spurn them evermore." The vitriolic tone of "The Holy Office" suggests that Joyce regarded the nationalist movement as more deserving of ridicule than support; yet Joyce submitted the earliest known draft of the *Portrait* to W. K. Magee for publication in *Dana*, just as in this episode Stephen proposes an article on Shakespeare to Eglinton and Russell for the same magazine. In *Ulysses* Eglinton says to Stephen, "—You are the only contributor to *Dana* who asks for pieces of silver," and Stephen replies, "—For a guinea you can publish this interview" (*U*214). Not coincidentally, Joyce received a guinea for a poem published in *Dana*. Thus in trying to sell an article to the nationalists, Stephen is doing no more than Joyce himself had done, and in asking for payment he dissociates himself from the spirit of the movement.

Stephen's action does, however, represent a compromise of principle: earlier he had scorned Mulligan for being willing to traffic with an English "usurper," but now he himself tries to abet a nonsensical cause. Stephen seems aware of his compromise, for he finds it difficult to carry out his salesmanship effectively, and throughout the episode he berates himself for having stooped so low. "Folly. Persist," he says to himself. And later, "I am tired of my voice, the voice of Esau," and "What the hell are you driving at? . . . Are you condemned to do this?" (*U*185, 211, 207). Stephen's misgivings suggest that the nationalists represent a threat to his independence of thought and that he is playing a dangerous game in attempting to profit from them while disdaining them. In the symbolic terms of this episode, he is playing a far too Aristotelian, materialistic game; and he risks detaching himself altogether from his idealistic notions of the true artistic role. Joyce himself flirted briefly with the nationalists, and Stephen's misgivings are no doubt reproductions of Joyce's own. But eventually Joyce broke loose, kept to himself, and hurled "The Holy Office" at the nationalists as a final gesture of scorn and of escape. He must have subscribed to Stephen's assessment of the nationalist movement as a "Gulfer of souls, engulfer. Hesouls, shesouls, shoals of souls. Engulfed with wailing creecries, whirled, whirling, they bewail" (*U*192). Stephen's immediate, practical dilemma is how to remain free and not betray his ideals for materialistic gain, while at the same time avoiding wholly unrealistic idealism. In the *Portrait* Stephen veered too much toward idealism, while here in *Ulysses* he veers too much toward materialism. Eventually he must find the open seas of Joycean independence—cognizant of reality yet uplifted by moral idealism.

The arguments of Stephen's proposed essay supply further evidence of his materialistic, Aristotelian bent. He suggests that Shakespeare was cuckolded by his brother, and that therefore *Hamlet* is an autobiographical play: old King Hamlet, the cuckold, is Shakespeare himself, and Prince Hamlet is Shakespeare's son, Hamnet. Furthermore, Shakespeare in a sense deserved to be betrayed by his wife, because their union began illicitly in a cornfield some months before bride and groom were joined in holy matrimony. Stephen's is surely the most down-to-earth interpretation of both *Hamlet* and its author's life ever concocted. It is a theory more remarkable for its ingeniousness than for its plausibility, and the reader is dissuaded from belief in the theory by the cavalier manner in which Stephen expounds it. Like any good Irishman, he seems more intoxicated by the verbiage tumbling sonorously from his mouth than by any sense he might be making. And as if to confirm one's suspicions, he replies to the query, "Do you believe in your own theory?" with an unhesitating "—No" (U213-14).

The theory is more interesting and important as a window on Stephen's mind than as a serious critique of Shakespeare.[33] What Stephen says about Shakespeare and the Elizabethan Age offers little to the Shakespearean scholar but much to the student of Stephen's preoccupations—and hence much to the student of Bloom, Mrs. Bloom, and the whole world of *Ulysses*. Consider first the label Stephen affixes to the reign of Elizabeth I: "It is an age of exhausted whoredom groping for its god" (U206). This statement befits the Stephen we have observed strolling dejectedly along the strand in "Proteus," depressed by the nightmare

[33] For a discussion of the theory's possible origins, see William M. Schutte, *Joyce and Shakespeare* (New Haven, 1957), especially pp. 153-77.

of history, by the womb of sin from which all men spring, and by his own remorse of conscience—"agenbite of inwit." In fact Stephen associates his own sense of guilt with his adverse moral judgment on the Elizabethans, for the sequence of his thoughts actually runs thus: "Agenbite of inwit: remorse of conscience. It is an age of exhausted whoredom groping for its god" (U206). Stephen sees in Shakespeare's age all of the vices which he recognizes in his own age and in himself. These are the melancholy thoughts of the disillusioned Stephen; the Stephen who has found his idealism, his worship of chaste feminine beauty, inadequate; the Stephen who laments to himself in "Scylla and Charybdis," "Fabulous artificer, the hawklike man. You flew. Whereto? Newhaven-Dieppe, steerage passenger. Paris and back. Lapwing. Icarus. *Pater, ait.* Seabedabbled, fallen, weltering. Lapwing you are. Lapwing he" (U210). Thus Stephen, while condemning the age of Shakespeare as degenerate, remembers his own naïveté and thinks of himself as a fallen Icarus, soiled by the snotgreen sea of Ireland, and as a lapwing, a bird which prematurely flies the nest with the shell still clinging to it.[34]

It is only natural that Stephen should turn so harshly against himself and against the world: the sublimest sort of optimism has been shattered. He is obsessed with sin and guilt and remorse, and so he says of Shakespeare's London years: "Twenty years he dallied there between conjugal love and its chaste delights and scortatory love and its foul pleasures" (U201). He asserts that Shakespeare married a whore: "Sweet Ann I take it, was hot in the blood. Once a wooer twice a wooer" (U202). And finally he accuses Shakespeare of being no more than an

[34] This aspect of lapwing behavior, symbolically apt for Stephen, is referred to by Horatio in *Hamlet* v.ii.181; and since Hamlet is on Stephen's mind, this is the probable reference. Equally pertinent is the fate of Daedalus' nephew, who, according to Ovid, was pushed off a tower by Daedalus and turned into a lapwing, a bird which fears heights, remembering its fall.

opportunistic, chauvinistic, possessive hack: "He drew Shylock out of his own long pocket. The son of a malt-jobber and moneylender he was himself a cornjobber and moneylender with ten tods of corn hoarded in the famine riots. . . . He sued a fellowplayer for the price of a few bags of malt and exacted his pound of flesh in interest for every money lent. How else could Aubrey's ostler and callboy get rich quick? All events brought grist to his mill. Shylock chimes with the jewbaiting that followed the hanging and quartering of the queen's leech Lopez, . . . The lost armada is his jeer in *Love's Labour's Lost*. His pageants, the histories, sail fullbellied on a tide of Mafeking enthusiasm. . . . The sugared sonnets follow Sidney's. As for fay Elizabeth, otherwise carroty Bess, the gross virgin who inspired *The Merry Wives of Windsor*, let some meinherr from Almany grope his life long for deephid meanings in the depth of the buckbasket" (U204-205).

These rantings illustrate Stephen's troubled conscience; they are a natural outgrowth of the melancholy soliloquies of "Proteus." They are the distorted fantasies of an enraged moral vision which perceives all creation as rank, gross, sinful—and Stephen himself does not take them wholly seriously. He is play-acting here, telling half-truths simply by allowing the seeds of discontent and disillusion within him to blossom into an indictment of the universe. "I think you're getting on very nicely," Stephen thinks. "Just mix up a mixture of theolologicophilological" (U205). Stephen's kind of misanthropy represents what *Ulysses* might have been had Joyce not added his humorous perspective; it also represents the extent of Stephen's anguish and the difficulty of his dilemma in "Scylla and Charybdis." He must not allow his mordant and melancholy kind of Aristotelianism, his materialism, to snuff out idealism altogether. Neither must he have any truck with the otherworldliness of the Irish poets and intellectuals around him, who favor aesthetic formulas similar to those of Stephen's now-discarded theories: "Art has to reveal to us ideas, formless spiritual essences" (U185). This kind of idealism represents the Platonic Charybdis of this episode.

To escape his dilemma, to shun neither facts nor ideals, to remain the morally committed interpreter of the "ineluctable modality of the visible," Stephen must learn the comic spirit. Not the mocking spirit of Buck Mulligan, that amoral comedian: of Mulligan Stephen thinks, "My will: his will that fronts me. Seas between" (U217). Stephen's will is to despairing indignation; Mulligan's will is to morality-destroying acceptance; the open seas of freedom lie between, and Stephen must take to them. Just as Stephen formulates this opposition between himself and Mulligan, Bloom appears: "A man passed out between them, bowing, greeting" (U217). Bloom—the kind, sentimental, narcissistic, masochistic, sensual, factually-minded Bloom. Not an evil man: a good man, in his weak, ineffectual way: unheroic, unsubstantial, Bloom. To him Stephen must adjust his perspective if he is to survive as a thinker and as an artist. Bloom must become to Stephen what he is to Joyce: the quintessence of Irish life, perhaps of life itself: a quintessence not to be taken tragically, but comically. Accept Bloom as you find him, Joyce seems to be saying. Accept him as practically paralyzed by his sensual longings, as a prime example of all that is stultifying about Irish life, yet ultimately comic, ultimately amusing, and you will be able to accept life. Only through such equanimity can one hope to avoid despair and the irreparable loss of idealism. If Joyce's conception of human nature seems none too generous or optimistic, at least it no longer partakes of the lugubrious kind of moralizing in which Stephen, like the younger Joyce, finds himself mired. In addressing itself to Bloom, the Joycean conscience has become almost amiable.

· 8 ·

"Scylla and Charybdis" is an island of intellect in mid-

Ulysses, and when Joyce transports us there abruptly the effect is a bit startling: suddenly the cerebral serenity of the National Library replaces a world of urine-scented kidneys, warm feminine flesh, the rising odor of feces, hot spicy pig's blood—the Bloomian world. Outside in the streets of Dublin draymen rattle about their business, trams "krandlkrankran" along; in pubs the porter and the blather flow endlessly. And in "Wandering Rocks" Joyce brings us back into the ordinary life of Dublin. This fragmented episode, which affords glimpses of the simultaneous doings of several Dubliners, broadens the scope of *Ulysses* beyond the immediate spheres of either Stephen or Bloom. It testifies to the comprehensive nature of Joyce's satiric intent, for while he considered the individual mind and soul to be the primary sources of human folly, Joyce envisioned Stephen and Bloom as parts of a generally decaying social fabric.

In his most vituperative, Stephen-like moments, Joyce could write violently of "the farce of Irish Catholicism": ". . . warrens full of swarming and cringing believers . . . an island the inhabitants of which entrust their wills and minds to others that they may insure for themselves a life of spiritual paralysis, an island in which all the power and the riches are in the keeping of those whose kingdom is not of this world, an island in which Caesar confesses Christ and Christ confesses Caesar that together they may wax fat upon a starveling rabblement which is bidden ironically to take to itself this consolation in hardship 'The Kingdom of God is within you' " (*SH*146). In "Wandering Rocks" Joyce attacks the Church in a more subtle and comical way in the person of "The Superior, the Very Reverend John Conmee, S.J.," who strolls through Dublin's warrens indifferent to the sufferings of its believers. Does a parishioner look downcast? Has there been a disaster in New York, hundreds killed and maimed? Father Conmee is not alarmed. A perfect act of contrition, a donation to the Church—these balms soothe, irrelevant though they may be to the sufferings of the poor. Father Conmee is not an evil man. His demeanor is in fact kindly. But he illustrates Joyce's contention that Ireland "has served only one master well, the Roman Catholic Church, which, however, is accustomed to pay its faithful in long term drafts" (CW213). Later in the episode, when Stephen encounters his starving sister, who has just been cheated out of a coin by her besotted father,[35] the complacency of the Reverend Conmee becomes still more disturbing, and the little girl intones mockingly, "—Our father who art not in heaven" (U227). Joyce blamed Irish religious subservience more than English oppression for the nation's ills. "I do not see what good it does," he once wrote, "to fulminate against the English tyranny while the Roman tyranny occupies the palace of the soul" (CW173). The episode ends, however, with a sardonic description of the warm welcome which Dubliners accord the parading English viceroy—"most cordially greeted on his way through the metropolis" (U252).

The drinkers, clerics, boasters, self-indulgers, the innocent victims too—these are the "wandering rocks" which any potential Irish Ulysses must avoid. These are the hazards which threaten to impale Stephen and to drown him in a sluggish Irish sea. Joyce escaped these rocks, writing of them, "Dublin is a detestable city and the people are most repulsive to me."[36] But what of our Irish Ulysses? How does Bloom fare in this episode fraught with threats to his heroism? He fares characteristically. We catch sight

---

[35] Simon Dedalus appears in Ulysses as an ambiguous figure. As a father he fails miserably, almost criminally; yet he exudes Irish music and wit and charm. Joyce's mingled admiration for and resentment of his own father is mirrored here. Stanislaus Joyce, by contrast, was far less indulgent of the father. His bitterness matched Stephen's toward Simon. See The Dublin Diary of Stanislaus Joyce (London, 1962), p. 113.

[36] 2 September 1909, Letters, II, 243.

of him panting over and then purchasing a pornographic novel. "—*Sweets of Sin*," the bookseller observes. "That's a good one" (*U*237).

· 9 ·

Joyce adjusts his focus again to Bloom in the "Sirens" episode and in so doing heightens our compassion for the unfortunate cuckold. The word alienation has become something of a twentieth-century catchword, but particularly in this episode Bloom does seem to fit the common conception of the alienated modern man.[37] An anomalous Jew in Dublin, he eats a meal in silence at the Ormond Hotel diningroom, while in the adjoining bar a congenial group of stage Irishmen, led by the mellifluous Simon Dedalus and rendered ethnically complete by the presence of a piano-playing priest, empties tankard after tankard and fills the air with laughter and song. Bloom can only chew on his fried liver, gaze wistfully at the siren-like barmaids, write a letter to his unseen pen pal sweetheart, listen to the singing, and contemplate with great uneasiness the impending violation of his marriage bed by Blazes Boylan. No wonder that he thinks to himself, "I feel so sad. . . . So lonely blooming. . . . I feel so lonely Bloom. . . . I feel so lonely" (*U*256, 287, 290). No wonder we want to lavish pity upon him and label him the alienated, isolated, uncommunicating, sociologically disinherited twentieth-century man.

But a more comprehensive analysis of the "Sirens" episode reveals the limitations and inadequacies of this approach to Bloom. We must be wary of an overly sentimental interpretation of Bloom's actions and inactions. In other episodes we have noted Bloom's tendency to indulge himself, to pity himself, to engage in narcissism and masochism. As should be expected, Bloom's behavior in the "Si-

[37] For arguments along this line see Douglas Knight, "The Reading of *Ulysses*," *ELH*, xix (March 1952), 64-80; and Mark Schorer, "Technique as Discovery," *Hudson Review*, i (Spring 1948), 79-80.

⟨   144   ⟩

rens" episode is consistent with his previous behavior. Joyce's tone here is consistent as well: surely there is an element of pity present in his treatment of Bloom, but there are still stronger elements of comedy and gentle satire which should condition our critical judgment, preventing us from emphasizing the pathos of Bloom's alienation to the exclusion of more prominent factors.

Consider first of all the reason for Bloom's presence at the Ormond. Earlier in the day he had scurried in fear from Molly's current suitor, Blazes Boylan, but now, at four in the afternoon, he espies Boylan jingling across Essex Bridge and along Ormond Quay. "Follow," Bloom urges himself. "Risk it. Go quick" (U264). Has Bloom finally plucked up courage for a confrontation with his rival? No—instead he wants merely to watch Boylan, for he takes a table in the dining room of the Ormond, while Boylan steps into the bar. Bloom thinks: "Sit tight there. See, not be seen" (U265). This is an important fact, because it demonstrates that Bloom sits sadly unseen in the dining room out of deliberate, conscious choice: he wants to observe, to see and not be seen. The Irish Ulysses worries about the supposed chance he is taking—"Risk it," he says to himself—but all he really worries about is being seen and thus being embarrassed. As his interest in Boylan testifies, Bloom is far from indifferent to Molly's infidelities;[38] in fact he seems to take a curious kind of pleasure, a self-indulgent and perhaps masochistic kind of pleasure in coming as close as he can to observing these infidelities: for now, the best he can manage is a close look at the jaunty Boylan, but in the "Circe" episode his imagination will take over and he will be able to delight in the *non plus ultra* of his masochistic voyeurism, the spectacle of Molly in bed with Boylan. By that time Bloom's masochistic delight in cuckoldry will be obvious; here at

[38] These remarks suggest an alternative to seeing Bloom as a rational pacifist; that is, his pacifism is irrational.

the Ormond he watches Boylan without, significantly, any apparent desire to interfere with him.

When Boylan quits the Ormond bar and departs for Bloom's bed, Simon Dedalus and his cronies begin singing in earnest, and the sentimental crooning puts Bloom in an unhappily amorous mood. The barmaids, of course, correspond to the Homeric sirens in this episode; but with devilish irony Joyce permits poor Bloom to become aroused initially not by the bronze and gold allure of the barmaids but by the alcoholic tenor of Simon Dedalus, siren of the Ormond. Simon somehow warbles Bloom into an erection: "Tenderness it welled: slow, swelling. Full it throbbed. . . . Throb, a throb, a pulsing proud erect. . . . Bloom. Flood of warm jimjam lickitup secretness flowed to flow in music out, in desire, dark to lick flow, invading. Tipping her tepping her tapping her topping her. Tup. . . . The joy the feel the warm the. Tup. . . . Flood, gush, flow, joygush, tupthrop. Now! Language of love.

"— . . . *ray of hope* . . ." sings Simon obligingly and sentimentally (U274). His song is an aria from Von Flotow's mawkish opera *Martha*, in which Lionel laments the departure of his beloved; and in an ineffectual attempt to compensate for his marital indignities, Bloom is inspired to compose a letter to his own Martha, that writer of sadomasochistic love-notes. In writing her, Bloom recalls one of his private masochistic fantasies, that of a sturdy girl whacking away lustily at a carpet: "You punish me? Crooked skirt swinging, whack by" (U280).[39]

The Bloom of the "Sirens" episode is not, then, simply isolated and unable to communicate and victimized by his environment: he is an amiable, likable, but remarkably weak and self-indulgent little man, whose passivity results far more from a paralyzing self-indulgence than from either hostile, alienating social forces or from any com-

[39] Cf. U59 and my analysis of the *Calypso* episode, section 2, above.

mitment to calmness and rationality. His rather perverse following of Boylan is hardly rational, and at times in this episode he appears on the brink of what would be an extraordinarily humiliating sexual frenzy and release: Simon's singing brings him to the point of spontaneous ejaculation, but a certain manual gesture of Lydia Douce, satiny barmaid, is even more exciting to the frustrated Bloom. He tells himself, "Time to be shoving. Looked enough." But he looks a bit longer and "On the smooth jutting beerpull laid Lydia hand lightly, plumply, leave it to my hands. All lost in pity for croppy. Fro, to: to, fro: over the polished knob (she knows his eyes, my eyes, her eyes) her thumb and finger passed in pity: passed, repassed and, gently touching, then slid so smoothly, slowly down, a cool firm white enamel baton protruding through their sliding ring" (U286). Seeing a sexual caress in Lydia's seductive beerpulling, Bloom feels he has had enough and had better get out, but thinks, "Thanks, that was heavenly. Where's my hat. Pass by her." When the Greek Ulysses came within reach of the sirens' song, he bound himself to the mast so as not to become enslaved and destroyed by them. The sirens of the Ormond have no desire to enslave poor Bloom, but he has not been so prudent as Ulysses: he is held fast by his own sirens, women of all shape and sort, some real and some fancied. He hurries out of the bar "by rose, by satiny bosom, by the fondling hand . . ." but the rose and the bosom and the fondling hand will stick in his mind, along with the curious images of his other sirens, clouding his brain, contributing to the comic and tragicomic paralysis which so largely characterizes him. He manifests the same inertia common to Joyce's Dubliners as a whole.

The conclusion of the "Sirens" episode emphasizes Bloom's association with, rather than his alienation from, his fellow Irishmen by means of an extremely comical gesture. Having left the Ormond, Bloom proceeds along the quay, looking in shop windows and, to his discomfort, becoming conscious of a growing flatulence. Now the breaking of wind has from time immemorial been considered a laugh-provoking act; it results in the most ignominious sound known to man and may be said to connote the very opposite of solemnity or high seriousness. Thus Bloom is anxious to avoid making this sound within earshot of his respectable fellow Dubliners. With mock-Ulyssean guile he manages to release the gaseous pressure building up within him just as a noisy tram passes by— and the "Sirens" episode of this mock-epic ends with the following comment from its hero: "Pprrpffrrppfff."

In itself that peroration is eloquent enough: it might stand as an audible symbol of Joyce's mock-heroic treatment of this Ulysses; it poignantly evokes the quality of Bloom's life. But going one step further in his mockery, Joyce manages to juxtapose Bloom's noisome emission upon the heroic last words of Robert Emmet, the patriot who died in the cause of Irish independence in 1803, those words being, "When my country takes her place among the nations of the earth, then and not till then, let my epitaph be written." Bloom reads this beneath a portrait of the gallant Emmet, and while doing so releases his excretory theme-song, the Bloomian musical signature to this musical episode:

"Seabloom, greaseabloom viewed last words. Softly. *When my country takes her place among.*
"Prrprr.
"Must be the bur.
"Fff. Oo. Rrpr.
"*Nations of the earth.* No-one behind. She's passed. *Then and not till then.* Tram. Kran, kran, kran. Good oppor. Coming. Krandlkrankran. I'm sure it's the burgund. Yes. One, two. *Let my epitaph be.* Karaaaaaaa. *Written. I have.*
"Pprrpffrrppfff.
"*Done*" (U291).

Joyce accomplishes two thematic purposes by means of this ingenious cloacal counterpoint: the cause of Irish nationalism is made to look absurd, as the stout rhetoric of a patriot long dead mingles with the flatulence of a modern Irishman; and at the same time the flaccid character of Bloom is contrasted with the iron will of Emmet. When Ireland takes her place among the nations, Joyce seems to be asking waggishly, will Bloom lead the parade? And will be the trumpets sound, "Pprrpffrrppffff"?

· 10 ·

Laurence Sterne once observed to a friend: "I am persuaded that the happiness of the Cervantic humour arises from this very thing:—of describing silly and trifling events with the circumstantial pomp of great ones."[40] Whether or not Joyce was aware of Sterne's remark, he made use of the happiness of the Cervantic humor in the "Cyclops" episode, wherein silly and trifling events, and silly and trifling characters, are described consistently with the circumstantial pomp of great ones. The Irish, of course, have a great talent for exaggeration, and a good part of the humor of this episode lies in that national talent, as Joyce allows his readers to listen in on the typical Irish pub talk of a typical Irish pub, Barney Kiernan's. Here the imbibers do more than imbibe: they fill the air with their fantastic talk and relish every pint with a gusto unheard-of on the other side of the Irish Sea: "Ah! Ow! Don't be talking! I was blue mouldy for the want of that pint. Declare to God I could hear it hit the pit of my stomach with a click." This Irish penchant for exaggeration is the foundation of what Joyce identified as his technique in "Cyclops," gigantism. The unidentified Dubliner who narrates the main action of the episode starts things off on a properly amplified note, by letting a poor chimneysweep "have

40 Letter to * * * in *Works*, VII (London, 1802), 299.

the weight of my tongue" when he "near shove my eye out
with his brush" (U292).

But there is another narrator, a more mischievous narrator, who regularly intrudes with his own delightful and
more literary kind of exaggeration. We can readily detect
the gigantism of the talk at Barney Kiernan's, where the
most trifling occurrence becomes embellished with the
comical grandeur of Irish speech; but what appears to be
Joyce's own narrative voice finally places the bombast of
this tavern in its proper, Cervantean perspective. Thus the
Fenian citizen, whom we already know for a mere boor,
has his boorishness ultimately and perfectly characterized
when Joyce describes him as though he were Polyphemus
himself: "A powerful current of warm breath issued at
regular intervals from the profound cavity of his mouth
while in rhythmic resonance the long strong hale reverber-
ations of his formidable heart thundered rumblingly causing the ground, the summit of the lofty tower and the still
loftier walls of the cave to vibrate and tremble" (U296).
Thus Molly Bloom, whom we already know for a distinctly
lower- middle-class adulteress, is diminished further in stat-
ure when Joyce describes her gigantically as though she
were princess of Gibraltar: "Pride of Calpe's rocky mount,
the ravenhaired daughter of Tweedy. There grew she to
peerless beauty where loquat and almond scent the air. The
gardens of Alameda know her step: the garths of olives
knew and bowed. The chaste spouse of Leopold is she:
Marion of the bountiful bosoms" (U319). And thus Leopold himself, whom we already know for a fearful cuckold,
whose prudence has thus far consisted of remaining unseen by his rival, looks more comical than ever when
Joyce mischievously causes him to enter as an Irish-Jewish
Sir Lancelot: "Who comes through Michan's land, bedight in sable armour? O'Bloom, the son of Rory: it is he.
Impervious to fear is Rory's son: he of the prudent soul"
(U297). In all three of these instances of Joycean gigan-

tism, the effect is one of ridicule; while the farcical nature of this episode is immediately apparent from the talk of the Dubliners assembled at Kiernan's, it is Joyce's ludicrously gigantic, mock-heroic narrative interjections which extend this episode to the limits of satire.

We must keep in mind the gigantic ludicrousness of it all if we are to take the episode in its intended spirit of levity, because otherwise we may be tempted into an inappropriate gravity by the issue which dominates the latter part of the action—anti-semitism. Since Auschwitz and Buchenwald and Dachau, it has become impossible for anyone with a conscience to acquiesce to the slightest hint of anti-semitism; even the most faintly anti-Jewish joke, or the most vaguely anti-Jewish stereotype, calls up visions of corpse-filled ovens and gas chambers and human skeletons strewn about a prison yard. A performance of *The Merchant of Venice* is bound to bring two reactions: cries that the play be suppressed for its alleged anti-semitism and assurances from well intentioned critics that Shylock is actually the hero of the play. In this atmosphere an accurate perspective on the "Cyclops" episode is difficult to maintain: we can perceive Joyce's farcical intentions, but only up to the point that anti-semitism becomes an issue; at that instant we are likely to stop laughing and to start cheering in earnest for O'Bloom, bedight in sable armor, champion of an oppressed minority.

But we lose sight of the mock-heroic tone and technique of this episode at the cost of distorting Joyce's meaning. Bloom's confrontation with the chauvinistic, anti-semitic citizen represents one of Sir Leopold's best moments in *Ulysses*: for once he does not flee fearfully from opposition but stands his ground, condemning anti-semitic injustice, berating "Force, hatred, history, all that. That's not life for men and women, insult and hatred. And everybody knows that it's the very opposite of that that is really life.

"—What? says Alf.

"—Love, says Bloom. I mean the opposite of hatred"
(*U*333). Noble sentiments, these, with which no reason-
able man could quarrel; but the comic circumstances of
their utterance should make us wary of exaggerating their
significance to *Ulysses*. Opposing Bloom in this scene are
the quarrelsome frequenters of Kicrnan's pub, with the
awesomely chauvinistic citizen at their head. Bloom appears noble indeed in countering their belligerence with
a doctrine of universal love; yet in his own way he is as
ridiculous as they are—not hateful, not contemptible, but
simply ridiculous. Certainly our sympathies are with him
here: but it is a sympathy mixed with laughter and pity
for the bizarre figure he cuts. And when the eternally
ironic Joyce breaks in with this absurd commentary—
"Love loves to love love. Nurse loves the new chemist. Constable 14A loves Mary Kelly. Gerty MacDowell loves the
boy that has the bicycle. . . . Li Chi Han lovey up kissy
Cha Pu Chow. Jumbo, the elephant, loves Alice, the elephant. . . . His Majesty the King loves Her Majesty the
Queen. . . . You love a certain person. And this person
loves that other person because everybody loves somebody
but God loves everybody"—when Joyce breaks in with this
commentary, poor Bloom looks more foolish than ever,
playing the role of a mock-Christ as well as that of a mock-
Ulysses. The importance of all of the mock-epic gigantism
which precedes Bloom's love-sermon must not be under-
estimated: this gigantism establishes the comic tone which
should prevent us from taking too solemnly in this context
the profundity that "Love loves to love love."

As for Bloom's specific thrusts against anti-semitism,
when he reminds the assembled gentiles that Mendelssohn,
Marx, Mercadante, and Christ were all Jews, one can note
the contrast between Bloom's courage here and his timidity
elsewhere, and one can be gratified that Bloom has landed
a good verbal thrust at the scabrous citizen, but one need
not exaggerate Bloom's courage nor lose sight of the com-

edy. Joyce's presently most influential critic, Richard Ellmann, would have it that Bloom's performance in this episode embodies "the theme of *Ulysses*," which he terms
"simple": "Casual kindness overcomes unconscionable
power."[41] The idea that Bloom embodies pacifist ideals and
hence is the center of positive values in *Ulysses* has gained
such prominence, particularly in recent years, that it may
be said to lie behind a preponderance of Joyce criticism
today. To Mr. Ellmann, Bloom's weaknesses and aberra-
tions are far less important than his calmness and rationality. In an age of strife, Bloom offers reasonableness; in a
city alive with brawlers, blasphemers, and bloody-minded
bigots, Bloom lives his quiet, exemplary existence, a model
of gentlemanly perseverance. This line of reasoning cannot be denied; it must be taken into account in any assessment of Bloom—but it leaves out a great deal more than it
encompasses. Granted that Bloom's calmness looks admirable beside the bestial ravings of the Fenian citizen:
yet this same calmness appears comically weak when
Bloom carries it to the extreme of running in fear from
Blazes Boylan. Granted that, from the outside, Bloom looks
the picture of rationality: but through his various narrative techniques, Joyce allows us to gaze into Bloom's heart
and mind and soul, as well as to peer at him from the outside; and when we see him from the inside, we find him
aglow with frustrated desires, beset by fears real and imaginary, and deluded by comical, quite irrational schemes
and dreams for the supposed betterment of mankind and
of himself. The line of reasoning which would set up
Bloom as the bearer of Joyce's positive values overlooks
that Joyce had values other than pacifism and that his
ideals included a degree of moral courage which the
amiable but malleable Bloom never approaches, ideals
which perhaps no man ever fulfills completely, except in
the pages of—the *Odyssey*. But more than anything else,

[41] Ellmann, *James Joyce*, p. 390.

this reasoning minimizes the marvelous comic spirit which permeates the "Cyclops" episode—and indeed all of *Ulysses*. Joyce's comic spirit, while it is far too jovial to permit a mordant scorn of mankind, is at the same time far too mirthful to permit the reader to take Sir Leopold seriously. Surely one misses the puckish comic spirit of "Cyclops" to say, in effect, that the theme of *Ulysses* is that love loves to love love and that Sir Leopold O'Bloom is meant by Joyce to be the apostle to us heathen.

Aside from gigantism as a comic technique in "Cyclops," there is a further irony in Joyce's permitting Bloom to defend the Jews against the "unconscionable power" of that "brawny-handed hairylegged ruddyfaced sinewyarmed" anti-semitic citizen: the irony lies in the fact that O'Bloom isn't much of a Jew himself. One recent Jewish analyst of Bloom maintains that "there is not one iota of Jewishness about this character" except for the name Bloom;[42] without getting involved in ethnic distinctions, one can at least safely argue that a thrice-baptized, uncircumcised Jew is hardly a Jew at all, and thrice-baptized and uncircumcised Bloom is. A remark of Joyce's to Frank Budgen may suggest his attitude toward Sir Leopold's nominal Christianity: "I sometimes think that it was a heroic sacrifice on [the Jews'] part when they refused to accept the Christian revelation. Look at them. They are better husbands than we are, better fathers, and better sons."[43] Look at Bloom: thrice-baptized, he has unheroically accepted Christian revelation; and as for his family life, it might best be described as *un ménage à je ne sais combien*. If, as Frank Budgen tells us, Joyce admired the Jew as a family man, Bloom is a curious Jew by Joycean standards. Perhaps Joyce measures Bloom against his ideal of the proudly

[42] Alfred J. Kutzik, "Faulkner and the Jews," *Yivo Annual of Jewish Social Science*, XIII (1965), 218.

[43] "James Joyce" in *James Joyce: Two Decades of Criticism*, ed. Seon Givens (New York, 1948, 1963), p. 23.

unchristian and family-centered Jew, much as he measures Bloom against his idea of Ulysses as a hero.[44] Certainly it is a mistake to try to lump Joyce, as some critics have unconsciously done, with the Yiddish tradition of Sholem Aleichem, carried on in our own day and tongue by such writers as Bernard Malamud and, perhaps, Saul Bellow. The gentle Jewish humor of this fiction, with its silently suffering anti-heroes, whose virtue is the acceptance of misfortune with dignity, is as foreign to Joyce as the *Talmud*. Joyce's tradition is that of the impish, ribald, mocking, rather dotty Irish comic spirit.

Aside from the satire directed at Bloom as an individual character, Joyce very likely made his Ulysses a Jew in order to render absurd the comparisons so often drawn by Irish orators and poets between Ireland and ancient Israel. An example of such patriotic hyperbole is given in the "Aeolus" episode, and Joyce must have known Lady Gregory's play, *The Deliverer*, in which Parnell is the Irish Moses. And if doubts linger as to the comic tone of "Cyclops"—if our sympathy for Bloom and our hatred of anti-semitism work against the impulse to laugh at this episode—Joyce's final satiric touch should facilitate and even insure an ultimately comic interpretation. If Bloom is given a chance at heroism in his defiance of the citizen, Joyce quickly pulls the heroic rug from under him by means of the absurd apotheosis which closes the episode, when Bloom is taken into heaven aboard a fiery chariot. This ending is of course quite in harmony with the tone of the rest of "Cyclops," being simply the last instance of Joyce's ironic technique of gigantism; the ending is also consistent with a long tradition of English mock-heroic satire, of which Dryden's *MacFlecknoe*, Pope's *Dunciad*, and Field-

44 In the "Oxen of the Sun" episode it is suggested that Bloom's Jewish strength is sapped by the pervasive weakness of Ireland (see U409-10). This notion would square with Joyce's often-repeated contention that no man of spirit could survive in Ireland: hence his own self-exile.

⟨   155   ⟩

ing's churchyard battle in *Tom Jones* are venerable examples. When Joyce compares Bloom to Elijah, the effect is equally as ridiculous as when Pope compared Colley Cibber to Aeneas: "And they beheld Him in the chariot, clothed upon in the glory of the brightness, having raiment as of the sun, fair as the moon and terrible that for awe they durst not look upon Him. . . . And they beheld Him even Him, ben Bloom Elijah, amid clouds of angels ascend to the glory of the brightness at an angle of fortyfive degrees over Donohoe's in Little Green Street like a shot off a shovel" (*U*345). One cannot find a more apt nor more skillful example of what Laurence Sterne meant when he defined "the happiness of the Cervantic humour" as the art of "describing silly and trifling events with the circumstantial pomp of great ones."

If one keeps that Bloomian ascension in mind as the concluding instance of Joyce's Cervantic technique in "Cyclops," the significance of the entire episode becomes clear. Not a serious confrontation between chauvinism and rationalism, "Cyclops" is rather a particularly amusing extension of Joyce's comic purpose in *Ulysses*: the dramatization, by an author of conscience, of the foibles, affectations, self-deceptions, and hypocrisies of mankind, executed good-humoredly within a mock-heroic framework.

· II ·

One of the most obviously satirical episodes in *Ulysses*, "Nausicaa" combines a portrait of the comical self-indulgence of Bloom with a complementary parody of sentimentalism. Because of this satiric force, critics and readers who believe *Ulysses* to be an essentially affirmative book are often discontent with "Nausicaa," the satire of which stifles any affirmation save that of a guffaw. S. L. Goldberg, for example, who argues most effectively for the notion that *Ulysses* embodies primarily a philosophy of pacifism and affirmation—Mr. Bloom being a pacifist notable for the classical balance of his character—questions Joyce's judgment in satirizing at length the sentimentalism of Gerty MacDowell. Mr. Goldberg believes that Joyce's treatment of Gerty betrays the essentially benign spirit of the novel and displays a side of Joyce's talent better left unexpressed: "If once we think of Gerty with any compassion as a human being during those twenty pages (as Bloom does afterwards), we may conclude that Joyce's ironic parody is breaking a butterfly on its wheel."[45]

If Joyce is simply not humane enough to poor Gerty, then the whole of "Nausicaa" fails. The answer to this argument is twofold: first, the nature of parody and satire and comedy requires that we grant writers license to ridicule, as long as they have a sound satiric purpose in so doing and as long as they make us laugh; and second, Joyce's parody of Gerty's sentimentalism is germane to *Ulysses* in that it helps us better to understand Bloom's mind. To begin with the license we must grant to Joyce: once we start to think of all characters in plays and novels as human beings, we make comedy and satire and parody impossible. If we are going to cluck our tongues in "compassion" when a character is ridiculed upon the stage or within a book, we shall have to ban ridicule from Aristophanes to Ionesco—and Joyce. Allow much compassion for cross-gartered Malvolio as a human being to intrude upon the mischievous delights of *Twelfth Night* and indeed there shall be no more cakes and ale. No play or novel is big enough to accommodate more than a handful of fully realized human beings: the other characters are of necessity types, exaggerations of certain human tendencies, vices, or virtues. Gerty MacDowell is such a type: she is not a human being but a collection of pulp-fiction clichés, and as such she is used as a means of mocking certain

[45] S. L. Goldberg, *The Classical Temper* (London, 1961), p. 141.

ridiculously sentimental distortions of reality. And as for Bloom's momentary compassion for her, that too is gently mocked.

Joyce's treatment of Gerty is quite relevant to Bloom and to our understanding of him. In order to make the character of Gerty's thoughts unmistakable, Joyce adopted an astonishingly mechanical method of composition for "Nausicaa," a method which testifies more assuredly than any critic can to the satiric intent of the episode: Joyce simply recorded hundreds of cliché words and phrases in his notebooks and then, when it came time to write the episode, strung them together within the narrative. "He was too young to understand . . . love, a woman's birthright . . . a man among men . . . she was sincerity itself . . . a smile reinforced by the whitest of teeth . . .": these are among the phrases Joyce culled from ladies' confession magazines, putting them down as Gerty's own idiom until she herself became the essence of this sentimental pulp-fiction.[46] "*Nausikaa*," as Joyce wrote Frank Budgen, "is written in a namby-pamby jammy marmalady drawersy (alto la!) style. . . ."[47] Gerty has no existence outside of this namby-pamby fictional world of oppressively innocent children, handsome strong-willed men, and "softlyfeatured" maidens made even more softlyfeatured with the help of eyebrowleine and "ivorylike" with the aid of iron jelloids. Once Joyce has established her in all her mawkish gush, she and Bloom are brought together, and our comprehension of Bloom thereby expands. As one of Gerty's magazines might say, she and Bloom were meant for each other.

What an enlightening thing is this conjunction of Gerty's mind and Bloom's mind! They do not speak to one another, and of physical contact they know, alas, only the meeting

[46] An examination of Joyce's notesheets for *Ulysses* in the British Museum (MS no. 49975) led me to this analysis of the method of composition for "Nausicaa." The pages of notes for "Nausicaa" consist of huge lists of sentimental clichés.
[47] Budgen, *James Joyce and the Making of Ulysses*, p. 205.

of eyes. But through this mental conjunction—or shall we get really into the spirit of it and call theirs a "spiritual union"?—one discerns a fundamental similarity between Gerty's sentimental distortion of reality and Bloom's own more complex distortion of reality. Both try to escape from life: Gerty through the agency of hack writers and advertisers, Bloom through myriad dreams, imagined schemes, sexual fantasies, nervous eating, reminiscences, daily busyness, and an occasional spate of Gerty-like sentimentalism. Both try, often rather successfully, to avoid thoughts of the emptiness of their own lives and thoughts of the real spirit of Dublin, "the city of failure, of rancour, and of unhappiness."[48] Both revel in unreality. How appropriate it is, then, that Bloom should make love to Gerty. And still more appropriate is the way in which Bloom chooses to make love to this specimen of Irish girlhood: masturbation, the classic means of illusory escape, the classic symbol of sterility, the perfect method by which one self-deceived dreamer can make love to another.

Evidence exists for arguing that Bloom's masturbation is emblematic of not only his own escapism but of that of Ireland as well. Irish chastity has often been attributed, only half facetiously, to an Irish fondness for what the Church likes to term "self-abuse." Coarse jokes on this theme are common enough, as are songs:

> "There is a man who lives in Cork,
> A man of great renown,
> Because he has a maxim which
> He preaches round the town.
> He's been a family doctor ever
> Since his very 'teens,
> But he made his great discovery when
> A student at the Queen's.

> "O Dr. Dooley! O Dr. Dooley!
> The nation owes a great big debt to you,

---

[48] Letter to Nora, 22 August 1909, *Letters*, II, 239.

For 'It's masturbation
That kills a nation,'
Said Dr. Dooley-ooley-ooley-oo."

Stanislaus Joyce recorded this little ballad in his diary, and in the margin he commented, "A nasty fact not cleverly parodied," the fact being that the Irish nation was famed for masturbation.[49] In another place Stanislaus listed masturbation among the three chief Irish vices, along with drunkenness and lying.[50] The accusation may be heard frequently enough in pubs and, no doubt, in confessional boxes; but Dr. Dooley and Stanislaus Joyce have not been the only savants to immortalize in writing the "nasty fact": James Joyce gave it further circulation when he had Stephen Dedalus make the familiar allegation in *Stephen Hero*, thus:

"— . . . I fully recognise that my countrymen have not yet advanced as far as the machinery of Parisian harlotry because . . . *

"—Because . . . ?*

"—Well, because they can do it by hand, that's why!

"—Good God, you don't mean to say you think . . .*

"—My good youth, I know what I'm saying is true and so do you know it. Ask Father Pat and ask Dr Thisbody and Dr Thatbody. I was at school and you were at school— and that's enough about it.

"—O, Daedalus!" (*SH*55).

In *Ulysses* Joyce again echoed the "nasty fact" by permitting Buck Mulligan to announce his little play, with its *national* theme:

Everyman His own Wife

or

A Honeymoon in the Hand
(a national immorality in three orgasms).

* Joyce's ellipses.
[49] *Diary of Stanislaus Joyce*, p. 52.   [50] *Ibid.*, p. 36.

And in the *Dubliners* story called "An Encounter," Joyce had less lightheartedly made a pervert's exhibitionistic masturbation a repulsive symbol of Irish paralysis, sterility, and corruption. Bloom's more discreet autoeroticism is also a sign of paralysis and sterility, but like Buck Mulligan's national immorality play, it is far less repulsive than ludicrous: the comic spirit of the episode and of *Ulysses* as a whole, together with our knowledge of Bloom's benign character, keep the incident amusing. But the commonness of slurs against Irish sexual practices, and the fact that both Stanislaus and James Joyce made literary use of these accusations, suggest that Bloom's act may have national as well as personal satiric significance.

Whether nationally symbolic or not, Bloom's self-induced ejaculation certainly functions as a kind of epiphany of the quality of his life—lonely, frustrated, filled with futile attempts at escape. The masochistic fantasies, dreams of faraway places, and narcissistic bathtub reveries of the "Lotus-eaters" episode closely resemble "Nausicaa" thematically; and the two episodes are more closely linked when Bloom reflects in "Nausicaa" on the earlier episode: "Damned glad I didn't do it in the bath this morning over her silly I will punish you letter" (*U*368). His self-control (such as it was) in the morning made possible this silent, self-indulgent tryst in the evening, when an Irish Ulysses encounters an Irish Nausicaa and— masturbates. Sentimental language inflates their meeting to the absurd proportions of a confession-magazine romance, complete with bad grammar: "Yes, it was her he was looking at and there was meaning in his look. His eyes burned into her as though they would search her through and through, read her very soul. . . . He was in deep mourning, she could see that, and the story of a haunting sorrow was written on his face" (*U*357).

Aside from the overwrought quality of this prose, the reference to the "haunting sorrow" written on Bloom's face should provoke smiles, not tears; for Bloom's pained

expression results from his Priapus-like predicament, as
he has not yet been able to effect handily a release from
the agitated state into which this flower of Irish maiden-
hood has moved him. "The very heart of the girlwoman
went out to him, her dreamhusband, because she knew on
the instant it was him. . . . There were wounds that wanted
healing with heartbalm. . . . Mayhap he would embrace
her gently, like a real man, crushing her soft body to him,
and love her, his ownest girlie, for herself alone. . . . She
looked at him a moment, meeting his glance, and a light
broke in upon her. Whitehot passion was in that face,
passion silent as the grave, and it had made her his. At
last they were left alone . . . and she knew he could be
trusted to the death, steadfast, a sterling man, a man of
inflexible honour to his fingertips. His hands and face
were working and a tremor went over her" (U358, 365).
Not only honor touches Bloom's fingertips as, steadfast and
sterling, his "working" hands at last accomplish their purpose, releasing him from priapism. He will never "embrace her gently" or ungently: this entire encounter is but
another example of Bloom's ineffectual fantasy world,
wherein positive action rarely takes place, wherein comic
inaction characterizes his life. "Nausicaa's" intermingling
of sentimentalism and masturbation epitomizes the vacuity of Bloom's daily life even more graphically than his
analogously abortive romance with Martha Clifford.

The light spirit of "Nausicaa"—in which Gerty and Bloom
commit mere folly, not crime—elucidates the central problem of this entire study: the nature of Joyce's conscience
and of his relation to the Church. Roman Catholic doctrine indicts masturbation as a serious sin, as an abuse
of one's sexual powers comparable to fornication and
adultery, and like Catholic boys all over the world, Joyce
was unquestionably harangued by his teachers about the
evils of "self-abuse."[51] Self-exiled from the Church, Joyce

[51] The act is also often termed "solitary pollution" by the Church.

yet retains from his Catholic background a disapproving attitude toward masturbation: he certainly does not condemn Bloom's act with moralistic, missionary fervor; but neither does he adopt the beliefs of modern psychiatric medicine, which considers masturbation a natural and healthy outlet for sexual urges otherwise unsatisfied. Instead he treats Bloom's masturbation as an important symbol of a frustrated, paralyzed, sterile existence. Joyce disapproves not so much of the act itself as of the characteristic weakness and timidity for which it stands in Bloom's case. With artistic skill and design, he places the act in a pervasively comic atmosphere—the namby-pamby romanticizing of Gerty, punctuated with hymns from the nearby church of Mary, Star of the Sea—and thus urges his readers to interpret Bloom's tumescence and emission not as sinful but as an amusing sign of Bloom's sad paralysis and self-deception. To the conscience of the mature Joyce, then, masturbation still constitutes self-abuse: for on Sandymount Strand it serves as an animated sign of self-deception.

Joyce's purpose in "Nausicaa" appears to be abundantly clear, so effectively do the sentimental phrases culled from magazines control the comic spirit of the episode. But if the foregoing analysis of this comic spirit still leaves the reader skeptical, he can probe that repository of comic meanings, the Homeric parallel. Again in "Nausicaa" Joyce reverses the action of Homer's epic in his own mock-epic. In discussing Ulysses' conduct in Book VI of the *Odyssey*, in which the Greek hero approaches the princess Nausicaa as she plays with her attendants on the strand, Joyce once commented, "He [Ulysses] was the first gentleman in Eu-

---

There is unanimity among Catholic theologians on the teaching that masturbation is an evil, contrary to divine and natural law. The official teaching of the Church may be found in the condemnation by Innocent XI (1676-89) on 4 March 1678, of Proposition 49: see William Kevin Glover, *Artificial Insemination among Human Beings* (Washington, D.C., 1948), p. 71.

rope. When he advanced, naked, to meet the young princess he hid from her maidenly eyes the parts that mattered of his brine-encrusted body."[52] To Joyce, Ulysses is not only wise and courageous; he is also a gentleman, becomingly modest. Imagine Ulysses working himself into an auto-erotic ecstasy at the sight of the lovely Nausicaa: the absurdity of such a scene makes quite evident the ludicrous, mock-heroic nature of Bloom's performance before his own sentimentalized Nausicaa. Eventually Ulysses and Nausicaa exchange courteous greetings, while Bloom and Gerty exchange only furtive glances, until finally "Mr Bloom with careful hand recomposed his wet shirt. O Lord, that little limping devil. Begins to feel cold and clammy. Aftereffect not pleasant. Still you have to get rid of it someway. . . . My fireworks. Up like a rocket, down like a stick. . . . Lord, I am wet. . . . Did me good all the same. Off colour after Kiernan's, Dignam's. For this relief much thanks" (U370-72). Poor Bloom must take comfort in little pleasures indeed. In view of his action before her, how ironic Gerty's estimation of him sounds: "Passionate nature though he was Gerty could see that he had enormous control over himself. One moment he had been there, fascinated by a loveliness that made him gaze, and the next moment it was the quiet, gravefaced gentleman, selfcontrol expressed in every line of his distinguishedlooking figure" (U361).

Just as Bloom's masturbation shows his lack of self-control, the bat which flies in and out of this episode symbolizes the blindness of both Gerty and Bloom, neither of whom recognizes himself nor faces up to reality—Gerty blinding herself through sentimentalism and Bloom through sexual fantasy, in this instance. And so it is with the lot of us, Joyce seems to be saying: the episode is mocking but not malicious. And, as in the case of Bloom's correspondence with Martha Clifford, Joyce may have been

---

[52] Budgen, *James Joyce and the Making of Ulysses*, p. 17.

quietly parodying his own voyeuristic relationship with Martha Fleishmann, whom he addressed as "Nausikaa."[53] The reversal of the *Odyssey* neither shocks nor repels; it amuses, while telling us something about the way an ordinary man and an ordinary girl spend an hour of a summer evening, harmlessly deceiving themselves, a few moments pleasure the result. The only nasty, somewhat sordid note sounds when Bloom discovers Gerty's lameness and moves from a compassionate first impulse—"Poor girl!"—to a rather perverse second-thought: "Glad I didn't know it when she was on show. Hot little devil all the same. Wouldn't mind. Curiosity like a nun or a negress or a girl with glasses. . . . Anyhow I got the best of that" (*U*368). This trace of perverse fetishism alters but little the episode's light texture. And with typical care, underlining the comedy of Bloom's predicament, Joyce ends "Nausicaa" with a gay, familiar refrain, which for centuries has teased the cuckold. "O word of feare," Shakespeare called it, "unpleasing to a married ear":

> "Cuckoo
> "Cuckoo
> "Cuckoo."

Plaintively and humorously, that word of fear evokes the origin of this Irish Ulysses' sexual frustrations: his sadly unheroic union with a promiscuous Penelope.

· 12 ·

Bloom next appears in the doorway of the Holles Street Maternity Hospital. An Anglo-Saxon narrator tells us that "Stark ruth of man his errand that him lone led till that house," which translates as "The naked pity of the man led him unaccompanied on his errand to the hospital," but the jocular style of the narration itself suggests the comic overtones of Bloom's "errand." Ostensibly he arrives merely

[53] See *Letters*, II, li and 431-36.

to inquire about Mrs. Purefoy, who is in her third day of labor with her tenth child, but Bloom's real purpose is to soothe his own emotional wounds by bathing them in the sufferings of others. His concern for Mrs. Purefoy first became evident in the "Lestrygonians" episode, when he indulged himself sentimentally in an extravagant amount of pity for her, as well as for seagulls and the children of the poor. George Meredith's definition of the sentimentalist was found to apply to Bloom in "Lestrygonians": "The sentimentalist is he who would enjoy without incurring the immense debtorship for a thing done." The same kind of sentimentalism, through which Bloom can lessen the sting of his own troubles by immersing himself vicariously in the woes of another, brings him to the Holles Street Maternity Hospital, where the groans of expectant mothers echo through the corridors. One would not wish to condemn Bloom's sentimental journey, but as in "Lestrygonians" his sentimentalism must be recognized as largely self-indulgent and as an act singled out for our scrutiny by Joyce's conscience, which no longer rails at human weaknesses but which continues to probe and to satirize them. The comical extent of Bloom's self-identification with Mrs. Purefoy is not manifest until, in the "Circe" episode, he cries out "O, I so want to be a mother" and promptly bears eight children (U494). Here in "Oxen of the Sun" he hovers near Mrs. Purefoy, lingering in thought over the travails of motherhood without having to undergo them.[54] Significantly, Meredith's definition of the sentimentalist appears again in this episode (U412).

The chief source of Bloom's sentimentalism is sexual frustration. Other frustrations, of course, contribute to his morbidly extreme concern with the woes of others. His job is not particularly rewarding, and he puts up with rough treatment from his employers; he dreams of far-off

[54] Bloom, of course, is prevented by Molly from having any more children.

lands but never visits them; he devises schemes for every-thing from moneymaking to municipal reform, but he can never seem to enact them. Sex is his one constant obses-sion, however, and hence his constant frustration. If he is not thinking of the "heaving embonpoint" of that smutty novelette he has bought, *The Sweets of Sin*, he is likely to be thinking of Molly, who dominates him, or of Martha, whom he will never meet, or of Gerty, a source of merely autoerotic pleasure for him. All of these women stimulate him but yield him at best an illusory satisfaction, holding their sensual allure out to him like the proverbial carrot before the jackass. And so frustrated Bloom, sad and lonely Bloom, consoles himself by commiserating with seagulls, paupers, and pregnant women, his quest for emotional balm leading him finally to the Holles Street Maternity Hospital, "woman's woe with wonder pondering" (*U*388). The fact that Bloom is, to his great grief, a father without a son makes all the more appropriate his sentimental trip to the maternity hospital. He is unable to incur the pleas-ant responsibility of a son of his own, so he involves him-self emotionally in someone else's childbirth. Bloom, as we learn in the "Ithaca" episode, has not completed sexual in-tercourse with his wife for the past ten years, five months, and eighteen days. This maritally abnormal situation re-sults directly from Mrs. Bloom's domination of Mr. Bloom—another marital abnormality—since Mr. Bloom continually expresses his desire for a son to replace the deceased Rudy, while Mrs. Bloom prides herself on her expertness in the art of contraception.[55] Joyce even tells us the contraceptive method employed by the Blooms—and presumably by Molly in her extramarital frolics—*coitus interruptus*, which Joyce terms in "Ithaca" a "limitation of fertility" (*U*736).

By way of Bloom's sentimentalism, sexual frustration, desire for paternity, and limitation of fertility, we come

[55] Molly refers to her contraceptive ability throughout her mono-logue.

to the main theme of this episode: sterility. Joyce had his own allegorical interpretation of Book XII of the *Odyssey*, upon which this episode is based: "The companions of Ulysses," Joyce told Frank Budgen, "disobey the commands of Pallas. They slay and flay the oxen of the Sungod and all are drowned save the prudent and pious Ulysses. I interpret the killing of the sacred oxen as the crime against fecundity by sterilising the act of coition. And I think my interpretation is as sound as that of any other commentator on Homer."[56] That commentary reveals much about Joyce's attitude toward the *Odyssey*, his attitude toward sex, and his purpose in the "Oxen of the Sun" episode in *Ulysses*. So morally sober an interpretation of Book XII substantiates what considerable evidence has already suggested, namely, that Joyce took the *Odyssey* seriously as a moral epic and that he viewed Ulysses as an ideal hero—"prudent and pious" he terms him here. Second, the influence which Roman Catholic moral teachings continued to hold over Joyce is demonstrated by his considering contraception a "crime." Third, Joyce's commentary acts as a helpful gloss on his own "Oxen of the Sun" episode, which evidently must be concerned with "crimes" against fertility. Bloom's grief and frustration at his self-inflicted sterility have already been noted, and Joyce thereby continues to contrast Bloom with the "prudent and pious" Ulysses, who alone among his men was not guilty of any "crime against fecundity." But before the objection can be raised that there is no reason to apply Joyce's interpretation of the *Odyssey* to his own *Ulysses*, in a letter of Joyce's to Mr. Budgen Joyce himself does just that: "Am working hard at *Oxen of the Sun*, the idea being the crime committed against fecundity by sterilizing the act of coition. Scene, lying-in hospital. . . . Bloom is the spermatozoon, the hospital the womb, the nurse the ovum, Stephen the embryo."[57]

[56] Budgen, *James Joyce and the Making of Ulysses*, p. 215.
[57] Letter of 20 March 1920, *Letters*, I, 139.

A valid stricture against Joyce's art in this episode might be that no one could have figured all that out without the author's extratextual assistance. That objection registered, let us accept the author's aid and work things out. If the idea of the episode is sterility, Bloom is the natural spermatozoon, for by submitting to the wishes of his Penelope, this uxorious Ulysses has sterilized his marriage and, in effect, himself. Imagining Bloom as a frustrated spermatozoon may seem ridiculous, but that is all to the good in this mock-epic, which in more than one place is a test of the reader's risibility. Whether one thinks of Bloom with Molly, Martha, or Gerty, a sterilized spermatozoon he is. In this episode Bloom recalls still another sterile sexual relationship, that with Bridie Kelly, who dared "not bear the sunnygolden babe of day. No, Leopold! Name and memory solace thee not. That youthful illusion of thy strength was taken from thee and in vain. No son of thy loins is by thee. There is none now to be for Leopold, what Leopold was for Rudolph" (*U*413-14).

The hospital as a womb is easy enough to see, as is the nurse as an appropriately sterile ovum: the nurse in this episode is a nun, who is "left after long years a handmaid. Nine twelve bloodflows chiding her childless" (*U*386). She and Bloom thus have sterility in common, and so they stand together "both awhile in wanhope, sorrowing one with other," sentimentally commiserating (*U*386). Bloom's sterility is of course more than physical. He is a good man, a well-meaning man, but his comically extreme weaknesses cause a spiritual sterility in him which is more significant than his frustrated physical paternity. Many commentators have maintained that Bloom's kindliness is enough to set him apart as spiritually superior to most of his compatriots, but much of his pitying is only sentimentalism, caused by his personal failings, and there is a great deal of self-pity about this Ulysses as well. He occupies so prominent a place in this Irish mock-epic precisely because of Joyce's conviction that mental and spiritual paralysis—or sterility—was the great Irish affliction.

In terming Stephen the "embryo" of this episode, Joyce suggests that this would-be artist is the great unknown, undeveloped quantity of the book. Whether this embryo will grow strong enough to escape the Irish womb remains an unanswered question. Bloom has not the will to extricate himself, but Stephen may. At the moment, "Boasthard" Dedalus grows sodden with drink, sinking deeper into the Dublin morass, and the paternal Bloom is probably right to grieve "for young Stephen for that he lived riotously with those wastrels and murdered his goods with whores" (*U*391). This sentence touches, of course, on the theme of the episode—sterility.

Also touching on sterility is the conversation of Stephen and his wastrel-friends, which consists mainly in an argument over contraception: "But, gramercy, what of those Godpossibled souls that we nightly impossibilise, which is the sin against the Holy Ghost, Very God, Lord and Giver of Life? For, sirs, he said, our lust is brief. We are means to those small creatures within us and nature has other ends than we. . . . Preservative had given them a stout shield of oxengut . . . that they might take no hurt neither from Offspring that was that wicked devil by virtue of this same shield which was named Killchild" (*U*389, 396). As is the case with Bloom, the young men's sexual practices, while they result in what Joyce termed "the crime against fertility," are less important than the symbolic sterility inherent in their purposeless daily activity. Their real crime is against the potential fertility of their spirits, which conceivably might lift Ireland out of its paralytic bog.

As the students' drunken debate about contraception rages downstairs, Mina Purefoy and others bring forth babies upstairs: a comic diagram of Irish life. The debate itself is termed "an epitome of the course of life" (*U*417), and in Joycean terms it is, for it goes round and round and never gets anywhere, beginning in Anglo-Saxon and ending finally in a barely decipherable, *Finnegans Wake*-like babble of a thousand tongues. This confusion implicitly mocks the notion that any progress has been made since the first savage grunted. No progress characterizes the Joycean view of the world; there are only the constants of human nature, which make history a nightmare to Stephen but to Joyce something of a joke, as well: "The aged sisters draw us into life: we wail, batten, sport, clip, clasp, sunder, dwindle, die: over us dead they bend" (*U*394).

Bloom is scarcely detectable amid the obscene cacophony of this episode, but what we know of him ties him to Stephen and his companions. For like them he permits himself a sterile existence, too often wasting instead of creating. Stephen and Bloom draw close together here, sitting down at the same table, giving us a chance to see how much alike they are in terms of sterility: both indulge in narcissistic, inherently sterile self-love; both are thus figurative slayers of the oxen of the sun. If the sterility of poor Bloom's existence happens to slip from our minds in this episode, it should not. For in addition to the sentimental, self-indulgent nature of his very presence at the hospital, there is in "Oxen of the Sun" an even more overt mocking of Bloom's actions, perhaps somewhat obscured by the language of Edmund Burke. Bloom has been silently critical of the coarse talk of Stephen and his companions, and at last he says something to his neighbor at the table about the heartlessness of these young men, who seem to be altogether unmoved by the fruition of Mina Purefoy's long confinement. But the Burkean narrator turns on Bloom at this point and ridicules him for being so presumptuous as to criticize anyone for taking a light attitude toward conception and birth: "He says this, a censor of morals, a very pelican in his piety, who did not scruple, oblivious of the ties of nature, to attempt illicit intercourse with a female domestic drawn from the lowest strata of society"

⟨   171   ⟩

(*U*409). Bloom was rebuffed with a scouringbrush in this instance; but his most frequent dereliction of husbandly duty is also recalled and mocked. Bloom, it seems, is fond of preaching against landlords who allow their fields to lie fallow or to be used as pasture, while the commoners starve: but "It ill becomes him to preach that gospel. Has he not nearer home a seedfield that lies fallow for the want of a ploughshare?" Here the narrator teases and chides Bloom for not having completed intercourse with Molly for ten years. A contributing factor to this sterile conjugal relationship is found to be Bloom's fondness for masturbation, another "crime against fecundity," which we have just witnessed in "Nausicaa": "A habit reprehensible at puberty is second nature and an opprobrium in middle life. . . . His marital breast is the repository of secrets which decorum is reluctant to adduce" (*U*409). The tone here continues to be light, but it keeps the reader from setting up Bloom as a paragon of benignity, as against the vice of his compatriots. Bloom seems unaware of the pervasiveness and the cause of his sentimentalism, but if he is thus self-deceived, he should not deceive us as well. As the Burkean narration suggests in the form of a question, "Is it that from being a deluder of others he has become at last his own dupe as he is, if report belie him not, his own and his only enjoyer?" (*U*409). It is indeed: Bloom is his own dupe. Amiable, good-natured Bloom is for all his kindness a sentimentalist, a self-loving masturbator who is his own and his only enjoyer, who has pity for all but most of all for Bloom.

Stephen looks similarly inward, seemingly incapable of more than a sterile despair and damnation of the universe. If Stephen is ever to advance from a sterile to a fertile, creative existence, he must transcend not only Irish life but himself. Comedy enabled Joyce to transcend himself and his past, enabled him to banish brooding with laughter. His treatment of the "crimes" of "Oxen of the Sun" is not harsh: he judges the "criminals" for their sterility, but he sentences them only to eternal ridicule. In the comic world of *Ulysses*, where oxen of the sun are metaphorically slain again and again, the artist's task is less to preach than to rise above the slaughter and perceive the mockery of it all.

· 13 ·

The "Circe" episode is the most obscene, the most imaginative, the most humorous, and the most significant part of *Ulysses*. In it the diverse thematic strands which have been lengthening for fourteen episodes unite at last, and Leopold Bloom stands psychologically and morally unveiled—a spectacle no less meaningful than hilarious. As this investigation of Joyce's conscience should by now have led us to expect, the most significant episode of *Ulysses* is replete with sex and its attendant subdeities—voyeurism, contraception, transvestism, hermaphroditism, homosexuality, masochism, sadism, infantilism. For Joyce never ceased to view sexual conduct as an index of moral conduct. The letters to Nora of 1909 reveal his disgust with what he regarded as the bestiality of sexual passion. At that time the frenzied, disordered state to which his own sexual desire transported him was to Joyce evidence of human weakness, of man's regrettably bestial side: "Ah not lust, dearest, not the wild brutal madness I have written to you these last days and nights, not the wild beast-like desire for your body, dearest, is what drew me to you then and holds me to you now. No, dearest, not that at all but a most tender, adoring, faithful love for your youth and girlhood and weakness. . . ." If a man feels so powerful a revulsion toward sexual passion at the age of twenty-seven, he is not likely to expunge that revulsion by the time he is thirty-two; and Joyce did not abandon his essentially negative attitude toward "wild beast-like" desire from 1909 to 1914, when he began *Ulysses*. Nor had he abandoned it by 1920, when he was writing the "Circe" episode.[58] But we have already observed the mellowing of Joyce's treatment of the moral climate of his native land: we have witnessed a change in the tone of his writing from indignation to mockery sometimes mordant but often mild. And thus the "Circe" episode, in which the sexual force which has been propelling Bloom through four hundred pages finally reaches maximum intensity in a whorehouse, reflects Joyce's adoption of a less acrid attitude toward the bestial, brutish side of man.

The extent to which "Circe" treats the animal side of man was indicated by Joyce when he stated flatly to Frank Budgen that "Circe" is "an animal episode, full of animal allusions, animal mannerisms. The rhythm is the rhythm of locomotor ataxia."[59] Locomotor ataxia is a chronic nervous disease, caused by syphilis and resulting in a loss of muscular coordination. Thus the animality of "Circe" helps to convey its moral atmosphere, which might be described as one of syphilitic decay. One cannot improve upon Mr. Budgen's analysis of the meaning of the bestiality of this episode: "The essence of the animal into man metamorphosis seems to be that man becomes an animal when he loses his many-sided wholeness. One of his functions gets out of hand and usurps the powers belonging to the governing authority of his virtuous republic. Beastliness is onesidedness. A man may be like a lion, a bull, an eagle or a serpent, but not for long or make a habit of it without losing his integrity."[60]

Words like "virtuous" and "integrity" continued to have meaning to Joyce, and the beginning of "Circe" conveys the extent to which he considered virtue and integrity to have given way to moral degeneration, to bestiality. The landscape of nighttown is bestrewn with "*stunted men and*

[58] See the timetable of composition in Litz, *The Art of James Joyce*, p. 144.
[59] Budgen, *James Joyce and the Making of Ulysses*, p. 228.
[60] *Ibid.*, p. 229.

women. . . . A deafmute idiot with goggle eyes, his shape-less mouth dribbling, jerks past, shaken in Saint Vitus' dance. A chain of children's hands imprisons him. . . . On a step a gnome totting among a rubbishtip crouches to shoulder a sack of rags and bones. . . . Figures wander, lurk, peer from warrens. . . . In an archway a standing woman, bent forward, her feet apart, pisses cowily. . . . The navvy, swaying, presses a forefinger against a wing of his nose and ejects from the farther nostril a long liquid jet of snot" (U429-30, 449-50, 433).[61] Cissy Caffrey, who in "Nausicaa" doted mawkishly but innocently on a baby in her care, here appears chanting an obscene ballad:

> "I gave it to Nelly
> To stick in her belly
> The leg of the duck
> The leg of the duck" (U430).

Such is the corrupt atmosphere of the episode. During the first few pages of it, one staggers beneath such a quantity of gruesome detail. One becomes prepared for the worst.

But the worst never comes. After so carefully sketching in a milieu the horrors of which Zola might have found excessive, Joyce permits his comic muse to take over, and the syphilitic rhythms of the episode begin to convey the humor so characteristic of *Ulysses*. "Circe" continues to display the bestial, degenerate side of man, but in a gro-tesquely humorous way. Scarcely five of "Circe's" one hundred eighty pages contain the revolting details de-scribed above. These five pages remind us of the treatment Joyce might have given his material, had he never evolved from the somewhat uncontrolled indignation of *Stephen Hero* to the comedy of *Ulysses*. And significantly it is the entrance of Bloom ("puffing Poldy, blowing Bloohoom") which changes "Circe" from an attack into a burlesque.[62]

---

[61] Italics Joyce's.
[62] Naturally, the bitterness is not eliminated, but it is overbalanced by comedy.

In Bloom, Joyce gives us a portrait of the animal side of man that is as funny as it is revealing. Bloom stumbles into nighttown and meanders through a bizarre series of debaucheries, some real and some hallucinatory, each displaying the comic magnitude of his sensual weaknesses. Bloom has been led into the red-light district of Dublin by his paternal urge, thwarted by his unnatural subservience to his wife's desire for sterility. Three incidents dominate his mental and physical meanderings through nighttown: his imaginary trial, his visit to Bella Cohen's whorehouse, and the kindly assistance he lends Stephen at the close of the episode.

The proceeds of the trial have the effect of reducing Bloom to a sex-mad absurdity. When Mary Driscoll, the scullery-maid, tells the judge that Bloom surprised her "in the rere of the premises, your honour . . . I was discoloured in four places as a result. . . . I remonstrated with him, your lord, and he remarked: Keep it quiet!"—when Miss Driscoll thus accuses in her delightful scullery-maid brogue, we ought to have no difficulty in complying with Joyce's stage direction: "(*General laughter*)" (*U*461). General laughter ought also to accompany Bloom's embarrassed account of his furtive bowel movement in a plasterer's bucket (*U*462). And equally ludicrous are the reports of Bloom's letters to three ladies:

"He said that he had seen from the gods my peerless globes as I sat in a box of the *Theatre Royal* . . . I deeply inflamed him, he said. . . . He lauded almost extravagantly my nether extremities, my swelling calves in silk hose drawn up to the limit, and eulogised glowingly my other hidden treasures in priceless lace which, he said, he could conjure up. He urged me . . . to commit adultery at the earliest possible opportunity. . . . He implored me to soil his letter in an unspeakable manner, to chastise him as he richly deserves, to bestride him and ride him, to give him a most vicious horsewhipping" (*U*465-67).

The writing of provocative letters to strange women has been termed "graphomasochism" by sexologists,[63] and Bloom's career as an epistolary Don Juan expands our conception of him as a masochist, a conception for which there is a great deal of evidence prior to "Circe."[64] But the psychosexual terminology of Bloom's habits is less important than the picture which those habits convey of Bloom as a weak little man, driven by his uncontrolled lust to degrade himself in a most comical fashion. That Joyce relied heavily in "Circe" upon the case histories of sexual deviates and the works of Leopold von Sacher-Masoch is well known.[65] Less well known is that Joyce was no doubt satirizing certain masochistic tendencies he had noted in himself. The requests from Bloom which Mrs. Talboys paraphrases above—"to soil his letter in an unspeakable manner" and "to give him a most vicious horsewhipping"— were foreshadowed in letters from Joyce to Nora in 1909. On 9 December of that year, Joyce in a somewhat frenzied state of mind asked Nora to break wind upon her next letter to him, presumably not as a token of reproach but of affection. And six days earlier he had confessed an unquestionably masochistic urge: "Tonight I have an idea madder than usual. I feel I would like to be flogged by you. I would like to see your eyes blazing with anger." It would be easy to conclude from this evidence that since Joyce recognized masochistic tendencies in himself, Bloom's masochism cannot be a sign of weakness but is rather a sign of the author's sympathy and self-identification with his protagonist. Such reasoning not only ignores the consistent irony with which Joyce treats Bloom, it ignores as

63 See Hirschfield, *Sexual Anomalies*, Chapters XIX and XX, especially pp. 347ff., where a series of letters very much like Bloom's, even in language, provides case histories of masochism. William York Tindall was the first to point out Joyce's use of Sacher-Masoch's *Venus im Pelz*.

64 See especially the "Calypso" episode, but also "Lotus-eaters," and "Lestrygonians": Chapter IV, sections 2, 3, and 6, above.

65 See Ellmann, *James Joyce*, pp. 380ff.

well the possibility of self-satire. Joyce undoubtedly put much of himself into Bloom: he put his own weaknesses into his sympathetic but comical and satirical portrait of an Irish Ulysses. And Bloom's masochism—his Joycean masochism, if you will—is an instance of Joyce's fondness for self-satire. In the letter quoted above, Joyce commented on his own masochistic desires, characterizing them, as we might expect, as a sign of his own guilt and weakness: "I wonder is there some madness in me. . . . Are you disgusted with me? . . . I want you to say to yourself, Jim, the poor fellow I love, is coming back. He is a poor weak impulsive man and he prays to me to defend him and make him strong.

"I gave others my pride and joy. To you I give my sin, my folly, my weakness & sadness."

But we do not need Joyce's self-accusing comments on his own masochism—comments wholly consistent with what we know of his moral conscience—to see that Bloom's self-degrading letter-writing contributes to the satire of "Circe." Masochism is in Bloom's case only the extreme of the ridiculous servility which more than any other trait characterizes him and makes of him a quavering symbol of Irish paralysis. When Mrs. Bellingham demands that he be whipped, gelded, and vivisected, Bloom strikes a self-defining pose: "(*Shuddering, shrinking, joins his hands with hangdog mien.*) O cold! O shivery! It was your ambrosial beauty. Forget, forgive. Kismet. Let me off this once. (*He offers the other cheek.*)" (*U*468). In permitting Bloom to turn the other cheek in so humiliating a fashion, Joyce makes of him a mock-Christ—a satiric touch repeated later in the episode. As Freud remarked, ". . . the true masochist always holds out his cheek wherever he sees a chance of receiving a blow."[66]

[66] "The Economic Problem in Masochism," *Collected Papers,* Joan Riviere, trans., Vol. 2 (New York, 1959), p. 262. An enlightening contrast could be drawn between Freud's analysis of masochism

The fundamental controlling mockery of "Circe," however, like that of all the other episodes, lies in the comic comparison of Bloom with Ulysses. In the *Odyssey*, Ulysses was able to vanquish the sorceress Circe by means of an "herb of virtue," called Moly, given him by Hermes: "Lo, take this herb of virtue [advised Hermes], and go to the dwelling of Circe, that it may keep from thy head the evil day. And I will tell thee all the magic sleight of Circe."[67] Ulysses, then, triumphs over Circe. She turns his men into beasts, but through his herb of virtue he avoids their fate and in the end rescues them. Joyce has supplied his mock-hero with a ludicrous Irish version of Moly—a potato plant. And continuing with his comic reversal of the action of the *Odyssey*, Joyce arranges for Bloom to surrender his herb of virtue to one of Circe's attendants, Zoe, a whore whose name ironically means "life."[68] Bloom's humorously symbolic loss of his potato plant prefigures his enslavement to that Irish Circe, the whoremistress Bella Cohen, and opens the floodgates of Joycean mirth in the "Circe" episode. From this point on, until Stephen Dedalus smashes the chandelier and brings this *Walpurgisnacht* to a halt, Bloom threads his way through an increasingly humiliating and increasingly humorous series of diversions, some hallucinatory and some real, all of them stripping his character bare.

In Bloom's most absurd hallucination, he becomes Em-

---

and Joyce's use of it for comic and satiric purposes. Freud argues that the most extreme form of masochism occurs in a person whose highly sensitive conscience (or, in Freudian terms, superego) activates an unconscious feeling of guilt and a demand for punishment. Along with self-pity, guilt, shame, and self-contempt exist in Bloom, but to Joyce, Bloom's masochism is only one of many kinds of comical weakness. Stephen, not Bloom, is obsessed with guilt, and Stephen is not made masochistic. Freudians are free to conclude that Joyce was a better artist than psychologist.

[67] *Odyssey*, x, 117-18.

[68] *Zoe* is the Greek word for life. Thus Bloom gives up his Moly— or virtue—to a whore called life: an indirect bit of satire, consistent with Joyce's frequent bitterness toward the sexual aspects of life.

peror of all Ireland, crown prince of Nova Hibernia, the new Bloomusalem, invested with his sacred powers during ceremonies the foolishness of which mocks both Irish and Bloomian foibles. His coronation is a bizarre religious-political goulash of Hebraic and Catholic ritual, symbolizing the apotheosis of—Bloom, and the amiable mediocrity for which he stands. It is the awesome moment of his swearing-in:

"BLOOM

(*Placing his right hand on his testicles, swears.*) So may the Creator deal with me. All this I promise to do" (*U*482). So may Bloom, in that pose, be remembered. He reigns supreme in all Ireland, wearing green socks, distributing loaves and fishes and contraceptives to the multitudes, proclaiming the new nine muses, muses suitable to his lower-middle-class mind: "*Commerce, Operatic Music, Amor, Publicity, Manufacture, Liberty of Speech, Plural Voting, Gastronomy, Private Hygiene, Seaside Concert Entertainments, Painless Obstetrics and Astronomy for the People*" (*U*490). The Irish, Joyce seems to be saying, may have deserted Parnell, but they have got Bloom as their Hibernian Moses.

Before being aroused from this wish-fulfilling reverie by the crass voice of Zoe, Emperor Bloom receives a medical examination from a corps of royal physicians. Their diagnoses are truly choice. Dr. Mulligan terms Bloom "bisexually abnormal"; Dr. Madden notes an enlargement of the genitalia and advises that they be preserved in spirits in a museum for biological monstrosities; and Dr. Dixon proclaims Bloom "a finished example of the new womanly man"—and pregnant. These diagnoses are marvelously, mischievously funny in themselves, but in Bloom's case they carry added thematic weight, and for all their absurdity, they apply quite nicely to him. For while Bloom does exhibit an extraordinarily active sexual drive, of which his enlarged genitalia are symptomatic, he satisfies this drive in a most curious fashion—not by completing intercourse with his wife but by watching a girl whack a carpet, writing provocative letters, searching out the posterior orifices of plaster goddesses, gazing at himself in the bath, masturbating, and so forth. He lacks the masculine assertiveness which might make more normal sexual habits possible: and this womanish timidity, coupled with his powerful love of the flesh, lies at the root of his character. How apt, then, is Dr. Dixon's analysis of Bloom as a "new womanly man." And Bloom's cry—"O, I so want to be a mother"—followed by his giving birth to eight male children, is likewise befitting this Hibernian Emperor, who may never again beget a son in any other way.

Bloom imagines himself proclaimed the Messiah and performs such miracles as hanging by his eyelids from Nelson's pillar, eclipsing the sun by extending his little finger, and turning each foot simultaneously in different directions (*U*495). More than one commentator has insisted that Bloom is actually intended to represent Christ, opposed to Stephen as Satan, but the obviously comic effects of Bloom's Messianic pretensions preclude so reverent a view of him. And when the Daughters of Erin recite a litany which recounts the principal mockery of each of Bloom's episodes, the satiric intention should be clear enough: "Kidney of Bloom, pray for us. . . . Sweets of Sin, pray for us. . . . Friend of all Frillies, pray for us. . . . Potato Preservative against Plague and Pestilence, pray for us" (*U*498-99). The protean Bloom manages to be not only a mock-Ulysses but a mock-Parnell and mock-Messiah as well.[69]

[69] Foster Damon surely misses the joke, the mockery of the Bloom-Christ parallel in his "The Odyssey in Dublin," in *Two Decades*, pp. 203-42. Mr. Damon complains that no critic has followed up the implications of his suggestion of a Bloom-Christ parallel (see p. 239). I have followed up these implications and have gotten many laughs out of them, as, I believe, Joyce intended: they work with the same degree of mockery as the Bloom-Ulysses parallel or the Bloom-Parnell parallel.

Bloom's versatility proves still more remarkable in the events which follow. Within the sanctuary of a ten-shilling house of prostitution, he allows his fancy full play, his twisted libido gains complete control, and he becomes the cowering slave of Bella/Bello Cohen, an immense, sadistic whoremistress replete with sprouting moustache. Bello treats Bloom with total disdain and with ingenious brutality—and Bloom loves every minute of it. For him Bello's domination is a moment of truth. No longer must he sublimate his masochism. In the whorehouse inhibitions vanish. He is "infatuated" with Bello's scorn, "enthralled" at her crushing weight; he allows her to ride him, to squeeze his testicles, to break wind upon him; and bowing to her/him, she/he exclaims: "Master! Mistress! Mantamer!" (U527-38). When Bello commands Bloom to swab latrines, "empty the pisspots in the different rooms," fetch, carry, smile, and swell his bust, Bloom can only mutter his thanks. He becomes a beast of burden, and the aptness of this animal metamorphosis should be noted well. For this episode thereby comically reverses the action of the *Odyssey*, wherein Ulysses alone escaped such degradation at the hands of Circe. Bella-Circe holds absolute sway over Bloom-Ulysses; and this reversed relationship mirrors in a comically exaggerated way Bloom's unfortunate lack of willpower and, more directly, the upside-down nature of his marriage to Molly, who plays Circe to him daily.

While the "Circe" episode is full of Bloom's hallucinations, much of the action is real. Fantasy and reality overlap so as to be frequently indistinguishable, but Bella's tyranny over Bloom is probably meant to represent the actual practices of a madam specializing in sadomasochistic diversions. Jean Genet, in "The Balcony," has made familiar to the world the extent to which Parisian brothels once catered to the exotic sexual anomalies and fantasies of their clients; and the madams of Anglo-Saxon countries often specialized in the satisfaction of masochistic cravings, one renowned London proprietress having gone so far as to invent a machine which could whip several men simultaneously with indefatigable efficiency.[70] Joyce's reliance in the composition of "Circe" upon the case histories of such works as Krafft-Ebing's *Psychopathia Sexualis* is probable, and he may also have drawn upon his own firsthand investigation of the more exotic establishments of Dublin and Paris.[71] Whatever his sources, the degradation which Bloom undergoes so willingly, even joyfully, has the important thematic purpose of exposing Bloom's psychological state to the extent that even the casual reader cannot mistake the loss of dignity exhibited. In a word, Bloom is unmanned. And in the broadest thematic sense, his unmanly weakness epitomizes the slavishness Joyce so lamented in his countrymen. At the age of twenty-two Joyce had proclaimed, "I am an enemy of the ignobleness and slavishness of people. . . ."[72] Sixteen years later, writing "Circe," he took a more sanguine view of the world and probably would not have considered himself an "enemy" of the slavishness Bloom represents; but he did find slavishness a ready target for his comedy and satire.

Cuckolds have long been a source of amusement in literature, but Joyce carries the comic degradation of Bloom to what would seem to be the ultimate extent. This is a curious fact, since there are places in *Ulysses* where the author's sympathies are obviously on the side of his beleaguered mock-hero, and the nature of Bloom's weaknesses would be quite clear even without many of the detailed indignities of "Circe." Perhaps Joyce sensed the pitiful appeal which Bloom would have to many readers and wanted to make sure that even the most sympathetic reader could not ignore the satire of "Circe." If so, Joyce

---

[70] See Hirschfield, *Sexual Anomalies*, Chapters XIX and XX.

[71] Stephen describes some of the diversions of Parisian bordelloes in *U*569-70.

[72] Letter to Nora, 29 August 1904, *Letters*, II, 48.

was correct in his anticipations of a rather excessive degree of sympathy for Bloom, a sympathy which often
obscures the comedy. It has been argued, for example,
that Bloom regains his self-control the minute his trouser-
button snaps off (U_{552}) and never loses it again in the
episode.[73] This rather ludicrous button-popping does snap
Bloom out of his indignity—but only momentarily. Briefly,
he even brings himself to berate the tyrannous Bella,
branding her a "Pox and gleet vendor!" (U_{554}). But in a
trice Bloom lapses back into masochistic fantasy, and
Joyce thereby safeguards against any excessive indulgence
of or admiration for Bloom on the reader's part. The
trouser-button snapping simply will not serve as a symbol, however bizarre, of an awakened Bloom. In fact, the
indignities which Joyce has still in store for Bloom surpass any yet endured by this transigent Ulysses. Anyone
looking to Bloom for pacifistic guidance in the modern
world would presumably admit that pacifism is carried
to excess when Bloom acts imaginatively as a chambermaid at Blazes Boylan's romp with Molly:

"BOYLAN

(*To Bloom, over his shoulder.*) You can apply your eye
to the keyhole and play with yourself while I just go
through her a few times.

"BLOOM

Thank you, sir, I will, sir. May I bring two men chums to
witness the deed and take a snapshot? (*He holds an oint-
ment jar.*) Vaseline, sir? Orangeflower? . . . Lukewarm
water?" (U_{566}). At the moment of Mr. Boylan's and Mrs.
Bloom's sexual climax, Mr. Bloom, so the stage directions
inform us, "*His eyes wildly dilated, clasps himself*": that
image of Bloom gleefully hugging himself at the precise
moment of his cuckoldry functions splendidly as a *tab-*

[73] Goldberg, *The Classical Temper*, pp. 183ff.

leau vivant of his narcissism, masochism, and general paucity of willpower.

Like Bloom, Stephen Dedalus experiences hallucinations in "Circe," and Stephen's visions are as evocative of the state of his mind as are Bloom's of his mind. The ghost of Mrs. Dedalus appears and reminds Stephen of his guilt, of his troubled conscience. Anguished at this apparition, Stephen loses control of himself and reveals his desperate struggle to retain a sense of superiority when he screams, "No! No! No! Break my spirit all of you if you can! I'll bring you all to heel!" (*U*582). He then smashes the chandelier, ending the bacchanal. In his own way, Stephen is as irrational as Bloom cowering beneath the heel of Bella or hugging himself at his wife's promiscuity. The two characters are united by a curious bond of irrationality, that beast in all men's souls. Stephen represents an extreme of intransigence, refusing to accommodate himself at all to the way of the world, while Bloom represents an extreme of transigence, giving way without much struggle beneath the pressures of his weaker side. "Jewgreek is greekjew. Extremes meet" (*U*504). And thus meeting, these extremes expose one another, joined by the bestial, irrational bond which caused Joyce to complain, "All men are brutes . . . but at least in me there is also something higher at times."[74]

There is something higher in Bloom and Stephen as well. In Bloom this higher potential remains largely buried, manifesting itself occasionally in a small act of courage or kindliness, as when he takes care of Stephen outside Bella Cohen's. His motives for helping Stephen are somewhat ambiguous, as we shall see in "Eumaeus"; but in the main, he aids young Dedalus because his paternal urge finds an outlet in such protectiveness. On the whole a rather sad and lonely figure, his pattern of life is set, his

[74] Letter to Nora, 11 December 1909, *Letters*, II, 273.

habits ingrained, his will largely broken, his higher potential only occasionally approached. So it is with most men,
in the Joycean view. Floundering in immaturity, Stephen
still has time to extricate himself from the common rut,
but he is paralyzed by guilt, doubt, and fear. As Joyce
wrote of Stephen in an early notebook, "He dreaded the
sea that would drown his body and the crowd that
would drown his soul."[75] Thus dreading, he cannot act.
Curiously united here with Bloom, Stephen ought to take
a close look at this specimen of ordinary humanity—weak
but amiable, often kindly if more often sentimental, on
the whole a harmless, comic specimen. Stephen needs to
stop trying to bring humanity to heel: for he cannot, and
as long as he tries, he remains as far from the Joycean
world-view as despair from laughter. He may retain his
ideals of beauty and of innocence, as Joyce retained his.
But flawed mankind, as Stephen must come to recognize,
is not Satanic but only Bloomian.

· 14 ·

In Book XVI of the *Odyssey*, Ulysses finally discloses
himself to Telemachus in Eumaeus the swineherd's hut.
Father and son embrace, shed many a tear of joy, and this
recognition scene marks the final turning point in the
fortunes of Ulysses. Keeping to his comic reversal of
Homer's story, Joyce brings his Ulysses and Telemachus
together in a cabman's shelter and permits them, in the
"Eumaeus" episode, to enact a nonrecognition scene which
marks no turning point in the fortunes of Bloom. Joyce
adds to the absurdity of this un-Homeric meeting by describing it in a wearisome, circumlocutionary style, sodden
with clichés and debased by bad grammar.[76] This style

---

[75] Alphabetized notebook, Cornell Collection. The notebook is
undated, but it contains material relevant to both the *Portrait* and
Ulysses, and I would guess its dates as 1904-14.
[76] The clichés are obvious enough, but as an example of delib-

mirrors more than the exhaustion of the pair: it also mirrors the ineffectual nature of their union, brief and superficial.[77] Stephen is too drunk to recognize anything at all, and Bloom, while "disgustingly sober," can offer Stephen not Ulyssean fatherhood but only momentary solicitude, a touch of self-interest, and fatuous homosexual advances. Such is the comic nonrecognition scene depicted in "Eumaeus."[78]

Much of the comedy of the episode stems from the quality of Bloom's mind, which is displayed at length through both meditation and conversation. Most of the conversation is one-way, since Stephen's alcoholic haze is nearly impenetrable; but a lack of response does not tie the tongue of Bloom, who in an apparent effort to impress his befogged companion ranges redoubtably over a score of subjects, each duller than the next. Bloom seems to favor a combination of the kind of pseudoscientific fact usually found on the back pages of newspapers and the kind of practical advice usually associated with a petty-bourgeois mind. Thus he deluges Stephen with the laws of electricity, the dangers of drink and fast women, the amount of water on the globe, the benefits of solid foods, the bowlegged cramps of squatting Aztecs, programs for the reform of Ireland. To the question of national reform Stephen gives a rare but pertinent answer:

"—We can't change the country. Let us change the sub-

---

erate solecism, which underlines the episode's comedy, I might cite ". . . neither of them were particularly pressed for time" (U614).

[77] Stuart Gilbert has argued that the style mirrors only the exhaustion of the pair. See his letter to Richard Ellmann (Ellmann, *James Joyce,* p. 322n.), with which Mr. Ellmann concurs.

[78] Stanley Poss, "Ulysses and the Comedy of the Immobilized Act," *ELH,* xxiv (March 1957), 65-83, shows the union of Stephen and Bloom in "Circe" to be ineffectual and without lasting significance. I have treated "Eumaeus" as the chapter in which one might expect mutual recognition and union—since this episode parallels the recognition-scene of the *Odyssey.* But Mr. Poss seems to me to be correct in denying the effectiveness of Bloom and Stephen's meeting: its symbolic value lies in its impermanence.

ject" (U645). Listening to Bloom, Stephen knows the country can never be changed. The artist must write his moral history from a comic distance, without anticipating any moral revolution.

Bloom, as was suggested above, attaches himself to Stephen partly out of a friendly paternalism but for other, less praiseworthy reasons as well. He feels somewhat flattered by the companionship, however benumbed by drink, of a poetical B.A. from University College; and though this fellowship has already cost him several shillings, he reflects, "Still, to cultivate the acquaintance of someone of no uncommon calibre who could provide food for reflection would amply repay any small . . . Intellectual stimulation as such was, he felt, from time to time a firstrate tonic for the mind" (U646). The irony here is that Stephen's drunken mumblings may hardly be described as intellectual tonic: but Bloom seems so entranced by the sound of his own voice that he needs little response from his acquaintance of uncommon* calibre. So pleased is Bloom with this tête-à-tête that he contemplates a handsome profit—in the distinctly nonintellectual form of guineas—by writing up *My Experiences in a Cabman's Shelter.*

That Bloom looks for intellectual and monetary gain from his befriending of Stephen may be considered innocent enough. But Bloom also engages in a more sordid—though no less amusing—kind of profit-seeking when he pulls out a picture of Molly and invites Stephen's comment on the female amplitude therein displayed. This raffish gesture, transparently homosexual in nature, resembles one of Bloom's wish-fulfilling fantasies in "Circe," when he requested permission to "bring two men chums to witness" the debauchery of his wife and then hugged himself with pleasure as the deed took place. In providing Stephen with this gratuitous glimpse of Molly, "in evening

---

* Bloom says "no uncommon" but this is a slip due to tiredness.

dress cut ostentatiously low for the occasion to give a liberal display of bosom, with more than vision of breasts, her full lips parted . . ." Bloom again gives way to the weakness which consistently compromises what virtues he does possess. In this instance his virtuous kindliness in helping a drunken young man is compromised by the kind of action one might expect from a seedy pervert in Times Square, Piccadilly—or Dublin's nighttown. Bloom goes so far as to act as a pander to his own wife,[79] assuring Stephen that Molly "would have the greatest of pleasure in making your acquaintance as she is passionately attached to music of any kind" (U662-63). The musical allusion is to Stephen's fine tenor voice—but also to any other kind of melody he might be able to make with Molly. Perhaps Stephen senses Bloom's weakness when he "thought he felt a strange kind of flesh of a different man approach him, sinewless and wobbly and all that" (U660). Spiritually and physically sinewless and wobbly, Bloom presents himself as a personification of Joyce's moral view of man. The artist, Stephen, has encountered his subject matter at last. He is too drunk to understand it.

Joyce was fond of ending many of the episodes of *Ulysses* with epiphanies which crystallize the preceding action in a single gesture. Thus "Lotus-eaters" ends with Bloom's gazing narcissistically at his own genitalia; "Sirens" with Bloom's gaseous "Pprrpffrrppfff" superimposed upon the heroic words of Robert Emmet; "Cyclops" with a mock-heroic apotheosis of ben Bloom Elijah; "Nausicaa" with a symbolic "Cuckoo" for the cuckold; and "Eumaeus" ends, just as Stephen and Bloom begin to walk off toward Eccles Street together, with the bowel movement of a horse: "The horse . . . added his quota by letting fall on the floor, which the brush would soon brush up and polish,

---

[79] Bloom's pandering, mingled with his homosexuality, was noted specifically by Joyce in conversation with Frank Budgen. See Budgen, *James Joyce and the Making of Ulysses*, p. 315.

three smoking globes of turds. Slowly, three times, one after another, from a full crupper, he mired" (U665). This gesture epitomizes, equally as eloquently as the endings of any other of the episodes, the preceding action of "Eumaeus," a nonrecognition scene in which nothing more valuable than the substance of that equine gesture transpires. If one were inclined to hunt zealously for symbols in a book known to be full of them, one might point out, at the risk of indelicacy, that the number of turds mired from the crupper of that horse corresponds exactly to the number of principal characters in Ulysses: Stephen, Bloom, and Molly Bloom. But one need not be quite so zealous to perceive the richly comic aptness of a horse's miring as an epiphany of "Eumaeus."

· 15 ·

The structure of Ulysses, like that of Finnegans Wake, is circular. For Bloom begins his day at home and ends it at home. This circular structure contrasts with that of the Odyssey, a tale whose hero begins in exile and ends having achieved his goal—the homeland, Ithaca. As Joyce himself phrased Ulysses' achievements, "He was subjected to many trials, but with wisdom and courage came through them all."[80] No goals are achieved in Ulysses, no quests fulfilled, no obstacles overcome, no joyful reunions celebrated; and the trials to which Ulysses-Bloom is subjected, comically reduced from Homeric scale, are more often failed than passed, and if passed are done so less with wisdom and courage than with fear and trembling. But with even greater authority than the various comic reversals of its episodes, the structure of Ulysses distinguishes it as a mock-epic. Where the Odyssey ends on a note of joy and hope, with Ulysses reestablished at the head of his family and kingdom, Ulysses ends on a note of resignation, with Bloom climbing back again into his violated

[80] Ibid., p. 16.

marriage bed, ready to give the last word to the true monarch of his home, an unfaithful Penelope. By the time the "Ithaca" episode is reached, Joyce's pattern of comic reversal should be unmistakable.

Since departing from the soothing proximity of Molly's flesh in the morning, Bloom has undergone numerous frustrations and humiliations—rebuffs from females, rudeness from his employer, insults from acquaintances, real and imagined debasements in nighttown, the omnipresent awareness of his cuckoldom. Had Joyce treated them differently, these ignominies would have been the substance of a tragedy; or, more precisely, they would have been the ingredients of another one of those extended literary exercises in pathos so common in our day, in which the anti-hero is affronted, flouted, defiled, and generally outraged until the apogee of misery is reached and the curtain rung down. Joyce keeps Bloom from the company of these contemporary anti-heroes by treating him ironically, by putting him through an elaborate series of mock-heroic episodes which on the whole make him look quite foolish. Joyce cuts short any extravagant amount of sympathy or reader-identification with Bloom by providing him with a generous dose of masochism, so that he rather enjoys the indignities heaped upon him. Trod upon by Bello, he is "enthralled" (U531). And as for his wife's infidelity, he invites an extension of it by showing other males a photo of Molly's décolletage. What might have been tragic or at least pathetic is thus transformed into comedy remarkable for its variety—high, low, sometimes subtly amusing, sometimes uproariously slapstick. Behind all this comedy is Joyce's conscience which, without hoping or intending to reform mankind, invites the reader to find both amusement and instruction in the antics of Bloom.

More than any other Bloomian characteristic, the absence of willpower offends the Joycean conscience. As one who risked everything to change his environment and to assert his own artistic freedom, Joyce could not approve of needless resignation: what others might term wise acceptance, he was likely to call slavishness. And in order to make his point in the most pleasant yet, so he thought, unmistakable way, he created in Bloom a comic character who epitomizes paralysis of the will to the extent of being enthralled by debasement and who manages to survive by the distinctly un-Ulyssean means of risking nothing:

"He had not risked, he did not expect, he had not been disappointed, he was satisfied.

"What satisfied him?

"To have sustained no positive loss" (*U*676).

Bloom is a player who avoids total defeat only by refusing to enter the game.

Bloom solaces himself with the absurd notion that he has brought "light to the gentiles" in Barney Kiernan's tavern by reminding them that Moses, Marx, Mendelssohn, and Christ were Jews and that love loves to love love: in providing this startling information, he tells himself, he has "brought a positive gain to others" (*U*676). How positive a gain Joyce considered it was indicated by the mock-apotheosis and ascension of ben Bloom Elijah. Bloom does give aid to a gentile, Stephen, and one would not wish to take credit from him for this act of charity, however modified by homosexuality and other factors it may be. Bloom and Dedalus, so dissimiliar in background and character, yet linked by a bond of common human moral frailty, are brought together in temporary union. They share the weaknesses of all men, but they share little else save a few common acquaintances.[81] Apart from the universal bestiality in which both partake, they are quite dissimilar, one the embodiment of submissiveness, the other of defiance. With his fondness for symbols, Joyce writes of their separateness in terms of water—that same water which since

[81] See *U*680, 682.

the *Portrait* Stephen has feared, trying to build break-waters against the sordidness of which it has been symbolic. Predictably, Bloom is a water-lover. "What in water did Bloom, waterlover, . . . admire?

"Its universality: its democratic equality and constancy to its nature in seeking its own level . . . its capacity to dissolve and hold in solution all soluble substances including millions of tons of the most precious metals . . . its ubiquity as constituting 90% of the human body: the noxiousness of its effluvia in lacustrine marshes, pestilential fens, faded flowerwater, stagnant pools in the waning moon" (*U*671-72).

To Bloom, water is a great leveler, emblematic of the universal equality of man. The power of water to dissolve precious metals suggests to him the power of the masses to dissolve anyone who might consider himself more precious than the rest. And that Bloom admires its repugnant, noxious stench when it lies stagnant completes the symbolic sense of his waterloving: as a masochist, Bloom loves what is vile and base, is allured by the scent of urine, enamored of female excrescences—or even "faded flowerwater." Stephen, by contrast, is "hydrophobe, hating partial contact by immersion or total by submersion in cold water . . . disliking the aqueous substances of glass and crystal, distrusting aquacities of thought and language" (*U*673). This much we know from the *Portrait* and from the opening chapters of *Ulysses*, when Stephen expressed fears of drowning in the "snotgreen sea" of Irish life. But now the full symbolic import of Stephen's hydrophobia becomes apparent. Thrown together with a waterlover—a man of the masses, a man who seeks not to rise above what he considers his own level, a man fond of water even in its most putrid state—Stephen cannot mingle with the aqueous Bloom. The two are incompatible, artist and commoner, because of "the incompatibility of aquacity with the erratic originality of genius" (*U*673).

After our extended examination of the relation of his conscience to Stephen and Bloom, it is not difficult to see where Joyce himself stood in this aqueous debate. Probably he believed in the political rights of man, and he sometimes referred to himself as a socialist. But Joyce was an apolitical writer: *Ulysses* does not deal with politics but with the human spirit, and in matters of the spirit Joyce was an aristocrat. He himself engaged in a constant struggle against what he regarded as his lower self, his common self, his bestial, weaker self. Leaving Ireland to protect his personal and artistic integrity, he sacrificed material comfort in order to preserve that integrity and to rise above the mass through his art. Thus he chose to satirize in *Ulysses* a man who had all of the Joycean personal weaknesses but none of the Joycean virtues: Bloom, a good man, well-intentioned, amiable, but lacking the fortitude to rise above the ordinary, content instead to rest at his own undistinguished level, like the water he so admires. This Bloomian "aquacity" is indeed "incompatible with the erratic originality of [Joycean] genius."

One would hope that the differences between Stephen and Joyce are already clear enough: similar in their commitment to a struggle for excellence and genius, they differ in approach, Stephen still lacerating himself and others with the outraged conscience of youth, Joyce preferring to gibe and mock with the better-humored conscience of maturity. Neither wishes to be dissolved by the Bloomian, Irish sea; and when Stephen and Bloom urinate together just before parting, this act serves as a final liquid symbol, a suitably ridiculous symbol, of both their bonds and their disparities.[82] They may urinate, excrete,

[82] William York Tindall, *A Reader's Guide to James Joyce* (New York, 1959), p. 225, somehow sees urination as a creative act: "Bloom and Stephen make water as if, by making it, acknowledging the water of life—as if by this inconsiderable creation celebrating all creation. . . . Compare Mrs. Bloom on pot." Making water seems

eat, drink, and whore together, but life to Stephen—and to Joyce—is more than bodily functions.

Once Stephen leaves him, Bloom is left to face alone the unpleasant reality of his home. The mock-epic has come full circle and this comic Ulysses has returned to the little house where first we encountered him, when he was playing something very close to the role of chambermaid to his Penelope. As Joyce once said of Bloom: "He romances about Ithaca . . . and when he gets back it gives him the pip."[83] That remark translates roughly as "There's no place so lonely as home for poor old Bloom." His consolations are few: as always, he schemes and dreams as a method of attempted escape, conjuring up a dream-cottage for himself, elevating himself to Shakespearean country squirehood, devising absurd social reforms, trying to imagine the perfect advertisement. These fantasies console Bloom to some extent, taking his mind off the day's humiliations and the greatest ignominy, his debased position in his own home. Most soothing of all to Bloom, throughout this day and throughout his life, has been his narcissistic self-indulgence; and as if to hammer that point down once and for all, Joyce goes so far as to place a statue of Narcissus in Bloom's living room: "What caused [Bloom] consolation in his sitting posture?" the narrator asks in the sober, catechetical style of "Ithaca." And the response: "The candour, nudity, pose, tranquillity, youth, grace, sex, counsel of a statue erect in the

---

less than an "inconsiderable creation" to me. Mr. Tindall here demonstrates the lengths to which one must go to try to find some kind of positive value or hope in the meeting of Stephen and Bloom. The two characters acknowledge nothing more here than the fullness of their bladders, and the water which they make will probably destroy the grass or flowers on which it falls—but I have no desire therefore to call it a symbol of destruction. If the urination has any symbolic weight at all, it corresponds in value to the defecation of the horse at the end of "Eumaeus." And everyone knows the symbolic value of horse manure.

[83] Budgen, *James Joyce and the Making of Ulysses*, p. 225.

centre of the table, an image of Narcissus purchased by auction from P. A. Wren, 9 Bachelor's Walk" (*U*710).

Bloom's relationship with Molly is the kernel of his weakness. To call him uxorious understates the case. Consider the rites he performs upon entering the marriage bed: they serve as a final epiphany of Bloomian acquiescence. He enters the bed with prudence, circumspection, solicitude, and reverence, for it is the bed of conception and of birth and of consummation. But in Bloom's case it is also the bed of "breach of marriage" (*U*731). Bloom recognizes that he is not the first, nor will he be the last, to feast on Molly's flesh here; the narrator lists twenty-five of Molly's lovers, Blazes Boylan being the last mentioned.[84] Crawling gently beneath the covers, Bloom notices "new clean bed-linen, additional odours, the presence of a human form, female, hers, the imprint of a human form, male, not his, some crumbs, some flakes of potted meat, recooked, which he removed" (*U*731). Certainly the experience of finding in his marriage bed the leavings of Molly's lover humiliates Bloom every bit as much as the real and imaginary degradations of the "Circe" episode. He at first feels envy, but ultimately he submits to the necessary rationalizations of a weak and ineffectual character. His ire, momentarily aroused, is quickly subdued. For Bloom does not wish to endanger, by protesting, what sexual pleasure he does get in life from the mere presence and sexual glow of his adulterous spouse. It would be inaccurate to see Bloom here as "a hero of Reason" who "triumphs over the temptations of the passions,"[85] because his motivation in not protesting his wife's adultery is not rational but

---

[84] On p. 388 of *James Joyce*, Richard Ellmann tries to lower the number of Molly's lovers from twenty-five to two: Bartell D'Arcy and Blazes Boylan. He dismisses the others because they are "extraordinary": two priests, a mayor, an alderman, a gynecologist, a bootblack, a professor. The respectable professions of some of these men only make their affairs with Molly the more amusing—not more unlikely—but the list of twenty-five may be an exaggeration. The number doesn't matter: Molly is far from chaste. Cf. Robert Martin Adams, *Surface and Symbol* (New York, 1962), pp. 35ff.

[85] Goldberg, *The Classical Temper*, p. 117.

lustful: as a sensualist, masochist, narcissist, and perhaps, homosexual, why should he risk destroying a source of pleasure? We know from his reactions to Blazes Boylan throughout the day that cuckoldom causes him great anguish and humiliation; we know too that he takes perverse pleasure in Molly's debauchery.

Joyce's own thoughts and actions in regard to adultery were as different as possible from Bloom's: the gulf between author and protagonist is sufficiently evident in *Ulysses*, in which every conceivable comic device is employed to deflate its mock-hero. But one aspect of Joyce's personal conduct stands as an additional ironic comment on that willing cuckold, Bloom. As Mary and Padraic Colum, who considered Joyce their friend, have written: "In spite of his visits to Nighttown and his student and poststudent days in Dublin, [Joyce] had fixed ideas of faithfulness in marriage, and nothing shocked him more than to hear that somebody he knew was commiting adultery."[86] If that somebody happened to be his own wife, Joyce's reaction was a mixture of shock, anger, and misery. As it happened, Nora was no Molly Bloom—despite the persistent attempts of many critics to draw a neat equation between Nora and Molly.[87] Joyce's only suspicion of her was ill-founded: in 1909, during a trip to Dublin,

[86] *Our Friend James Joyce* (New York, 1958), p. 134. As the Colums point out, the fact that Joyce's marriage to Nora was not made official until long after the birth of their children does not affect the reverence he held for the idea of sexual fidelity. Joyce did not need Church or State to tell him he was married.

[87] In her "Joyce and Nora: The Indispensable Countersign," *Sewanee Review* (Winter 1964), 29-64, Mary T. Reynolds strongly implies an equation between Nora and Molly. Her article's title, for example, refers to Joyce's remark that Molly serves as the "indispensable countersign" to Bloom, and the idea that Nora is Molly and Joyce is Bloom is suggested throughout. And as another example of this attempt to equate Bloom and Joyce, here is Richard Ellmann's interpretation of the significance of Joyce's meeting Nora: "June 16 was the sacred day that divided Stephen Dedalus, the insurgent youth, from Leopold Bloom, the complaisant husband" (*James Joyce*, p. 163). The implication is that Joyce was as complaisant in his marriage as Bloom was in his. As Joyce's reaction to the possibility of his being cuckolded shows, he was no Bloom.

he was erroneously informed that Nora had cheated on him five years earlier, during their courtship. Before discovering his error, he wrote to Nora in the most anguished terms: "I loved you only: and you have broken my faith in you. . . . I am crying for my poor unhappy love. . . . I have been a fool. . . . How old and miserable I feel! . . . I cannot call you any dear name because I have learnt that the only being I believed in was not loyal to me."[88] Joyce was obviously far from acquiescent to the idea of sexual infidelity. After he learned that Nora actually had been wholly faithful to him, he expressed his sorrow at having mistrusted her, but he continued to make clear his belief in sexual fidelity and his hatred of anyone who might try to violate the trust between husband and wife: "My darling, forgive me. I love you and that is why I was so maddened only to think of you and that common dishonourable wretch."[89]

Three years later, Joyce again provided evidence of his personal dissociation from Bloomian permissiveness. An Italian journalist had attempted to initiate an affair with Nora, who—unlike Molly Bloom—told her husband of the matter and sought to avoid any extramarital entanglement. Joyce reacted in a distinctly un-Bloomian manner by accosting the would-be paramour in a piazza and reducing him to tears by the vehemence and earnestness of his expostulations.[90] Evidently Mary and Padraic Colum were quite correct in their assessment of Joyce's ideas on faithfulness in marriage. We should be wary of the attempt of many critics to depict Joyce as a Leopold Bloom who wrote great novels on the side.[91]

[88] Letters to Nora, 6 and 7 August 1909, *Letters*, II, 231-33.
[89] Letter to Nora, 19 August 1909, *ibid.*, p. 235.
[90] See Ellmann, *James Joyce*, pp. 327-28.
[91] See note 87, above. Other critics following this line include William York Tindall and S. L. Goldberg. Mr. Goldberg argues throughout his *The Classical Temper* that Leopold Bloom embodies Joyce's belief in rational moderation, the *via media*, the golden mean. This may be a good description of Joyce, but not of Bloom.

In his treatment of Bloom, as in all else he attempted, Joyce's great skill lies in irony, an ability simultaneously to show things as they are and as they ought to be. By means of irony, Joyce brings his conscience to bear upon this timid advertising canvasser, who acquiesces to the paralyzing forces of his lower nature, rarely giving his higher potential a chance, floundering far from the ideal, almost submerged in the waters of reality. The extent of Joyce's ironic detachment was indicated one day in 1922, when he asked a sculptor friend of his, "What sort of monument would you make for me?" "I suppose—Mr. Bloom," said the sculptor. "Mais non! Mais non!" Joyce cried out in protest. For he had put much of himself into Bloom—but mainly those parts of himself he would sooner have done without. Something of Bloom exists in all of us, Joyce calls upon us to admit. Thus when we laugh at Bloom, we are laughing at ourselves—a merriment not easily endured. Joyce's judgment of Bloom is comic but not damning, negative but not vitriolic. Finding the weaknesses of human nature immutable, Joyce turned to comedy—to self-satire instead of self-laceration.

Throughout this chapter, the word "reversal" has been used as a description of Joyce's ironic, comic technique of judgment.[92] In relation to the *Odyssey*, Bloom's actions and inactions constitute a comic reversal of those of the heroic Ulysses; and in an even more fundamental way, the progressive development of the *Odyssey* from lonely exile to familial reunion and joy is reversed in *Ulysses*, in which a circular structure takes the mock-hero from an unhappy home back to an unhappy home. Aside from the *Odyssey*, Bloom's personal psychology is reversed from the Joycean ideal, with instinctive weaknesses ruling virtuous strengths. The life within Bloom's unhappy abode

92 Lawrance Thompson's *A Comic Principle in Sterne—Meredith—Joyce* shows that this "comic principle" has been a favorite of many writers in the comic mode, including Sterne and Meredith.

is itself also a kind of reversal, for the topsy-turvy relationship between Mr. and Mrs. Bloom, in which wife rules husband, reverses the ideal domestic order: whether one believes that the husband should dominate or that marriage should be an equal partnership, neither is the case at 7 Eccles Street. The combination of Bloom's masochistic weakness and Molly's tyranny represents the opposite of ideal married love. In writing about the Bloom household Joyce had in mind the kind of domestic malaise which he described in a letter of 1904: "There is no life here—no naturalness or honesty. People live together in the same houses all their lives and at the end they are as far apart as ever."[93] That kind of life was to Joyce, ever the idealist, the reverse of ideal love and marriage; and so it is with Bloom and his Penelope.

In a final Bloomian epiphany, Joyce carries his technique of reversal to new comic heights—or depths—as Bloom climbs at last deferentially into bed, reverses his position, and—"He kissed the plump mellow yellow smellow melons of her rump, on each plump melonous hemisphere, in their mellow yellow furrow, with obscure prolonged provocative melonsmellonous osculation" (U734-35). A tableau of inversion, of reversal, this final sycophancy of Bloom's figuratively evokes the panoramic pattern of comic reversal upon which Ulysses is based and through which Bloom's nature has been exposed. As Bloom fades from view, and Molly begins her surging monologue, we can remember him with amusement as he kisses his way into oblivion, appropriately upside-down.

[93] Letter to Nora, 16 September 1904, Letters, II, 53.

v. the conscience and
molly bloom

"One of Joyce's . . . dreams . . . caused considerable
chuckling each time he thought of it. This was a dream
the climax of which was the titanic figure of Molly Bloom,
seated on the side of a high hill. 'As for you, James Joyce,
I've had enough of you,' she shouted. His reply he never
remembered."[1]

Molly had good reason to be miffed with Joyce. He had
imperilled her reputation by allowing anyone to eaves-
drop on her thoughts for the price of a copy of *Ulysses*.
Yet she has not fared badly. For the most part her reputation stands higher now than it did in the days when
she was only the adulterous spouse of an advertising canvasser. Her monologue has been found "symbolic of the
divine love of Nature for her children . . ."[2] and more
frequently, if less effusively, "an affirmation of life."[3] But
not all readers have been so kind to Molly. Mary Colum
considered Molly's thoughts "an exhibition of the mind
of a female gorilla."[4] Perhaps if all her critics had been
females, Molly's exasperation with Joyce for exposing her
would have been justified. But most have been males, and

[1] Eugene Jolas, "My Friend James Joyce," in *James Joyce: Two
Decades of Criticism*, ed. Seon Givens (New York, 1948, 1963), p. 16.
[2] Stuart Gilbert, *James Joyce's Ulysses* (New York, 1955), p. 403.
[3] William York Tindall, *A Reader's Guide to James Joyce* (New
York, 1959), p. 232.
[4] "The Confessions of James Joyce," *Freeman*, v (19 July 1922),
451. J. Mitchell Morse, "Molly Bloom Revisited," *A James Joyce
Miscellany, Second Series* (1960), ed. Marvin Magalaner, pp. 139-49,
takes a similarly dim view of Molly.

on them Molly has worked her considerable powers of seduction, bringing the scholars under her spell, until in 1959 she achieved her greatest conquest when Joyce's most influential critic and biographer wrote of her: "Molly . . . acknowledges, though with considerable reluctance and appropriate feminine indirection, the importance of mind as opposed to body, the importance of decency, and the bonds of the family."[5] What Irish Catholic wife and mother could ask for greater praise than that? If Joyce were still dreaming, and if Molly should appear to him again, she'd have to say, "James Joyce, I was wrong about you. So God is me Judge, you've made me respectable!"

One can be susceptible to Molly's charms without being entirely swayed by them. Her animal vitality is engaging, but her crudity repulsive. Her husband's sexual neglect of her invites sympathy, but the virulence of her contempt for him seems malignant. And her narcissism is of such proportions that one is hard pressed to discover amid her effusions any kind of love—be it divine, maternal, romantic, or marital—except self-love. One certainly does not envy Bloom for being married to her. But these may be subjective reactions; tastes in wives differ. And the question is not how well or how little we like Molly but rather how she appears in the light of Joyce's conscience, that arbiter of meaning in *Ulysses*.

The Homeric parallel functions well as an initial approach to the problem of Joyce's own attitude toward Molly. For 2,500 years Penelope has stood as the classical model of the chaste wife. Her ingenuity in putting off the suitors and her adamantine loyalty to Ulysses marked her as the epitome of marital fidelity, and so she has remained. Joyce's idea of Ulysses as a hero has already been discussed at length; Joyce seems also to have revered the idea of Penelope as a chaste wife. Frank Budgen tells us that Joyce had pinned upon a wall of his Zurich flat a

[5] Richard Ellmann, *James Joyce* (New York, 1959), pp. 388-89.

photograph of a Greek statue of Penelope, representing "a woman, draped, seated, looking at her upheld forefinger." One evening, when Budgen and Paul Suter were visiting, Joyce pointed to the photograph of Penelope and asked, "What is she thinking about?"

"She is weighing up her wooers," Budgen said, "trying to decide which one of them will make the most manageable husband."

"To me," said Suter, "she seems to be saying: 'I'll give him just one week more.' "

"My own idea," said Joyce, "is that she is trying to recollect what Ulysses looks like. You see, he has been away many years, and they had no photographs in those days."[6]

Joyce's comment is revealing. His two friends had displayed the modernity of their temperaments by suggesting either that Penelope had already decided to accept a suitor and to forsake Ulysses or that she was about to forsake him. Penelope to them was obviously not prey to any outmoded ideas of marital fidelity. But to Joyce no such novelty occurs: Penelope waits faithfully, even for a husband whose face she has forgotten, so many years has he been away. And if we compare Joyce's Irish Penelope, Molly Bloom, to that old-fashioned idea of the faithful Greek Penelope, the contrast between the two is obvious. Joyce's favorite comic technique in *Ulysses*, that of reversal or inversion, again establishes a controlling irony.

One need not make extravagant claims for the Homeric parallel to argue its helpfulness here, as elsewhere in *Ulysses*. The parallel simply suggests that a satiric contrast is about to be drawn. If one wishes to be especially cautious, one can set it up as a merely tentative hypothesis for Joyce's attitude toward Molly, admitting that it actually tells us very little about her, and then test it

6 Frank Budgen, *James Joyce and the Making of Ulysses* (Bloomington, 1960), pp. 183-84.

against her character as set forth in her monologue. The more one tests, the more the contrast between Molly and Penelope proves a reliable first step. For if one trait is dominant in Molly, it is a narcissism of which Penelope would have been incapable. Penelope's devotion to someone or something—a principle of loyalty, perhaps—keeps her faithful. Molly's devotion to herself prevents her from being faithful to any other person or value. She places self-love above marital love or even maternal love.

Molly is not therefore some kind of monster—or gorilla, as Mary Colum would have had it. Such is not the Joycean way, not the style or tone or tenor of *Ulysses*, a book meant to amuse but not to horrify. She is a comic example of a self-loving woman, even as Leopold Bloom is a comic example of a narcissistic man. Bloom, to be sure, is better-intentioned than Molly: he has his moments of kindness, though they usually degenerate into sentimentalism and self-pity. But Bloom's narcissistic devotion to the cravings of his own flesh motivates the bulk of his actions in *Ulysses*, as we have seen; and it is not by accident that Joyce arranges for him to gaze with consolation at a statue of Narcissus. Molly accuses Bloom of narcissism. Deprecating his performance in bed, she says of him, "he does it all wrong too thinking only of his own pleasure" (*U*773). But poor Bloom is dominated by Molly in everything—even in self-love. Her concern for herself knows few bounds, and Joyce manages to express, to symbolize this gargantuan narcissism of hers in one extraordinary passage. Again that little statue of Narcissus plays a leading part. For Bloom it was significantly an object of consolation. Molly goes considerably further: "that lovely little statue he bought I could look at him all day long curly head and his shoulders his finger up for you to listen theres real beauty and poetry for you I often felt I wanted to kiss him all over also his lovely young cock there so simply I wouldnt mind taking him in my mouth if nobody was looking as if it was asking you to suck it . . ." (*U*-775-76).

Suffice it to say that Molly equals Narcissus in the symbolic intensity of her self-love, and Narcissus' aberration eventually led to self-destruction. This remarkably salacious passage demonstrates the care which Joyce took and the interest he had in establishing Molly's self-love: he was willing to stretch the boundaries of realism to accomplish his symbolic purpose, because one certainly must tax the imagination to accept a woman so fond of a statue that she wishes to engage in oral copulation with it. But in many other passages in Molly's monologue Joyce takes care that her narcissism is expressed in less symbolic, perhaps more direct terms. "I bet he never saw a better pair of thighs than that," she thinks, referring to her own. "Look how white they are the smoothest place is right there between this bit here how soft like a peach easy God I wouldnt mind being a man and get up on a lovely woman . . ." (*U*770). Those sentiments and desires, while hardly shocking, unusual, or terribly perverse, contribute to the general pattern of Molly's self-centeredness and narcissism when they are taken together with all of the other overt instances of her self-love. Perhaps the most distinctly expressed instance comes in the form of a reminiscence of her Gibraltar girlhood: "I used to love myself then," she muses, referring in particular to her physical allure, "stripped at the washstand dabbing and creaming . . ." (*U*763).[7]

One would expect someone who cares so much for herself to care very little for others, and Molly's self-loving contempt for Bloom is monumental. Of course any wife might be dissatisfied with a husband whose chief means of sexual satisfaction is the embracing and kissing of her posterior—"better go easy not wake him have him at it again slobbering after washing every bit of myself . . . I

[7] On *U*739 Molly refers to "the usual kissing my bottom."

⟨   205   ⟩

wish hed sleep in some bed by himself . . . its a wonder
Im not an old shrivelled hag before my time living with
him so cold never embracing me except sometimes when
hes asleep the wrong end of me . . . any man thatd kiss a
womans bottom Id throw my hat at him after that hed
kiss anything unnatural . . ." (U763, 777). But even in
view of Bloom's multiple weaknesses, of which we have
read so much in previous episodes, Molly's contempt for
him appears excessive when, in thinking of his unreligious
materialism, she accuses him of lacking a soul: "he says
your soul you have no soul inside only grey matter because he doesnt know what it is to have one . . ." (U741-
42). To Molly, Bloom's lack of "soul" means his inability
to feed her voracious sexual appetite. Perhaps Bloom
would be incapable of sexually satisfying even a timid,
frigid wife, so encumbered is he by his masochism, narcissism, voyeurism, homosexuality, and what have you;
but he is certainly inadequate for Molly, who measures a
man's soul by the size of his—sexual capacity. So vexed is
she by his lack of virility, she even wishes he'd "smoke a
pipe like father to get the smell of a man" (U752). She
views with disdain Bloom's homosexual displaying of her
picture to Stephen: "I wonder he didnt make him a present of it altogether and me too after all why not . . ."
(U774). She does not share his predilection for sado-
masochistic perversion—"hed like me to walk in all the
horses dung I could find but of course hes not natural like
the rest of the world" (U745)—but she often becomes so
exasperated with him and scornful of him that she admits
sadistic impulses toward him: "Id like to have tattered
[his trousers] down off him before all the people and give
him what that one calls flagellate till he was black and
blue do him all the good in the world" (U765).

Such is the alarming degree of this self-loving woman's
contempt for her husband. We cannot blame the admit-
tedly impuissant Bloom altogether for the sad state of

this marriage. Molly would devour any man. Only this afternoon she had a most productive visit from Boylan, her current lover, but now in the early hours of the morning she squirms again with desire—or as she so indelicately phrases it, remembering Boylan, "my hole is itching me always when I think of him" (U763). With Bloom a somnolent lump beside her, she thinks again of Boylan, "I wished he was here or somebody to let myself go with and come again like that I feel all fire inside me . . ." (U754). And in one meaningful exclamation she reveals to us the depth of her religious faith, and her personal definition of the human heart: "O thanks be to the great God I got somebody to give me what I badly wanted to put some heart up into me . . ." (U758).[8]

Molly's one great wish is to satisfy herself. Her narcissism, sexual appetite, and contempt for Bloom all go together, since Bloom does not contribute to her self-satisfaction. If she praises him, it is faintly, as when she admits he does try to look after his family financially and does show politeness to old women and beggars, or sarcastically: "he ought to get a leather medal with a putty rim for all the plans he invents . . ." (U738, 765). If he were unable to keep her in room and board and bring her breakfast in bed, one cannot but conclude that she would leave Bloom, for no bonds of unselfish love hold this pair together. And as for any maternal love Molly might have for her daughter, it is not in evidence in her monologue. Molly's attitude toward young Milly seems compounded of the same elements as her attitude toward Bloom: contempt and exasperation. She seems even to resent the pain of giving birth to her child (U742) and now that

[8] Of course Molly cares nothing for Boylan as a person: one might say that she considers him an extremely useful household appliance. Several times during her monologue, she looks forward to his return on the following Monday. See, for example, p. 754, which should counter the notion sometimes advanced that hereafter Molly and Bloom will experience a felicitous reconciliation.

the girl is sexually blossoming, Molly considers her something of a slut and certainly a brazen nuisance: "her tongue is a bit too long for my taste your blouse is open too low she says to me the pan calling the kettle blackbottom and I had to tell her not to cock her legs up like that on show on the windowsill" (U767). Molly would begrudge Milly even the normal motherly attention: "well I hope shell get someone to dance attendance on her the way I did when she was down with the mumps her glands swollen wheres this and wheres that . . ." (U767). Not that every mother hasn't entertained similar thoughts about her sometimes vexatious offspring. But for Molly this querulous tone toward her daughter dominates, to the exclusion of either tenderness or the indulgence and parental pride one hopes to see in a mother. Significantly, Milly scarcely crosses her mind during her monologue: she is too taken up with Bloom's inadequacies and Boylan's adequacies. Molly is not a woman easily given to solicitous thoughts, maternal or otherwise.

One wishes to give Molly her due: as this analysis progresses, she appears to be looking more and more like Mary Colum's female gorilla and less like a human being. Molly probably would survive nicely in the jungle—but this very animality is her most engaging quality. The ferocious energy of her sexuality, even of her narcissism, is somehow awe-inspiring, at least to the male reader and presumably to her male creator. Her tidal wave of thoughts can easily drown one's moral objections to her self-centeredness. Just as Nietzsche preferred the vitality, however corrupt, of a Caesar Borgia to the emasculated ideal of a Parsifal, so we may be inclined to prefer the vitality, however self-centered, of a Molly Bloom to the emasculated timorousness of a Leopold Bloom.

But Joyce carefully constructs a formidable barrier between Molly and her readers, a barrier designed at least to discourage any great enthusiasm for her and to diminish the effect of her seductive powers. That barrier consists of Molly's extraordinary crudity, combined with her essential venality. By crudity, one does not mean so ordinary a matter as her breaking wind in bed; nor can one blame Molly, certainly, for beginning to menstruate two-thirds of the way through her monologue—"the clean linen I wore brought it on too damn it damn it" (*U*769). These are natural processes from which only a hypocritical prude—which Joyce was not—could turn away in disgust, although Joyce presents them in such detail that they have a certain repulsive air about them. By her crudity I mean both the paucity of any delicacy or tenderness of feeling in her monologue and also her consistent use of the most disgusting possible language to describe her emotions, cravings, lusts. When Swift spreads his *Gulliver's Travels* with excrement, he is trying to remind mankind of human baseness, lest we entertain an exalted view of ourselves. And when Joyce puts in Molly's mouth such a phrase as "my hole is itching me always when I think of him," he is trying to remind us of Molly's baseness, lest we entertain an exalted view of her. On the surface Molly might appear as a warm, vital, attractive mound of female flesh. But once we see her basic crudity for what it is, refusing to let our romanticism obscure it, then the effect is something like discovering that an attractive woman whom one has admired is infected with syphilis. One passage in particular brings out this crudity as well as the venality which together show Molly to be less a wife or mother or mistress than a kind of egocentric force, willing to employ even the most sordid means to the end of self-aggrandizement. Molly is somewhat puzzled and vexed by Bloom's highly unusual request that for once she make breakfast for him. But she resolves to turn the occasion to her own distinct advantage and at the same time to demonstrate both her domination of and contempt for poor old Poldy: "Ill throw him up his eggs and tea . . .

I know what Ill do Ill go about rather gay not too much
singing a bit now and then mi fa pietà Masetto then Ill
start dressing myself to go out . . . Ill put on my best shift
and drawers let him have a good eyeful out of that to
make his micky stand for him Ill let him know if thats
what he wanted that his wife is fucked yes and damn well
fucked too up to my neck nearly not by him 5 or 6 times
handrunning . . . Ive a mind to tell him every scrap and
make him do it in front of me serve him right its all his
own fault if I am an adulteress . . . then if he wants to
kiss my bottom Ill drag open my drawers and bulge it
right out in his face as large as life he can stick his tongue
7 miles up my hole as hes there my brown part then Ill
tell him I want £1 or perhaps 30/– Ill tell him I want to
buy underclothes then if he gives me that well he wont
be too bad I dont want to soak it all out of him like other
women do . . . Ill let him do it off on me behind provided
he doesnt smear all my good drawers . . . Ill tighten my
bottom well and let out a few smutty words smellrump
or lick my shit . . . then Ill wipe him off me just like a
business . . ." (*U*780-81).

This passage demonstrates the extent to which Molly
is ready to take advantage of the sensual hold she has over
Bloom. She is quite willing to sell herself to her own husband for a pound or a pound and a half: that makes her at
least ten shillings more expensive than the whores at Bella
Cohen's, but Bloom will no doubt be willing to pay the price.
She is prepared to flaunt her unfaithfulness before him, to
cater to his peculiar sexual habits, to throw him up his
breakfast once or shout a bit of provocative filth—anything he wants, if the price is right. Of course Molly throws
a sop or two to her own conscience, blaming Bloom for
her adultery and priding herself on not soaking him for
all he's got, "like other women do," but these asides hardly
detract from the powerful crudity and venality of the
passage. Joyce provides us here with a bit of foreknowl-

edge of the morrow, letting us in on Molly's plans for starting the day, and provides us as well with rather depressing insight into both Molly and the tenor of Bloomian married life. For all of Molly's attractive vitality, for all of her fleshly charms and engaging bravado, she is at heart a thirty-shilling whore. In view of the pleasure she takes in activities such as those she plans for the morning, how ironic sounds her remark—"of course a woman is so sensitive about everything . . ." (U742).

Why did Joyce choose to end *Ulysses* with Molly's monologue? Why did he select a passion-driven woman to speak the last several thousand words of his comic epic? And why do so many of those final words—the words which are bound to stick in the reader's mind more than any others—deaden the often jovial, comic spirit of the book with their crudity and venality? The answer to each of those questions lies in the fact that *Ulysses*, as well as being a highly amusing and entertaining comedy, is a book with a conscience—the peculiar, stringent, idealistic conscience of Joyce. In a letter to Joyce in 1928, H. G. Wells showed deep understanding of this conscience: "Your training has been Catholic, Irish, insurrectionary," he wrote to Molly's creator. "You began Catholic, that is to say you began with a system of values in stark opposition to reality. Your mental existence is obsessed by a monstrous system of contradictions. You may believe in chastity, purity and the personal God and that is why you are always breaking out into cries of cunt, shit and hell. . . ."[9] Wells went on to say that his own values were so different from Joyce's that he could not follow Joyce's "banner," though wishing him well. Our values too may be quite different from Joyce's. But Joyce believed in chastity and purity and heroic ideals—in Ulysses and Penelope—and so when he permits Molly to break out into "cries of cunt,

[9] Letter to Joyce of 23 November 1928, quoted in Ellmann, *James Joyce*, p. 620, and *Letters*, I, 275.

shit and hell" he is pointing out how far she is from the Joycean ideals. He chooses Molly to end his mock-epic precisely because her values are the values of reality, as Joyce perceives it, while his own values are, as Wells wrote, "in stark opposition to reality." The energy and sheer length of her monologue raise her to the level of a symbol, expand her significance until she appears to be more a relentless force than a mere woman—perhaps a symbol of the life force. Many readers have noted this symbolic quality in Molly, and Joyce himself wrote that the "Penelope" episode "turns like the huge earth ball slowly surely and evenly, round and round spinning, its 4 cardinal points being the female breasts, arse, womb and cunt expressed by the words because, bottom . . . woman, yes."[10] But if Molly is a symbol of the life force, as irresistible as gravity, as pervasive as the earth itself, she is an ironic symbol, like so much else in *Ulysses* the amusing reverse of the ideal. Thus she is "Gaea-Tellus," the Earth Mother—but an Earth Mother who complains of birth pangs and who prides herself on her contraceptive skills: a sterile Earth Mother, a Joycean mockery of the very idea of the Earth Mother, a narcissistic Earth Mother who will debase herself for thirty shillings.[11]

For all her crudity and venality, however, Molly ends her monologue with a wave of lyrical beauty, drifting off to sleep at last amid memories of mountains, rivers, lakes, flowers, and a seduction far more romantic than has been typical of her. It is this final lyrical outpouring which has won so many admirers for Molly among her readers, for

[10] Letter to Frank Budgen, 16 August 1921, quoted in Ellmann, *James Joyce*, p. 517, and *ibid.*, I, 170.

[11] S. L. Goldberg, who believes that Joyce was essentially a humanitarian writer—a kind of pacifist-humanist—thinks that Molly's monologue is intended as an affirmation of all of life. But Mr. Goldberg finds Molly somewhat repulsive, too indiscriminate, and inadequate as a life-affirming symbol; he therefore concludes that Joyce has failed in the "Penelope" episode and that Joyce ought to have found a more suitable vehicle than Molly to convey his affirmations. *The Classical Temper* (London, 1961), pp. 298-300.

one can easily forget her narcissism, her contempt for Bloom and Milly, her crude language and actions, her venal plan for getting money in the morning, and remember only the apparently exultant lyricism of those famed final words, ". . . yes I said yes I will Yes." The objections to so selective a view of Molly seem obvious: one can no more interpret Molly's monologue by confining oneself to its last two pages than capture the spirit of a symphony by listening to the last few bars of the fourth movement. But there is a more serious objection to allowing Molly's final lyrical pulsations to govern one's ultimate view of her monologue, of her character, and of her significance in *Ulysses*, because underneath all this lyricism lies a depressing reality. And lest we be swept away altogether by Molly's affirmations, lest we conclude that somehow Joyce too affirms the entire grotesque panorama of *Ulysses*, we must confront the ironic and pathetic truths which compromise her apparent joy.

Molly's final reverie consists of her recollection of her initial yielding to Bloom, sixteen years before on Howth head, overlooking Dublin Bay. Whatever the present state of her marriage, one might expect Molly to recall that moment of seduction with unalloyed tenderness, for the first full embrace of lovers certainly ought to be a moment devoid of deception, no matter what corruptions set in as the years pass. But on the contrary, what Molly remembers is the initial deception of a union which has become rife with deception. Lying there with Bloom on Howth head, Molly, so she now recalls, was thinking of things poor Bloom knew nothing about; and had he been able to read her thoughts, Bloom would have noted how little Molly cared for him from the beginning. "I was thinking of so many things he didnt know of," Molly muses, and she reveals that her mind was not lingering on Bloom but had wandered far off to Gibraltar and thoughts of men other than poor Bloom and of the beauty of Gibraltar—its flowers and Moors and castanets, its Spanish girls and sleepy marketplaces and crimson sunsets. So from the very start of their life together, Molly and Bloom were far apart. From the start Bloom was led on and deceived by the resourceful Molly, and Molly herself was surrendering to a life quite different from her romantic dreams and memories—a life unalterably bound to be empty and frustrating for both of them. "I liked him," Molly says of Bloom, "because I saw he understood or felt what a woman is. . . ." That sounds nice enough—but Molly quickly adds: "and I knew I could always get round him . . ." (U782). There is the crux of their marriage: Molly always getting round Bloom, with Bloom either unaware or perversely pleased to be betrayed.

Molly's final affirmations must be seen entire to be seen at all—must be seen as a recollection of the first of countless marital deceptions, as affirmations of the emptiness of her life with Bloom. Sixteen years before she lay with him on Howth head, feeling his heart "going like mad" with desire for her, yet letting her mind wander off to better lovers than Poldy and more romantic climes than dirty Dublin. She yielded to him, said "Yes" to him—but why? Because, as she so pertinently recalls, "I thought well as well him as another" (U783). One would certainly not wish to deny the lyrical beauty of these memories of Gibraltar. Nor would one wish to minimize the seductive appeal of that marvelous "yes I said yes I will Yes." But taking into judicious consideration the precise circumstances of those lyrical affirmations does cast a shadow of Joycean irony over them. Viewed comprehensively, Molly's affirmations serve at least two purposes: they complete her self-characterization as an essentially narcissistic Penelope and Earth-Mother; and they serve as a final reminder that for all her brazen disregard of conventional morality, for all her lack of inhibitions, she has found neither love nor happiness. She must dredge up old memories to allay her own miseries.

Molly's monologue, then, provides a detailed picture not only of herself but of her life with Bloom as well. When first Molly got Bloom to propose to her so long ago—it was a leapyear, she tells us—she drew him down to her and permitted him to take his pleasure, while she took hers by letting her mind wander, thus commencing an endless chain of deceptions. Poldy, of course, has long since ceased to mind being tricked: now he demands to know the subject of Molly's thoughts as they lie together, enjoying the ignominy of his own inadequacy: "who is in your mind now," he asks Molly, "tell me who are you thinking of who is it tell me his name who tell me who the German Emperor is it yes imagine" (U740). Molly doesn't care for this inquisitiveness: "simply ruination for any woman and no satisfaction in it pretending to like it till he comes and then finish it off myself anyway" (U740). She prefers to keep her deceptions to herself, just as she did on Howth sixteen years before. Little has changed since then: she and Bloom are no closer together, no closer to the ideal of love Joyce had in mind by contrasting them to Ulysses and Penelope. How right Molly is when she complains, "Here we are as bad as ever after 16 years" (U772). And how prescient Joyce was about the themes of *Ulysses* when he wrote of Dublin in 1904, "There is no life here, no naturalness or honesty. People live together in the same houses all their lives and at the end they are as far apart as ever."[12]

If *Ulysses* ends on a note of romantic illusion and even of frustration, and if its characters wander aimlessly through this day and through all the days of their lives as prisoners of self-love, one might imagine that Joyce has written either a wholly mordant attack on mankind, or else a kind of modern tragedy, in which hero and heroine know only loneliness and are to be deeply pitied for their plight. But *Ulysses* is neither of these. Let anyone tempted

[12] Letter to Nora, 16 September 1904, *Letters*, ii, 53.

to read the book as either diatribe or tragedy take note of Joyce's puckish jibe at the psychologist Carl Jung: "He seems to have read *Ulysses* from first to last without one smile. The only thing to do in such a case is to change one's drink."[13] There was a time when Joyce might have written *Ulysses* from first to last without one smile—but evidently he changed his own drink, because the book as he has given it to us resounds with laughter. Joyce was certainly an idealist, and for years, as we have seen in previous chapters, he struggled violently and unhappily with the split in his nature between spirit and flesh. A man so struggling and so torn does write diatribe or tragedy. Such a man writes with the cold scorn of *Dubliners* or with the agony suffusing *Exiles*. Such a man writes a *Portrait* of himself and criticizes his own youthful attempts to obscure ugly realities with romantic idealism. And such a man confesses to his beloved his worship of the angel in her and his hatred of the beast in himself. But such a man cannot write *Ulysses* until he allows the spirit of comedy to leaven his pessimistic view of human nature. Rather than remain morosely intransigent, Joyce chose to chide such intransigence in the person of Stephen Dedalus, the "jejune jesuit" of *Ulysses*. And where he might merely have castigated human weaknesses, including his own, he elected instead to mock them outrageously and hilariously in the person of Leopold Bloom.

Binding all the thematic strands of *Ulysses* together is the figure, in Joyce's own words, of the "perfectly sane full amoral fertilisable untrustworthy engaging shrewd limited prudent indifferent Weib"—Molly Bloom. Again in Joyce's words, she is *"der* [sic] *Fleisch der stets bejaht"*:[14] the Flesh, which always says yes. She binds all themes together because of the nature of Joyce's conscience, that

[13] Ellmann, *James Joyce*, p. 641. The remark was made in response to an extremely sober appraisal of *Ulysses* by Jung.
[14] Letter to Frank Budgen, 16 August 1921, *Letters*, I, 169-70.

paradoxically apostate Irish Catholic conscience, which would have sex as the keystone of morality. To Freud, sex is simply the controlling force in man. To Joyce, sex is the controlling bestial force in man, the force which roots man to the earth and keeps him from being an angel; sex is the ineluctable force symbolized by that untrustworthy, indifferent, yet somehow engaging *Weib*, Molly Bloom. The flesh loves only itself, and thus Joyce depicts Molly as obscenely narcissistic. The flesh exerts inevitable control over all men, turning them into lumps of flaccid acquiescence, inversions of their proper moral selves, and thus Joyce makes Bloom the willing slave of his *Weib* and leaves Bloom comically upside-down, embracing with emblematic obsequiousness the posteriors of all-powerful Molly. The ideals of this pagan Irish Catholic writer remain exalted, even in his apostasy, for he gives us Ulysses and Penelope as analogues for Christ and the Virgin Mary. And so the comic epic ends, with Ulysses untriumphant and Penelope unfaithful.

vi. the conscience and shem and shaun

Elaborate technical development distinguishes James Joyce's later from his earlier work, and yet his thematic concerns endure. Not only was Joyce fond enough of his minor characters to transport them from book to book, along with the setting of Dublin itself, but he continually evoked the same kinds of experience and the same concepts from the *Portrait* to *Finnegans Wake*. As Joyce's literary career progressed, in fact, his books began to lean more and more heavily upon one another. Anyone can read *Dubliners* in isolation, but the *Portrait* may be read profitably with one eye on the first three chapters of *Ulysses*. Stephen's youthful experience cannot be fully evaluated without some consideration of its aftermath. Joyce's artistic technique may have changed from the *Portrait* to *Ulysses*, but his major themes remain intact.

For all its opacity, *Finnegans Wake* becomes somewhat less impervious to the reader who keeps the lesson of the relation of the *Portrait* to *Ulysses* in mind. Though Bloom has vanished by the time of the *Wake*, and Stephen is absent at least in name,[1] Joyce's mind continues to work in its own peculiarly consistent fashion. As only a single example, though an important one, the battle of the brothers Shem and Shaun in *Finnegans Wake* is largely an extension of a theme which lies at the heart of both the

---

[1] Adaline Glasheen identifies the word "crown" as a reference to Stephen, however, in her *A Second Census of Finnegans Wake* (Evanston, 1963), p. 63; some of her suggested correlations seem useful, others farfetched.

Portrait and *Ulysses*. Shem and Shaun are in conflict with one another throughout the *Wake* because each embodies an opposite tendency in the human soul or psyche. Their opposition is one of the few immediately apprehensible aspects of the *Wake*. But the precise meaning of this opposition remains elusive and the subject of tentative conjecture unless Joyce's earlier concern with Shem and Shaun is taken into account.

Shem and Shaun are as much a part of the *Portrait* as of *Finnegans Wake*. For the two brothers are Joyce's personification of a conflict central to the emotional and intellectual world of Stephen Dedalus—and of Joyce himself. We have seen how Stephen's own mind is troubled from earliest childhood by an irreconcilable opposition between the ideal and the actual, an opposition which foreshadows Joyce's later development of the Shem-Shaun theme. Stephen, one recalls, is shocked and dismayed by the ugliness, the bestiality of the life around him and of himself. Time and again he attempts to push sordid images from his mind, but he is unable to shield himself from them altogether. The result is a prolonged intellectual and emotional dilemma in which Stephen struggles vainly against divisive forces, never able to escape unpleasant reality. In the opening chapters of *Ulysses* Joyce brings Stephen to a full realization of the deficiencies of his narrow vision. While it may have been necessary for Stephen to leave Ireland because of the ensnaring nets of nation, family, and religion, his attempt to avoid realities which recognize no national boundaries must inevitably fail. It becomes no longer possible for him to fly above the gross earth on wings of beauty. The act of procreation itself he has come to recognize as tainted, and the apparently inescapable sinfulness of all existence presses in on his consciousness.

Neither Stephen nor the reader who wishes to encounter Joyce whole, to perceive both sides of the Joycean conscience, can avoid this unpleasantness. The alternative to an acceptance of what Joyce and Stephen view as the sordid tide of life is self-deception. In *Finnegans Wake*, the split between sordidness and beauty which plagues Stephen's mind emerges in Joyce's treatment of Shem and Shaun. In broadest terms, the Stephen of the *Portrait* is depicted in the Shaun stage of his development; in *Ulysses* Stephen has adopted a more Shem-like perspective. From Joyce's point of view, Shem represents self-knowledge, while Shaun represents self-deception and hypocrisy.

· I ·

Shem and Shaun hurry on and off stage throughout the *Wake*, but the first section which they wholly dominate is Book II, Chapter i. The brothers' names have been changed to Glugg (Shem) and Chuff (Shaun), and the chapter depicts the games in which the brothers engage with a group of lively young maidens, who are rainbow-tinted.[2] Joyce has deliberately chosen the most innocent of human endeavors—the fanciful games of childhood—as the activity for the brothers. The reader's initial response to the idea of childhood games is one of sentimental delight. And it is Joyce's intention that our initial reaction be an innocent one, so that he can then undercut our sentimentality through a complicated manipulation of irony. The reader begins with Shaun-like preconceptions: childhood is the time of ingenuous diversion, and innocent are the pastimes of youth. In the course of the episode, the comic undertones of these childhood games reverse our expectations, as we encounter not a sentimental celebration of youth but a Rabelaisian mockery of human motivation.

The childish recreation is rendered in the form of a

[2] Just why the girls are rainbow-tinted is a complex matter indeed, but not relevant to the present discussion. See Glasheen, pp. 231-32, under "Seven."

play, and as in all of *Finnegans Wake*, Joyce is careful to establish the action on a universal plane. There is much that is unclear about the book, but that Joyce intended even the most seemingly insignificant action to resound with universal implications is beyond question. From the beginning this particular episode embraces mankind in general. The little drama is said to take place "every evening at lighting up o'clock sharp and until further notice in Feenichts Playhouse" (*FW*219). HCE's house, where the scene is set, is near Phoenix Park, but "Feenichts" refers not only to the incidental fact that no fee is charged for admission at this performance, but that any man might see the same drama enacted at all times in the history of mankind, in "humpteen dumpteen revivals," at no charge save the effort of self-recognition. Joyce undermines the apparent innocence of these diversions from the start, for they are "newly billed for each wickeday perfumance." The perfume of the assembled maidens, though sweet to the smell, cannot erase their basic wickedness, toward which Joyce is about to turn a discerning if laughing eye.

Joyce further universalizes the play by terming it *The Mime of Mick, Nick, and the Maggies*—the battle between St. Michael and the Devil. This title also establishes the antipodal nature of the forces involved. A list of the cast of characters, containing short descriptions of each of the players, reinforces the immutable opposition of Glugg and Chuff, for Chuff is "the fine frank fairhaired fellow of the fairytales, who wrestles for tophole with the bold bad bleak boy Glugg." Glugg, we are told, is rejected by the maidens "because he knew too mutch" (*FW*219-20). What Glugg knows is the focal point of not only this episode but of *Finnegans Wake* itself. His knowledge is Joyce's knowledge, and it acts eventually to deflate the sanctimonious pose of both Chuff and the sentimental reader.

The substance of the brothers' contention in this chap-

ter is Izod, "a bewitching blonde who dimples delight-
fully," who has cast Glugg aside in favor of the angelic
Chuff. The reason for Izod's jilting of Glugg is clear:
Glugg is unabashedly sexual in his aims, while Chuff is
able to flatter the maiden and her friends through his
innocent demeanor. "Chuffy was a nangel then and his
soard fleshed light like likening." Izod cannot bear the
bluntness of Glugg's advances; her vanity will not allow
the thought of a man's pursuing her for blatantly sexual
ends, though both she and the rest of the rainbow-colored
maidens are slyly coquettish in their airs. The total action
of the episode is a contest between Glugg, who proclaims
the sexual truth behind these innocent childhood games,
and Chuff, who protests his innocence, whilst flattering
the maidens with his gentlemanly manners. The maidens
themselves are anything but childlike: "How pierceful in
their sojestiveness were those first girly stirs, with zitter-
ings of flight released and twinglings of twitchbells in
rondel after, with waverlings that made shimmershake
rather naightily all the duskcended airs and shylit beacon-
ings from shehind hims back" (FW222). Never has flirta-
tiousness been so sojestively described.

The games begin, and poor Glugg is led through a series
of defeats. His first task is to "cometh up as a trapadour,
sinking how he must fand for himself by gazework what
their colours wear as they are all showen drawens up"
(FW224). This comical troubadour must sneak around
underneath the rainbow-colored maidens and, as if from
a trapdoor, determine the true colors of the girls through
their drawn-up drawers. Unfortunately, he is plagued by
a full bladder, and in "a little tittertit of hilarity" the girls
whisper, "holding their noises," that Glugg "make peace in
his preaches and play with esteem" (FW225). Humiliated
by the suggestion that he has wet his pants, or is playing
with "his stem," Glugg scurries off stage to the amusement of the maidens.

Soon he is back guessing their colors gleefully, but again they drive him off amid hoots of amusement. And in Glugg's absence, the girls turn to "the kerl he left behind him," Chuff. They begin to "chant en chor" a hymn in his honor, "prositating their selfs eachwise and combinedly. . . . For the sake of farbung and of the scent and of the holiodrops. Amens." The maiden sing to the angelic Chuff in adoration, and he is elevated to the position of a god of innocence. The girls assure him that in future years, when "after desk jobduty" he finds himself a middling bank manager, living in a mansion in the midlands, he will be welcome in their homes and will be greeted along with the most renowned personages of a childlike society: "Lady Marmela Shortbred will walk in for supper with her marchpane switch on, her necklace of almonds, and her poirette Sundae dress with bracelets of honey and her cochineal hose with the caramel dancings, the briskly best from Bootiestown, and her suckingstaff of ivorymint. You mustn't miss it or you'll be sorry. Charmeuses chloes, glycering juwells, lydialight fans and puffumed cynarettes. And the Prince Le Monade has been graciously pleased. His six chocolate pages will run bugling before him" (FW235-36).

The purpose of all this ice cream parlor imagery is to emphasize the apparent innocence, the childishness of these maidenly fancies. How charming, one thinks, the little girls are, and what a lucky fellow Chuff to be blessed with their candy-sweet approval. But as might be expected, Joyce is employing the same trick here which characterizes the episode as a whole: sentimentality is undercut by a humorous intrusion of reality, often in the person of Glugg, but this time sometimes in the voice of the narrator. As Chuff watches the maidens sing and caper before him, Joyce advises his readers that "the tot of all the tits of their understamens is as open as he can posably she and is tournesoled straightcut or sidewaist, accourdant to the

coursets of things feminite, towooerds him in heliolatry."
The little darlings, one perceives, are falling out of their
dresses, and the saintly Chuff "can espy through them, to
their selfcolours." "O my goodmiss!" he cries. "O my
greatmess!" The maidens are delighted with Chuff's cries
of apparently ingenuous exultation and they begin another round of inflated praise of him: "You are pure. You
are pure. You are in your puerity. You have not brought
stinking members into the house of Amanti. . . . Return,
sainted youngling, and walk once more among us!"³

Meantime, of course, the sainted youngling can delight
in espying feminine "selfcolours." Joyce has enabled us to
view simultaneously the saccharine façade and the libidinous undertones of these childish fooleries. The maidens,
moreover, are themselves occupied with less than saintly
thoughts. Amid all their hymns of praise to Chuff, they
are actually begging him to lead them into more satisfying pastimes: "Pleasekindly communicake with the original sinse," they plead with Chuff, and the "original sinse"
of their communication is sinful indeed, though hardly
original. They are not sure of Chuff's own desires, but
"Master of snakes," they offer, "we can sloughchange in
the nip of a napple solangas we can allsee for deedsetton
your quick. By the hook in your look we're eyed for aye."
"I'm ready when you're ready," would be the familiar
translation of these passages. "And whenever you're tin-
gling in your trout we're sure to be tangled in our tice-
ments." The maidens look ahead hopefully to that day when
words will cease and desire will be quenched: "To these
nunce we are but yours in ammatures yet well come that
day we shall ope to be orea. Then shalt thou see, seeing, the

³ FW237. Note that Chuff is "posably" able to see—indicating that
he is already posing, anticipating later conduct. John Henry Raleigh
has established that Joyce intended this and subsequent passages in
the chapter to act as a gentle joke on Stanislaus Joyce. See Mr.
Raleigh's article " 'My Brother's Keeper'—Stanislaus Joyce and Finnegans Wake," *Modern Language Notes*, LXVIII (February 1953),
107-10.

sight. No more hoaxites!"[4] It is worth noting here that Joyce is not simply using familiar Freudian notions in his own comic way. The maidens are not *unconsciously* indulging in sexual play; they are not the victims of prolonged Freudian slips. Their wordplay is meant as a demonstration of the *conscious* mind's ability to garb its earthy desires in the costume of ingenuousness. Joyce's doubts about modern psychological theory are quite relevant to the case of the rainbow-girls: "Why all this fuss and bother about the mystery of the unconscious?" Joyce once remarked to Frank Budgen. "What about the mystery of the conscious? What do they know about that?"[5]

Thus the saintly Chuff and his innocent maidens are left "waltzing up their willside" in a grand crescendo of mutual titillation, all beneath the guise of a propriety as pure as sugar candy. The woeful Glugg, meantime, has been brooding in "a place where pigeons carry fire to seethe viands, a miry hill . . ." (*FW*239). But he returns to the scene of action. Glugg, the opposite of saintly Chuff, recants his heresies, and peace appears imminent. But before the end of the episode the two boys are battling again, as battle they must. For Chuff continues to represent the ingenuous yet often sanctimonious façade which conceals human motivation. Beneath that façade lies that humorous truth of which poor Glugg is conscious. A mock reconciliation closes the chapter, but Glugg can no more be allied with Chuff than truth with falsehood.[6] Glugg is

---

[4] *FW*239. "Ope" is the operative word here.

[5] Frank Budgen, "Further Recollections of James Joyce," reprinted in his *James Joyce and the Making of Ulysses* (Bloomington, 1960), p. 320.

[6] I cannot agree with Campbell and Robinson's assertion that upon the awakening of Finnegan, "all contraries will have found their resolution in the eternal"—*Skeleton Key to Finnegans Wake* (New York, 1961), p. 142. Shem and Shaun are irreconcilable, as this essay attempts to demonstrate. Campbell and Robinson take a generally more affirmative view of the figures and events in the *Wake* than I have come to think warranted by the text. Clive Hart, in what is surely the most comprehensive and informed study of the structure of the *Wake* yet published, shows that Shem and Shaun

aware of the hidden delights engaged in by the children—
"knows for he's seen it in black and white through his
eyetrompit. . . . Prettimaid tints may try their taunts:
apple . . . zaza . . . What are they all by? Shee" (*FW*247-
48). Beneath the rainbow-tints of innocence, the maidens
were making Chuff a common proposition, while he took
pleasure in their selfcolors. The falsity of Chuff's position
is comparable to that of the young Stephen Dedalus, who
allowed the slums of Dublin to remind him of the prose
of Cardinal Newman. Stephen, however, was simply a
character undergoing one phase of his artistic development: when we encounter him again in *Ulysses*, he is
fully cognizant that all men are "wombed in sin darkness."
Chuff is not a character at all in the usual sense of that
term; he is Joyce's amusing personification of the tendency in human nature toward a denial of the frankly
physical basis of life. Chuff's negation of what Glugg
"knows" takes the form of an angelic demeanor analogous
to the childish frolicking of those somewhat unchildish
maidens. The two brothers—one bold and bleak, the other
defiantly angelic—will oppose each other unalterably "till
tree from tree, tree among trees, tree over tree become
stone to stone, stone between stones, stone under stone

---

do "meet" when the orbits of their world travels cross; but Mr. Hart
points out that their conjunction is only momentary. See *Structure
and Motif in Finnegans Wake* (London, 1962), pp. 129-33.

J. Mitchell Morse, *The Sympathetic Alien* (New York, 1959), p.
66, also argues that the twins are joined; and William York Tindall, *James Joyce: His Way of Interpreting the World* (New York,
1950), p. 83, writes that Joyce reconciles opposites in *FW* by making HCE the embodiment of "balance among them." Mr. Tindall argues that the reconciliation of opposites is the central effort of Joyce's
art (p. 81): I hope that this chapter counteracts this extremely
widespread assumption about Joyce's writings. So far is HCE from
maintaining a balance between opposites that he is unable to read
the Shemian facts of life written on the letter scratched up from a
dung-heap, though he sees it time and again. HCE, like every
Joycean man, is compounded of irreconcilable twins who are unceasingly at war. Cf. Edmund Wilson, "The Dream of H. C. Earwicker," in *James Joyce: Two Decades of Criticism*, ed. Seon Givens
(New York, 1948, 1963), p. 337n.

for ever" (*FW*259). It would be Chuffian to deny that this is indeed a pessimistic picture of human affairs. No lasting integration of the divisive forces in human nature is possible. Yet Joyce leaves no doubt as to the comic tone of his drama: "Loud, heap miseries upon us yet entwine our arts with laughters low!" (*FW*259).

· 2 ·

The second chapter of Book II is at once the most difficult and the most direct section of *Finnegans Wake*. Its language and allusions pose extreme barriers to understanding, and yet the thesis of the chapter could not be less complex. Joyce has thoughtfully, if uncharacteristically, even provided us with a diagram of that thesis. From the start the chapter is directed at the most basic and comprehensive of all philosophic questions: *unde et ubi*. One's initial impulse is to dismiss Joyce for being so pretentious as to pose that question at the beginning of a chapter, or anywhere outside the confessional. But if one remembers that Joyce's art is "entwined with laughter," one is then prepared to receive Joyce's inevitably comic answer to this monumental inquiry.

The chapter is structured on the problems of the study hour of Shem and Shaun—now termed Dolph and Kev, respectively. The first twenty-two pages establish the resonance of the question which has been posed—Whence come we?—and Joyce is bold enough to begin with a consideration of the primal act of creation, next passing through a series of parodies of anthropological and psychological attempts to explain the mystery of human origins. Eventually we return to the nursery, where Dolph-Shem and Kev-Shaun are studying geometry: "Problem ye ferst, construct ann aquilittoral dryankle Probe loom. . . . Concoct an equoangular trillitter. On the name of the tizzer and off the tongs and off the mythametical tripods. Beatsoon" (*FW*

286). Here Joyce's exasperating verbal play has succeeded in embodying within a few words the theme of the entire chapter, and indeed the major theme of the *Wake*. The construction of the geometric figure, an equilateral triangle, constitutes the action of this chapter; by referring to the figure as "ann aquilittoral dryankle," Joyce evokes Anna Livia Plurabelle, the watery mother of Dolph and Kev; and by concluding the passage with a mathematical mockery of the sign of the cross, Joyce reminds the reader of the universal nature of the questions posed in this chapter. One is, after all, searching for the mystery of creation. Apparently we are meant to look for that mystery in an equilateral triangle somehow associated with ALP. A quick recognition of the precise location of ALP's triangle may cause the same reaction in some readers that it will soon cause in the naive Kev. Can Joyce really take mankind so lightly—so obscenely? He can, and with Dolphish delight.

The reader has presumably caught on by this time to Joyce's triangular joke, but it is the task of Dolph, alias Glugg, alias Shem, to acquaint Kev with Joyce's irreverent explanation of man's origins. Dolph is about to make Kev "vicewise." Kev cannot manage the problem, so Dolph advises him of the proper approach: "First mull a muggfull of mud, son." Mud is found on the bottom of any river, and would therefore be found on ALP's bottom and is hence the prime ingredient of ALP's aquilittoral triangle—the source of not only ALP's sons, Dolph and Kev, but in a metaphorical sense, of all men. But the virtuous Kev shuns such a suggestion, even as he refused to acknowledge the prurient nature of his interest in those rainbow-hued maidens: "Oglores, the virtuoser prays, olorum! What the D.V. would I do that for?" (Why would I begin with a mugfull of mud?) Dolph advises Kev that fastidiousness will never do in these matters: the origins of man are not to be taken sacredly. "Now, sknow royol road to Puddlin. . . ."

Eventually Dolph constructs the following figure, "ann aquilittoral dryankle," for Kev's elucidation:

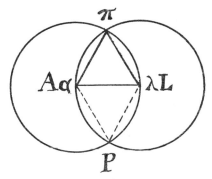

The triangle ALP is meant of course to represent the triangle of ALP, π being the navel and P the vagina, and the entire drawing resembling an amply buttocked woman wearing a small maid's apron. Dolph proposes to "lift . . . the maidsapron of our ALP" (*FW*297). Once this act is completed, the origin of mankind will be laid bare for even the saintly Kev to see. Dolph proceeds with the final operations and rejoices in the revelation of the "sixuous parts, flument, fluvey and fluteous, midden wedge of the stream's your muddy old triagonal delta, fiho miho, plain for you now, appia lippia pluvabille (hop the hula girls!) the no niggard spot of her safety vulve, first of all usquiluteral threeingles . . ." (*FW*297). This exultant tone is not shared by Kev, who after repeatedly failing to grasp the significance of the drawing, finally comprehends when Dolph exclaims, "Her trunk's not her brainbox." "Well, well, well, well!" is Kev's first reaction. He is soon furious with his brother over so scandalous an assertion, calls the drawing a hoax and tells Dolph, "You know, you'll be dampned, so you will, one of these invernal days . . . !" (*FW*300). And Kev eventually hits Dolph "where he lived. . . ."

The first problem, the question of the origins of mankind, has been solved in highly comical fashion. Joyce has exhibited to the world his answer, and Shauns of the world are to take heed. There is no place here for pious pronouncements upon man's sacred beginnings. Man is a foolish and ludicrous creature, originating at the apex of the triangle, self-divided between Shem-like perception and Shaun-like evasion of the comic truth about himself. Kev is shocked by Dolph's triangle in much the same way that Stephen Dedalus was shocked by the abrupt appearance of the word "foetus" on a student's desk. In the *Portrait*, however, the sordid vision bruises Stephen's still delicate consciousness; here Kev's reaction is laughable, a comic refusal to assent to a fact placed literally beneath his nose. Kev resorts to the convenient escape of self-deception or, possibly, hypocrisy.

The chapter closes with a "NIGHTLETTER" from the children of HCE and ALP:

"With our best youlldied greedings to Pep and Memmy and the old folkers below and beyant, wishing them all verry merry Incarnations in this land of the livvey and plenty of preprosperousness through their coming new yonks."

The land of the living was to Joyce a preposterous place, filled with merry incarnations every night of the week, palatable when taken with large doses of laughter.[7]

· 3 ·

By the end of Book II, Chapter ii, the nature of the

[7] Shem and Shaun are given still another set of names, Butt and Taff, respectively, when they appear again toward the end of Book II, Chapter iii. As this section does little to illuminate the nature of the brothers themselves, it does not have a major bearing on the subject of this essay. It is worth noting, however, that to Butt is assigned the task of recounting the particulars of HCE's misdemeanor. In view of the knowledge which Shem has been revealed to possess, it is only fitting that he should be allowed to tell us of HCE's crime, which stands for the fall of all mankind. Naturally, the fall is the result of an obscenity, just as the origins of mankind were an obscenity.

brothers has been clearly established. We have been given a more than thorough insight into the particular aspects of human nature which they symbolize. Yet Joyce felt it necessary, as one might expect, to elaborate further on the theme of Shem and Shaun. In Book III, the brothers, Shaun in particular, are depicted acting out their opposite roles in the public sphere. Here we can observe the public Shem and Shaun. Shaun dominates the action because Shaun has continuously represented the "public" aspects of the human personality. Shaun's creeds are those wholly acceptable in polite society, and his actions are always held up by those around him as saintly and worthy of emulation. *The Mime of Mick, Nick, and the Maggies*, however, revealed that Shaun was capable of the same basic lusts as Shem, just as the frolicking maidens were also found less than immaculate. Shaun's conduct, therefore, must be viewed as hypocritical at least in part. Even the indignation with which he reacted to Shem's diagram was probably not wholly sincere. Self-deception and hypocrisy are often so intermingled that a clear distinction between them is impossible. One is thus not surprised by the hypocritical role which Shaun is assigned in Book III, Chapters i and ii.

In Chapter i, Shaun appears before the people as a candidate for their approval. Joyce intends his readers to take Shaun's candidacy in a very personal sense. Every man, after all, must choose between Shem and Shaun for himself. Here is a decision between facing the comical truth about life and about the self, or electing to escape behind a Shaun-like piety.

Shaun tells the people his own version of a familiar fable, terming it "The Gracehoper and the Ondt," and casting himself, predictably, in the role of the prudent Ondt. He recites the fable as a moral lesson, just as he punched Dolph for reciting an immoral geometry lesson. The Shemian Gracehoper wastes his time in pursuit of young ladies, asking them "to commence insects with him, there mouthparts to his orefice and his gambills to there airy processes" (FW414). For Shem this activity is perfectly in character. But the Ondt, "not being a sommerfool," was prudently—and sanctimoniously—providing for the winter. "He was sair sair sullemn and chairmanlooking when he wore making spakes on his ikey, he ware mouche mothst secred and muravyingly wisechairmanlooking" (FW416). Shaun is every bit as pompous as His Ondtship, as he delivers the fable to the people and then castigates Shem for immorality and "lowquacity."

Shaun engages in the same kind of pedantic moralizing in Book III, Chapter ii, when once again he encounters the rainbow-tinted maidens. Shaun's extemporaneous sermon on this occasion, oozing hypocrisy, is surely one of the most amusing portions of the *Wake*, in addition to being a further illumination of Shaun's character: "Make a strong point," he advises the maidens, "of never kicking up your rumpus over the scroll end of sofas in the Dar Bey Coll Cafeteria by tootling risky *apropos* songs at commercial travellers' smokers for their Columbian nights entertainments like *White limbs they never stop teasing.* . . . First thou shalt not smile. Twice thou shalt not love. Lust, thou shalt not commic idolatry. Hip confiners help compunction. Never park your brief stays in the men's convenience. . . . Where you truss be circumspicious and look before you leak, dears. . . . Secret satieties and onanymous letters make the great unwatched as bad as their betters" (FW433-35). Significantly, Shaun is here termed (Don) Juan, and it becomes increasingly evident as his sermon continues that he is taking considerable delight in contemplating the sins against which he counsels. Grave as is his bearing, suddenly "something of a sidesplitting nature must have occurred to westminstrel Juanathaun for a grand big blossy hearty stenorious laugh . . . hopped out of his woolly's throat like a ball lifted over the head of a deep field, at the bare thought of how jolly they'd like to be trolling his whoop" (FW453).

Juan here betrays himself to the reader. Though his self-righteous behavior appears unaltered from the occasion of that highly informative geometry lesson, he is on the verge of breaking down with laughter. Perhaps, we wonder for a moment, he is ready to acknowledge the triangular truth upon which his brother has been so vehemently insisting. What a positive advance it would be, if Shaun-Juan could finally throw off self-deception and hypocrisy and accept the inevitable physicality of his nature. Juan is amused, it seems, by the thought of the highly sexual desires of the pious maidens grouped about him; they are just as eager now as they were during those "sojestive" games in Book II, and all of them are "just starting to spladher splodher with the jolly magorios, hicky hecky hock, huges huges huges, hughy hughy hughy, O Juan, so jokable and so geepy, O, Thou pure! Our virgin! Thou holy! Our health! Thou strong! Our victory! O salutary! . . ." (FW454). The scene is about to give way to a welcome acceptance of the sensuousness which lies beneath all piety.

But Juan remains true to his nature—to his hypocrisy, to his escapism. "Suddenly . . . swifter as mercury he wheels right round starnly on the Rizzies suddenly, and with his gimlets blazing rather sternish (how black like thunder!), to see what's loose. So they stood still and wondered. Till first he sighed . . . and they nearly cried . . . after which he pondered and finally he replied:" that they should be thinking of their "eternal retribution's reward (the scorchhouse)" (FW454). Juan's strategy is now clear. He is human; he is subject to the truth which Shem has proclaimed; but here in Book III he is using his knowledge of that truth for political gains. In the previous chapter he warned the people against his Gracehoper-brother, and now, in the manner of a priest, he intimidates the maidens through hypocritical moralizing. Though it is not an improbable suggestion, one need not maintain that Juan is here meant to represent the Church. Certainly the Church is included in the implications of Joyce's satire, but Juan's "character" is more coherent when taken in a general way as the personification of the pious side of human nature. Joyce does clearly imply that piety lapses easily into hypocrisy—as in this instance, when false piety is being used as a means to personal gain. But on both the private level of Book II and the public level of Book III, Shaun represents an evasion of Shem's boldly asserted knowledge.

As Shaun fades momentarily out of the picture at the end of Book III, Chapter i, the narrator delivers a rather ironic tribute to him, mocking him beneath apparent praise: "You were the walking saint, you were, tootoo too stayer, the graced of gods and pittites and the salus of the wake. . . . Winner of the gamings, primed at the studience, propredicted from the storybouts, the choice of ages wise!" We will think of you, dear Shaun, the tribute continues, "scrimmaging through your scruples to collar a hold of an imperfection being committed." And "when the natural morning of your nocturne blankmerges into the national morning of golden sunup . . . you will shiff across the Moylendsea and round up in your own escapology some canonisator's day or other . . ." (FW428). Shaun, in other words, will be back, though he disappears for now; he will return to castigate the imperfect, though he himself is far from perfect. He will return because of man's tendency to deny the comicality of the human race. As long as maidens proclaim their virginity, politicians warn of their subversive rivals, and churches threaten the consequences of the afterlife, Shaun will dwell among them all. Shem will return too, of course, to lead men into the dreadful regions of self-knowledge and to excoriate those who resort to "escapology." The brothers cannot be eluded, says Joyce, for they make up the nature of man:

"A locus to loue, a term it t'embarass,
These twain are the twins that tick *Homo Vulgaris*"
(FW418).

· 4 ·

This chapter began by suggesting a thematic continuity among the *Portrait, Ulysses,* and *Finnegans Wake.* It was argued that Stephen Dedalus' difficulty in reconciling the "sordid tide of life" with his search for the essence of spiritual beauty constitutes the initial appearance of the Shem-Shaun theme in Joyce's writings. In *Ulysses* Stephen finally accepts the unpleasant Joycean belief that life originates from a "womb of sin"; spiritual beauty is opposed by the "ineluctable modality of the visible." The opposition does not seem amusing to Stephen as we observe him in *Ulysses,* but Joyce himself chose to adopt a comic stance toward life's antinomies in his treatment of the Blooms and in *Finnegans Wake.* Laughter results from the spectacle of Shem-Glugg, crouching in his blunt way beneath the maidens to catch a glimpse of their self-colors; and saintly Shaun-Chuff is equally humorous, reacting like a prim bluenose at the sight of maidenly disarray.

In the tradition of satire, Joyce harbors a serious intent behind his "tittertit of hilarity." We suspect amid the ostensibly innocent children's games that Shaun-Chuff is not admitting all that he perceives: hypocrisy has ever been a favorite target of satire. When Joyce makes explicit the maidens' true desires, allowing them to proposition Shaun-Chuff through sly innuendo, the principal target of Joyce's mockery becomes clear: a Shaun-like piety and sentimentalism can conceal real motives, and thus Shem-Chuff-Dolph emerges as not only a libertine but a liberator of the truth. To Shem is assigned the Joycean task of unmasking comic realities. In Book II, Chapter ii, Shem-Dolph shocks both Shaun-Kev and the reader with his triangular revelations. The issue—What is the origin of man?—could not be more vital, nor could it be more sacred in the eyes of the sentimental reader. As children we were perhaps told that the stork brought us; as adults we prate, in Joyce's eyes, about the "miracle of creation" or of the manner in which our first parents were formed *ex nihil.* Shem-Dolph obliterates such rhetoric for the enlightenment of all of us Shauns. He leads us to the apex of the triangle, lifts the maid's apron and reveals to our everlasting indignation the true origins of mankind. Having mocked false piety in Book II, Joyce concludes his major treatment of the Shem-Shaun theme in Book III with an expansion of the motif of false piety into the public sphere. Here a pompous hypocrisy typifies the speechmaking and sermonizing of Shaun-Juan. He first slanders Shem in order to ingratiate himself with the people; and he then preaches chastity to the maidens, while secretly delighting in their desires for him.[8]

Like Shem the Penman, Joyce is a "sniffer of carrion, . . . seeker of the nest of evil in the bosom of a good word" (*FW*189), who reduces mankind to a laughing-stock.[9] To Joyce there are no heroes among men—only

[8] The scope of the present study does not permit a more lengthy treatment of *Finnegans Wake* than is undertaken in this chapter, but as an indication of how pervasive the concept of *irreconcilable* opposites is in the book, note the following remark of Joyce's: "Isn't it arbitrary of me to make use, as I do, of forty tongues I don't know in order to express the dream state? Isn't it contradictory to make two men speak Chinese and Japanese in a pub in Phoenix Park, Dublin? Nevertheless, that is a logical and objective method of expressing a deep conflict, an irreducible antagonism." Quoted by Jacques Mercanton in his "The Hours of James Joyce, Part I," *Kenyon Review,* XXIV (Autumn 1962), 708-709.

[9] Herbert Howarth, "The Joycean Comedy: Wilde, Jonson, and Others," *A James Joyce Miscellany, Second Series,* ed. Marvin Magalaner, pp. 179-94, analyzes Joyce's mocking attitude in *Finnegans*

mock-heroes. Shem the Penman himself is no hero, for Shem is only half a man, only one of the twins who make every man tick. The complete Joycean man is HCE, whose obscene misdemeanor in Phoenix Park is merely the type of a universal failing or fall, the Shemian fact of all human life, eternally recurring. Finnegan will wake again and fall again, over and over, world without end, and that is why *Finnegans Wake* begins in the middle of its last sentence and ends in the middle of its first. In Chapter II of this book, we observed Joyce's own moral and psychological struggles with this same Shemian fact. Unlike HCE, Joyce did not try to deny his fall and argue like a Shaun against inescapable truth. Joyce's conscience eventually would not permit such escapology: the Shem in him lifted the maid's apron and pointed bluntly. For a time Joyce reacted with Shaun-like horror, though without Shaun-like self-deception and hypocrisy. And in *Exiles* this conception of human nature is reflected in Joyce's sober treatment of Richard Rowan, a man who finds that his libertarian attitude toward sex is morally compromised by sordid, bestial motives. But gradually Joyce was able to adopt a more amused, comically satirical, Shemian attitude, and the first flowering of that attitude was Leopold Bloom.

Bloom, too, is a complete Joycean man by virtue of his very ambivalence. Poor Bloom, with his illusory dreams of fame and ardent conquest, his visions of escape and his inescapable fleshly ties to Molly—Bloom shows the unmistakable signs of Shem and Shaun at war within him, although he predates Joyce's formulation of the irreconcilable twins. Along with Molly, herself the apex of

---

Wake toward the sexuality lying beneath the proper exteriors of even the greatest of men. Mr. Howarth focuses particularly on Joyce's treatment in the *Wake* of "the love that dare not speak its name"—homosexuality, "the byways of pederasty," as he so amusingly terms Joyce's explorations in this realm. The tone of Mr. Howarth's article seems to me comically apt for *Finnegans Wake.*

Joyce's elemental triangle, Bloom enables Joyce to give voice to his moral conscience without preaching a sermon. Stephen Dedalus, if he is to come to endurable terms with the opposition between the sordid and the beautiful, must first observe the comicality of Mr. Bloom, must cast off his Jesuitical cloak of gloom, leaven his Joycean conscience with Joycean laughter and be amused by the battles of "the twins that tick *Homo Vulgaris*."

vii. the conscience in perspective

When Joyce was nineteen, he wrote a letter to Henrik Ibsen which, when we read it today, seems to prefigure much of Joyce's later life and thought. Ibsen's resolution and indifference to public disapproval inspired Joyce, and he praised the "inward heroism" which had enabled Ibsen to triumph in literary and personal battle.[1] Joyce himself was to go on to fight many a battle, both personal and public; and when he was unpublished or censored or almost blind, laboring over his extraordinarily arduous art, he no doubt looked to the example of Ibsen. It was Joyce's way to emulate his heroes and to strive after seemingly impossible goals, even at the cost of self-torture. Indeed, it is hard to imagine Joyce in comfortable circumstances, writing at his leisure, secure and serene. He was the sort of artist who thrives on conflict, poverty and neglect, not to say drink. In his letters he most often portrayed himself as a heroic figure, continually beleaguered by debt, illness, and disloyalty, determined to see his self-appointed labors through. The price of great art is always high, but Joyce was bent on heroism no matter what the risk to himself or to his family. Even after Harriet Shaw Weaver had made him financially independent, in 1924, he threw the money away on exorbitant tips, on drink and on expensive meals, all with such abandon that one can conclude only that he could not abide security. He fought battles to the end, and his eagerness to fight, his tenacity,

[1] Letter to Ibsen, March 1901, *Letters*, I, 51-52.

and his enormous pride enabled him to laugh at his weaker side and at those who seemed less heroic than himself.

Eugene Jolas, who knew Joyce well from 1927 on, once characterized him as "never an ebullient man. His moments of silence and introspection frequently weighed . . . on his immediate surroundings. Then a profound pessimism, that seemed to hold him prisoner within himself, made him quite inaccessible to outsiders. Usually, however, among his intimates, there finally came a festive pause, when he would begin to dance and sing, or engage in barbed thrusts of wit; when he would show flashes of gaiety and humor that could, on occasion, approach a kind of delirium."[2]

It is almost as though Mr. Jolas were describing Joyce's books along with their author. That "profound pessimism" manifests itself first in those studies of Irish moral paralysis, the *Dubliners* stories, written in a spare, almost reticent prose, which Joyce himself termed a style of "scrupulous meanness." When the snow begins to fall upon all Ireland at the close of "The Dead," falling, "like the descent of their last end, upon all the living and the dead," an icy Joycean pessimism descends simultaneously upon us, and as we look back over the sorry lot of Dubliners just encountered—the paralyzed and the perverse alike—we may be tempted to reflect upon the bleakness of the moralist who created them. In the *Portrait* that same pessimism, expressed this time in a different style, lurks beneath the many passages of soaring, silvery romanticism. A first reading of the *Portrait* is invariably an uplifting experience: we fly with Stephen by the restrictive nets of environment and join with him in his exultant, final "Welcome, O life!" But look again—like Stephen, we have ignored a part of reality; wretchedness rivals beauty; barriers of order and elegance will not hold back the sordid

[2] Eugene Jolas, "My Friend James Joyce," in *James Joyce: Two Decades of Criticism*, ed. Seon Givens (New York, 1948, 1963), p. 3.

tides of life; spiritual love cannot be fashioned from lust; and a glance at the first three episodes of *Ulysses* shows us a disillusioned Stephen and reveals that the moonlit strand of his artistic awakening is littered with decaying, chaotic debris. Meanwhile the lugubrious *Exiles* has been written: a dramatization of the irreconcilable conflicts between liberty and love. Truly this Joyce was not "an ebullient man."

But just as in Mr. Jolas' characterization, "there finally came a festive pause." Enter Bloom, and with him Joyce's barbed wit, humor, and sometimes delirious comic satire. Enter Molly Bloom as well, and later Earwicker and Anna Livia and certainly "the twins that tick *Homo Vulgaris*," Shem and Shaun.

Joyce's pessimism, of course, is never banished: but it requires redefinition, revaluation. It dresses now in cap and bells, covering a sad heart with a gay costume, even as a Shakespearean Fool. It is resigned to the doubleness or duplicity of life, recognizing the common reality co-existing with every vision of beauty, but choosing to laugh rather than to rail at life's irreducible antinomies. Adopting this ironic stance, Joyce directed his comic satire against a wide range of human follies, some truly reprehensible and others merely amusing: the venality of a Buck Mulligan, the weakness of a Bloom, the sentimentalism of a Gerty MacDowell, the vapid rhetoric of journalists, the narcissism of a Molly Bloom, the smugness of the Very Reverend Conmee, the poses of Stephen Dedalus, the bloody-minded bigotry of a chauvinist, the fawning subservience of Dubliners to an English Viceroy, the sterility of Irish life itself. Ever mindful himself of the disparity between the ideal and the actual, Joyce reserved many of his sharpest satiric barbs for man's most characteristic folly, self-deception, the capacity to believe himself far better than he is. Self-deception has always of course been a favorite target of satirists, from Lucian, Rabelais, Cervantes, Swift, and Sterne to Joyce. As Sterne once wrote, "To know one's self, one would think could be no very difficult lesson;—for who, you'll say, can well be truly ignorant of himself, and the true disposition of his own heart? If a man thinks at all, he cannot be a stranger to what passes there;—he must be conscious of his own thoughts and desires, he must remember his past pursuits, and the true springs and motives which in general have directed the actions of his life: he may hang out false colours and deceive the world, but how can a man deceive himself? That a man can, is evident, because he daily does so. . . . Most of us are aware of and pretend to detest the barefaced instances of that hypocrisy by which men deceive others; but few of us are upon our guard, or see that more fatal hypocrisy by which we deceive and over-reach our own hearts!"[3] Joyce was upon his guard, one might say, against self-deception, both in himself and in others; and he fashioned much of his most effective comic satire out of his awareness and observation of this vice. Thus the posing Stephen and the dreaming Bloom are made to seem absurd; thus the hypocritical and self-deceiving Shaun is made to see the truth about himself—however distasteful Shem's little geometry lesson may be. And thus Humphrey Chimpden Earwicker appears ridiculous to the reader precisely because he persists in self-deception, persists in denying the comical, obscene truth about his misdemeanor in Phoenix Park, a misdemeanor which Joyce intends to stand as a humorous type or symbol of the Fall of all mankind.

Every satirist, bitter or comic, Christian or pagan, must begin with the premise of a fallen mankind. Satire depends upon a view of man as a rather puny creature, who perhaps has great potential, but whose most characteristic folly consists in convincing himself of his own grandeur

[3] Laurence Sterne, "Sermon IV: On Self-Knowledge," *Works*, v (London, 1802), 54-55, 67-68.

despite overwhelming evidence to the contrary. How satirically appropriate it was, then, for Joyce to select as the subject of his greatest literary effort—if not his greatest literary success—the Fall of man and the self-deceiving, hypocritical attempts of man to deny that Fall. Beneath all the bewildering, bedeviling obscurity of *Finnegans Wake*, this is Joyce's subject: the ineluctable Fall of man and the ridiculous self-deceiving attempts of the Shaun in all of us to deny that Fall to ourselves and to others.

Whether Joyce thought that man had actually slipped from a state of perfection, to which someday he might return through the grace of God, is a question to which the answer is probably no: that was the kind of detailed dogma or myth in which Joyce ceased to believe when he left the Church. He retained from Irish Catholicism, however, an essential mistrust of human nature and, most significantly, a mistrust of sex, which both he and his rejected Church viewed as the most powerful element in man's moral degeneracy. If there is any similarity whatever between the Freudian and the Joycean conceptions of human life, it is that each considers sex the dominant force in man. At that point Joyce and Freud part company, Freud considering sex quite apart from any traditional moral scale of values, Joyce considering sex the primary evidence of the beast in man which rivals the angel in man.[4] To Joyce, sex was the great proof of man's Fall or original sin: hence the centrality of sex in his writings. To deny man's inescapable animality, to deny man's Fall, was in Joyce's view an act of self-deception. The sexless, spiritual

---

[4] I certainly do not mean to minimize the importance of Joyce's use of psychoanalytic theories in the construction of the unconscious reveries of *Finnegans Wake* and, to a lesser extent, of the reveries of *Ulysses*. Frederick J. Hoffman discusses the structural use of Freud by Joyce in "Infroyce," *Two Decades*, pp. 390-435; this article appears also as a chapter in his *Freudianism and the Literary Mind* (Baton Rouge, 1945). But Joyce was far from sympathetic to an amoral, scientific approach to human nature, and thus he does part company with Freud over the moral significance of sex.

love poems of *Chamber Music* were written, he said, as "a protest against myself,"[5] meaning as a protest against the sexual or lower part of his nature. He implicitly criticizes Stephen Dedalus in the *Portrait* for trying to deny or to escape this lower half of life. He expounds dramatically in *Exiles* upon the impossibility of reconciling sexual liberty with moral ideals. Softening his attitude without essentially altering it, he satirizes the mock-heroic trials and troubles of Leopold Bloom, a man enthralled by his senses, a man disposed to stare glassy-eyed at his own genitals; and the sexual center of Bloom's universe, Molly, emerges as a titanic symbol of sexual force itself, as powerful and as pervasive as the gravity of the earth. Finally, Joyce writes his dream-epic of the Fall of man, with a sexual misdemeanor, indecent exposure, as the playful Joycean equivalent of Edenic apple-picking. His point of view is in this respect as Irish as his impish kind of mockery and his obsessions with language, history, and myth. Everywhere one looks in Joyce, sex betrays or befuddles man—even in *Dubliners*, where sexual perversion lies at the heart of one story, and Gabriel Conroy's lustful sullying of his wife's spiritual love lies at the heart of another.

Stanislaus Joyce, who once described the Irish Catholic Church as "the accomplice of a form of religion which is more Puritan than Catholic and a vigilant and pitiless enemy of free thought and joyful living, . . . a cross between English Puritanism and the most unenlightened features of Catholic doctrine,"[6] detected the pronounced puritan strain in his brother's books and decried it. Anyone familiar with writings by and about Stanislaus knows him as a militantly apostate Catholic, whose hatred for his native Church knew no discernible bounds. Though James had no rival in his disgust with Irish Catholic clergy and his mischievous ridicule of ritual and dogma, he retained

[5] Richard Ellmann, *James Joyce* (New York, 1959), pp. 154-55.
[6] Stanislaus Joyce, *Recollections of James Joyce* (New York, 1950), p. 11.

a basically puritanical view of man which Stanislaus did not. Stanislaus might complain about his brother's drinking habits, but he did not consider James by any means a pagan. In fact he wrote critically to James in 1924: "To me you seem to have escaped from the toils of the priest and the king only to fall under the oppression of a monstrous vision of life itself. Where so much has been recorded [in *Ulysses*], I object to what has been omitted. There is no serenity or happiness anywhere in the whole book. . . . It is undoubtedly Catholic in temperament. This brooding on the lower order of natural facts, this re-evocation and exaggeration of detail by detail and the spiritual dejection which accompanies them are purely in the spirit of the confessional. Your temperament, like Catholic morality, is predominantly sexual. . . ."[7]

In substance Stanislaus was correct, though he seems to have missed the comedy of *Ulysses*, comedy which redeems Joyce's vision from the epithet "monstrous." Joyce does brood in *Ulysses* upon human weaknesses; he does evoke detail by detail what to him was the lower order of natural facts, enumerating relentlessly Bloom's little follies, perversions, and self-deceiving dreams. And as the letters to Nora show, *Ulysses* is certainly written in the spirit of the confessional, for many of Bloom's sins were Joyce's own. He would confess his sins to Nora, begging her forgiveness for them, and then he would make satiric sport of them in *Ulysses* and later in *Finnegans Wake*, confessing in a more oblique way to the whole world, flagellating himself with his own satire, yet certain that his errors were those of all mankind. Sex predominates in all these confessions, private and literary alike, even as Molly Bloom predominates in *Ulysses*. Joyce devoted his artistic life to setting down our sins and his own sins in his enormous books, like some tireless medieval monk at work on a sacred manuscript. And like those of a monk, his ideals were supernal, mythical, exalted, impossible. These ideals are somehow

[7] Letter from Stanislaus, 7 August 1924, *Letters*, III, 104.

present in all of Joyce's writings, functioning as standards beyond the possibilities of reality and as reminders of the shortcomings of ordinary lives. They include Stephen's several ethereal females, especially the dovelike, wading girl; and the dead Michael Furey, whose memory Gretta Conroy, herself a sinless Joycean example of ideal femininity, carries about in her heart almost as a talisman against the baseness of the world; they include as well the guiltless Bertha of *Exiles*, and heroic Ulysses and chaste Penelope. Each of these figures embodies something of Joyce's spiritual idealism. In his own life Joyce tried to make an equally exalted, equally impossible ideal out of his wife, to whom he proclaimed that his love was a kind of adoration and that she was to his manhood what the ideal of the Blessed Virgin had been to his boyhood.[8] Indeed Stanislaus said much when he called his brother's temperament Catholic.

Though we may marvel at Joyce's technical virtuosity and though we may applaud his revolutionary inclusion of life's everyday trivialities—Bloom within his outhouse, Molly upon her chamberpot—we may find it difficult to accept, let alone to approve, his curious ideals, his puritanical prejudices, his mistrust of sex. We have trampled sexual puritanism, and the style of our literature no less than our attire attests to the demise of Joyce's kind of morality. Though Joyce's technical innovations still seem new, it is D. H. Lawrence who proved to be more the prophet—Lawrence the worshipper of the dark gods of passion, who advises his readers to adhere to the rhythms of the earth, and who tells us that "when genuine passion moves you, say what you've got to say, and say it hot."[9] As one might expect, Joyce and Lawrence, the one an advocate of the old and the other of a new moral order,

---

[8] Letters to Nora of 27 October and 31 August 1909, *ibid.*, II, 255 and 242.

[9] *Studies in Classic American Literature* (New York, 1964), p. 17.

openly despised one another's works. To Lawrence, *Ulysses* was a manifestation of modern decadence: "There it is, in James Joyce . . . —in all the very modern novels, the dominant note is the repulsiveness, intimate physical repulsiveness of human flesh."[10] Lawrence found even Joyce's techniques symptomatic of a lamentable dissociation from physical life: "James Joyce bores me stiff—too terribly would-be and done-on-purpose, utterly without spontaneity or real life." And in Joyce's distaste for the physical, Lawrence detected old-fashioned values behind a merely technical experimentalism: "My God, what a clumsy *olla putrida* James Joyce is! Nothing but old fags and cabbage-stumps of quotations from the Bible and all the rest, stewed in the juice of deliberate, journalistic dirty-mindedness—what old and hard-worked staleness, masquerading as the all-new."[11] For his part, Joyce reportedly had only one word for *Lady Chatterley's Lover*: "Lush!"[12] Lawrence could hardly appeal to a man who liked to think of his wife as the Blessed Virgin.

But Lawrence turned puritanism upside-down and became a kind of puritan-in-reverse, worshipping the opposite of the customary end. He was a transitional figure. Contemporary writers seem to have rejected both physical and spiritual gods. The serious literature, drama, and cinema of today mirror a world in which codes and customs and values have vanished, and we are left with an exceedingly noisy, garish, and efficient society, with man no longer a creature of God, nor a pilgrim progressing toward heavenly reward, nor even a self-confident shaper of his own earthly destiny, but simply a consumer. The

[10] *Selected Literary Criticism* (New York, 1956), p. 411.
[11] *Ibid.*, pp. 149, 148. For a fuller treatment of the Lawrence-Joyce relationship, see William Deakin, "D. H. Lawrence's Attacks on Proust and Joyce," *Essays in Criticism*, VII (1957), 383-403.
[12] Ellmann, *James Joyce*, p. 628n. This was Joyce's first reaction. Later he made a typically mischievous Joycean remark about "*Lady Chatterbox's Lover*": ". . . a piece of propaganda in favor of something which, outside of D.H.L.'s country at any rate, makes all the propaganda for itself."

game appears to go on as before, but we play without racquets, even without a ball. We are still learning to be Joyce's contemporaries, as Richard Ellmann has said, but chiefly in terms of subject matter and technique. Even Joyce's melancholy, while profoundly moving, is not quite our own; it is the bitter fruit of his disappointment with mankind and with himself for not living up to standards in which we, it must be said, have ceased to believe. "A hundred cares, a tithe of troubles and is there one who understands me?" Joyce has Anna Livia lament, but surely she speaks for himself. "One in a thousand of years of the nights? All me life I have lived among them but now they are becoming lothed to me. And I am lothing their little warm tricks. And lothing their mean cosy turns. And all the greedy gushes out through their small souls. And all the lazy leaks down their brash bodies. How small it's all! And me letting on to meself always. And lilting all the time. I thought you were all glittering with the noblest of carriage. You're only a bumpkin. I thought you were great in all things, in guilt and in glory. You're but a puny. . . . And it's old and old it's sad and old it's sad and weary I go back to you, my cold father, my cold mad father, my cold mad feary father, till the near sight of the mere size of him, the moyles and moyles of it, moananoaning, makes me seasilt saltsick and I rush, my only, into your arms . . ." (FW627-28).

All the sadness of a lifetime is in that passage, enlivened by a wry, Irish lilt. Joyce's mind may be compared to one of those ruined abbeys scattered about the Irish countryside: soaring spires and vaults and archways; spiraling stairs; a view from the turrets of vistas green and gray; labyrinthine corridors; walls and tombs covered with angular carving and angular script, hinting mysteries unfathomable and secrets long forgotten; broad stone steps, with tufts of grass grown up between the cracks; a broken altar; and over all an air of sadness in this dead place, where the roof has vanished centuries ago and the rain falls free and the wind blows cold.

Joyce's comic spirit, however, saves his mature writing from the slightest moralizing tone, whatever its moral seriousness and underlying melancholy. While his conscience gives all of his works their point of view, the comic tone of his satire gives *Ulysses* and *Finnegans Wake* an atmosphere which is agreeable whether or not we accept Joyce's moral position. His uncompromising devotion to his art enabled him to triumph over the limitations of his ideas. Whatever our own moral, immoral, or amoral bias, we can take pleasure in his playful mockery of Bloom; we can take pleasure in the skill with which Joyce, in the tradition of great satirists, lays bare with an engaging laugh the myriad follies and sins of mankind. And even if we disagree with Joyce over the nature of sin, even if our own conscience differs from his, we can profit from his comic unmasking of our own Stephen-like, Bloom-like, Molly-like, Shaun-like self-love.

index